Those were the Days...

JUMPING JACK

MICHAEL GEGG

All profits from the sale of this book will be
donated to the Ruth Strauss Foundation

THOSE WERE THE DAYS…

FOREWORD

I was fortunate to play 100 Test matches for my country. There were highs (the centuries and series wins, particularly the victories in Pakistan and Sri Lanka) and there were the inevitable lows (missing some series and of course never winning the Ashes), but what was consistent throughout my career, were the many, many, ongoing memories that were created.

Michael (or Freddie as he is known in cricket circles) and I first spoke back in 2016, when we spent two hours on the phone talking through my career. It was unlike a typical interview I was used to as a player. There was no trying to trip me up with awkward questions. It was just a good, honest and open conversation between a former player and an interested supporter. And it felt good recounting memorable moments from my career.

Since that day, I've enjoyed reading the many other interviews that Michael has carried out through the excellent Addis Army newsletter - it's certainly been interesting reading the stories from some of my former team-mates and players from other eras. I'm particularly gutted to have missed Adam Hollioake's 'best drinking tour of all time' but on the flip side, thanks to Jack Russell I now remember how to make the perfect Weetabix and cup of tea!

When Michael told me he was looking to pull all of these interviews together into a book, I thought what a great idea. And when he asked me if I'd be happy to write a foreword, I was delighted to put pen to paper as it gives me a chance to say thank you to the many people who helped create many of my memories – the supporters.

I always have fond memories of 1994, which is when I heard my name being sung for the first time. When you hear that as a player it truly does help raise your game. I'm now part of the England set-up as a coach, and I know how thankful all of the current players are for the continued support that the likes of the Addis Army, their 'cousins' the Barmy Army and all of the England supporters that travel all over the world, give to the team.

Trust me, when you're playing in matches, thousands of miles away from home, the support we receive, particularly when the going gets tough, is unrivalled. When I took to the field, it genuinely felt like we had a 12th man – and yes, I'm still 'walking in a Thorpey wonderland'!

I hope all of you enjoy reading the stories in this book as much as my former team mates and I enjoyed sharing them.

Those, definitely were the days!

Graham Thorpe

INTRODUCTION

Anyone who knows me, will know that I'm a true cricket nut. If cricket is on television, I'll be watching it. If cricket is in the papers, I'll be reading about it. And if England are on tour, work permitting, I'll be there. This crazy passion has allowed me to travel the world and explore so many interesting cultures and it's this passion for touring, in particular, that has led me to write this book.

My first England tour abroad was the 2002/03 Ashes series – the tour when Michael Vaughan rose to prominence - and who can forget that terrific win in Sydney? Oh, the celebrations that occurred in the streets of Sydney that evening. A stranger wouldn't have realised we'd lost the series 4-1! Since then, I have undertaken 15 further tours (at the time of this book getting published).

Yet, it was the 2004 tour to South Africa that saw the birth of the Addis Army, a group of England supporters, that may not be known to all, but who travel all over the world to support the team. Why 'Addis Army'? There's a good question. For some strange reason – actually it wasn't strange at all, it was just a damn cheap flight option – a group of around 30 independent cricket fans flew to South Africa, via a stay in Addis Ababa. For many of us it was our first insight into a third world country. Apart from our accompanying travel partner, none of us knew each other. So, we did what all strangers do on tour, share a beer (around a swimming pool) and talk cricket. The Addis Army was born.

15 years on, the group has grown. We're all close mates, there's been marriages, a few children, Midnight's books and we've had members of the hard-core group on every England tour since. Yes, this includes Pakistan and Bangladesh. We've had many

highs watching England and A LOT of lows, but those highs
and lows are what make touring so much fun. We're good
friends with the Barmy Army and acknowledge the great work
that Andy 'Leafy' Burnham, Chris Millard, Andy Thompson and
Billy 'The Trumpet' Cooper have done over many, many years in
raising the profile of supporting England, Test cricket and
numerous charities.

In the middle of the dot com boom we launched our own
website www.addisarmycricket.co.uk and over the years the site
has evolved into what could now be described as an online
fanzine for England supporters. Primarily aimed at those
watching England overseas, it's full of supporters' blogs, a
monthly blog by an ex-county pro – which is always a fascinating
read - entertaining tour diaries from everywhere we visit,
supporter Q&A's, and much more.

We have a monthly newsletter/fanzine that has grown in
popularity in recent years and one of the evolutions of the
newsletter has been a regular interview with a former (and
sometimes current) England player, coach, administrator,
journalist, some great old county pro's; oh, and an Australian fast
bowler who wrecked some havoc against us in the 1980s.

As a self-confessed cricket nut, it has been a dream over the last
three years, spending hours on the phone with (and meeting in
person) some of my schoolboy heroes. Being able to ask them
questions on the highs and lows of their cricketing careers and
then just sitting there rivetted at the answers they provide, has
been a joy. Having undertaken over 30 interviews from both the
men's and women's game, I thought it'd be great to pull all the
interviews together into this book you have parted your hard-
earned money for – thanks again for doing that. All profits are
going to the Ruth Strauss Foundation, so, thank you for your
contribution to a worthy cause.
Throughout the book, you'll find some great stories and

hopefully some 'I remember that…', 'I didn't know that…' and 'those were the days…' (do you get the title now?!) moments. That's the aim anyway.

Now the confession. I'm not a journalist, so I'm sorry if you're after some sensational scoop – it's unlikely you'll find it in here – we're not a red top newspaper. Although… does Charles Dagnall's revelation that the TMS team enjoy savoury snacks as much as cakes, count as such a scoop?

What you will get is a host of cricketing favourites sharing some great stories from their playing days.

If you find a typo or grammar error, remember I'm just an England cricket fan not J.K. Rowling. So, no need for the grammar police, ok?

And finally, these are a collection of interviews, it's not a novel – so it may not all flow seamlessly, but I tried! – I've ordered the interviews by the year of a player's first-class debut, which hopefully gives it a degree of order!

Enjoy.

Michael Gegg
September 2019

THOSE WERE THE DAYS...

ACKNOWLEDGEMENTS

Before I get stuck into the interviews, I must say some thank yous.

Where do I start? There's a few.

The first has to be to Simon Tremlin, my regular room-mate on tour, who back in 2016 during the Centurion Test, suggested: 'Freddie, what would be interesting for the website, is to interview some former players.' And in fairness to Tremers, he didn't just put the idea forward and leave it there, month after month he's followed it up by continually opening up his little black book. "Freddie, I've secured you...., here's his number."

Thanks also to a good friend of mine and everyone's favourite umpire, Ian 'Gunner" Gould. "Geggy, I'm in Bangladesh, series finished, it's too hot, can't get a drink but I've lined you up an interview with their assistant coach." Cheers mate!

Their support in opening up doors to people has been fantastic.

A big thank you to all of the people who agreed to be interviewed. Your willingness and openness has been really appreciated. Thanks to Jack Russell for the kind offer of using some of his artwork.

A huge thanks to my favourite cricketer of all time – Graham Thorpe – who very kindly wrote the foreword. Thorpey was a fighter in England's middle order in the 1990s and early 2000s and I often think just how much he would have thrived in the current England set-up. In what is a World Cup and Ashes Summer, and being part of England's coaching team, I can't thank him enough for supporting me with this book, when his mind will so obviously be occupied with other stuff. Once a legend, always a legend.

To Ian Florance, my former boss from many years ago, a cricket-fan, author and poet who agreed to be chief 'proof-reader' and to Doug Norman, the creative genius, who designed the cover – thanks both!

Finally, to my partner, Marta, for all of her support and who for 95% of the time was 'happy' to switch off Love Island so I could interview 'another player'.

If I missed anyone, I'm sorry, it wasn't deliberate.

Thank you one and all.

CONTENTS

1

BOB TAYLOR
FORMER ENGLAND WICKET-KEEPER

I doubt that Bob Taylor's record of 2,069 dismissals will ever be broken. He was arguably one of the most accomplished wicket-keepers to have ever played the game.

When people talk about 1981, people inevitably think of Botham and Willis, but it is Bob Taylor who has the famous match-ball in his possession, proudly displayed at home, as a result of his seven catches in the match.

"When the final wicket fell, we all ran off the pitch. Geoffrey Boycott had picked up the ball and given it to Bob Willis," remarked Bob. "I didn't realise at the time, but when we were on the balcony watching Botham and Willis being interviewed by Peter West on BBC2, one of the press boys tapped me on the shoulder to ask if I realised that when I caught Geoff Lawson for my 4th catch, it gave me the world record. When we went back into the dressing room, Bob was sat there with the ball, so I told him what the press guy had just told me and asked if he minded if I could have the ball. Bowlers often get the balls for the best bowling analysis, but wicket-keepers never really got anything. So, he gave me the ball, and I have it my possession now."

We'll talk more about 1981 later. But there is so much more to Bob's career than just 1981.

Similar to my conversations with Jack Russell, Rob Turner, Neil Burns and Paul Nixon, I asked Bob what made him take up wicket-keeping as a youngster. "I used to love watching Godfrey Evans on my small 10 inch black and white television. He was always so lively behind the stumps; just a ball of energy. He took my eyes straight away. So much so, that when I got to school for my first cricket lesson, I remember asking the cricket master if I could have a go at wicket-keeping. I was always small as a kid and I hated the thought of being posted down to third man or fine leg boundary. A wicket-keeper, or back-stop as it was called in those days was always involved in the game, what with catches and stumpings; I wanted some of that. The school master said that if I grabbed the gloves out of the kit bag first the following week, I could be the wicket-keeper. There was no way I wasn't going to get those gloves! These days, whenever I coach, I tell kids that the wicket-keeper is the second most important man after the captain, no matter what the level. You're the king-pin of the fielding side and should inspire the rest of the team."

Yet, Bob's admiration for Godfrey Evans wasn't the only reason he wanted to become a wicket-keeper, there was also a hint of an ego in there as well! "In the Winter months I loved my football. I was a centre forward and my ego was often boosted on a Monday morning because the football master (who was also the cricket master) used to write a match report on his type-writer and underlined the goal scorers in red, then pin it onto the school notice board. I couldn't wait to get to school on a Monday morning to see that I had scored and my name highlighted. I genuinely got a boost! So, I thought as a wicket-keeper I would get a lot of catches and thus my name would get underlined in the Summer months as well!"

As with many cricketers in that era, football and cricket was always a difficult juggling act. Bob's goals as a centre forward saw him on the books of Port Vale. "I only played for the reserves, but I left there to go to Burton Albion, but that's when I started playing cricket for Derbyshire and the two clashed. I couldn't play mid-week games for Burton Albion and cricket for Derbyshire. Cricket was always my first choice so that was the end of my illustrious football career!"

But it wasn't his football skills that attracted the attention of Derbyshire, it was his form for Staffordshire in the Minor Counties League. "I was a 16-year-old schoolboy when I first played for Staffordshire. David Steele was also in the team and we were both fortunate that we had former Lancashire and England batsman John Ilkin who'd retired from first class cricket in the team. He must have seen something in me as he played for my club side and also captained Staffordshire. He gave me the opportunity to play Minor Counties cricket."

Bob's form for Staffordshire over a three-year period saw him picked up by Derbyshire at just 19 years of age on the back of his performance playing for a Minor Counties XI against a South African touring team in 1960. "After that game, I had a game for Staffordshire against Durham, which got rained off; I was in the pavilion at Wolverhampton Cricket Club when someone had said a couple of Derbyshire officials wanted a chat. I was then sat on the back seat of a car being offered a contract to play for Derbyshire in 1961. To my delight, in those days if you played in the Minor Counties League and was offered a contract by a first-class county in which you weren't born, they had to give you a 3-year contract. It was great for me as three years gave me the security and chance to really prove myself; if I had been born in

Derbyshire I would likely have just had a one year contract and, who knows, I could very easily have had a bad season and been on the scrap heap before I'd started."

Bob made his first-class debut for Derbyshire during the first year of that 3-year deal in a home fixture against Sussex. "I was on a king pair when I had to go in during the second innings trying to save the game. I had Don Bates at one end trying to bounce me out and Harold Rhodes at the other coming in to bowl in brown suede shoes!!"

In today's game bowlers tend to cut a hole in their boots if their big toes give them discomfort when running in to bowl - it was obviously very different back then! But Bob survived, Derbyshire drew the match and Bob's professional career was underway. It was the beginning of a happy 23-year spell for the county.

"I was always happy at Derbyshire. We weren't the best team, but it allowed me to drive a banger of an old car and they were great guys to play cricket with! We were the first winners of the NatWest Trophy in 1981. Prior to that, it was the Gillette Cup, but Gillette pulled out of sponsoring the Trophy and NatWest Bank took over. In the semi-finals we beat Essex, who had the likes of Keith Fletcher, Graham Gooch and John Lever, in a rain-affected match. With one ball to go we needed one run to level the score, the scores finished level and we won the game as we lost less wickets. Remarkably, the final was exactly the same. Geoff Miller managed to get the one run to equal the scores and we beat Northants as we'd again lost less wickets. That trophy was probably my biggest Derbyshire highlight, sadly we never got close to winning the County Championship."

Reflecting back on Bob's world record, what was more remarkable about this feat is that Derbyshire weren't one of the major counties challenging for the title, year on year. As such, they could often get bowled out cheaply and thus Bob would get only one chance to field as the opposition had racked up enough runs to win by an innings. Imagine how many more dismissals he could have had if he'd played for a more successful county; no disrespect to Derbyshire.

"To be honest it just made me extra pleased to get the record."

After eight years at Derbyshire, Bob was on the fringes of the England side. In 1969, he was selected for an MCC tour of Sri Lanka – his first representative tour. Bob played in a one off 'Test' match in Colombo where he scored seven and 19 not out, in a convincing win for the MCC. "Tony Lewis was captain of that tour. We should have gone to East Africa, but we pulled out because of the apartheid situation. Instead we went on a tour of South East Asia. The match in Sri Lanka was the only official first-class game. For the rest of the tour we went to Singapore, Bangkok, Kuala Lumpur and Hong Kong, just playing one-day matches, mainly against ex-pats. It was a fun tour, but amusingly Geoff Boycott, who was one of the experienced players on tour, scored hundreds against the amateurs, but in the only game that counted towards first class averages he got two low scores!!"

12 months later and Bob was finally given an opportunity at international level when he was selected for England's 1970/71 tour to Australia and New Zealand under the captaincy of Ray Illingworth. It was a tour that saw him make the first of what was to become a 57 Test match career for the great gloveman.

To many it should have been many more for someone of his ability, but the challenge for Bob was that there was another great gloveman in that era, Alan Knott. Both were highly regarded and to this day many debate who was the better keeper. Knott was, though, the better batsman.

"I guess it is like a goalkeeper in football, there is only space for one of them in the team. It's just the way it was."

Bob went on to that first tour knowing he was second fiddle to Knott. England won the Ashes series 2-0, our first Ashes win since 1956, and the New Zealand leg 1-0. Knott was excellent throughout, but in the first Test of the New Zealand tour, Bob was given the gloves in Christchurch; a Test match England won by eight wickets, with Bob taking two catches and a stumping.

"I knew I was going to be the understudy on that tour but I owe Ray Illingworth a lot for giving me my debut. I never dreamt I would be playing in New Zealand. I remember we had a team meeting and it came as a complete shock when Ray said he was giving Alan Knott a rest and I'd play the first Test. It was a great win and performance with Basil D'Oliveira getting a hundred and Derek Underwood a number of wickets."

With Knott coming back in for the final two Tests of the series, it would be six years before Bob was able to wear the gloves again in Test match cricket and this time it was Kerry Packer, who he had to thank. "I owe a huge debt of gratitude to Kerry Packer. He came along with World Series Cricket and took away a number of the super stars of cricket including Alan Knott. So, I owe Packer a lot as it helped me play 56 more times for my country."

And there was someone else Bob owed a lot to as well, the great all-rounder Sir Ian Botham. "Beefy was a genuine all-rounder who could win matches with both bat and ball; because he performed two roles it allowed the selectors to pick me for my wicket-keeping ability.

I don't think I'd have got in the England side these days as a wicket-keeper batsman, although I might have improved my batting now! I always did try to improve it, but I would never lose sleep if I wasn't batting well. However, I couldn't sleep if I wasn't keeping well. Wicket-keeping was the most important thing for me and the team. The game has changed now; selectors and captains will always go for batting all-rounders first."

Despite not getting the nod by the England selectors, Bob was selected for a Rest of the World squad to tour Australia in 1971. The tour was put on as a replacement series for South Africa who were now in international exile because of apartheid. It was a huge honour for Bob who got the opportunity to share a dressing room with the likes of Lloyd, Sobers, Pollock, Gavaskar, Greig to name just a few.

"Donald Carr, my first captain at Derbyshire, had become the assistant secretary of the MCC and asked me if I would like to go to Australia with a rest of the world side. There had been a lot of pressure on the Australian cricket board to replace the South Africa series. It was a unique tour and was fantastic to be among those players. It was a fantastic squad."

Bob played in the last 'Test' of the series, a win at Adelaide, which gave the touring side a 2-1 series victory. But it was the whole experience off the field that left Bob with many cherished memories.

"The start of the tour was chaos: there was total segregation. The West Indian players were in one part of the dressing room and others in the other half. Nobody mixed. There was no team spirit or anything. Norman Gifford, Richard Hutton and I suggested to our management team that we needed to build team spirit. We formed a Saturday night club, where we'd all get together, have a drink, and let our hair down and just enjoy each other's company. Our first 'club' saw Norman and I as barmen; I'd pinned a notice to the dressing room outlining the dress code: jock strap, white sock, black sock and a comb in your hair. Honestly you should have seen Clive Lloyd and Gary Sobers with a jock strap on, odd socks and a comb in their hair. It was funny to see the management team's faces with us all dressed the same as that! What I didn't realise was the Muslims in the group didn't drink. Richard noticed they weren't drinking so he fined them five dollars - they soon started after that! Everyone had a great time! Sir Donald Bradman who was chairman of the Australian Cricket Board thanked us for helping them out and I remember him saying Sobers' 250 in Melbourne was the best innings he'd ever seen – a huge compliment from the greatest batsman of all time."

When Knott was banned from international cricket in 1977 for turning to World Series Cricket, Bob was back in the selectors' thoughts and returned to Test cricket for the tour that year to Pakistan. Bob became a regular and was first choice keeper for the series that followed against New Zealand, Australia and India. Bob's performances behind the stumps were outstanding, but he missed the 1981 tour to West Indies – the selectors preferred the superior batting of Paul Downton and David Bairstow.

A 5-0 whitewash and some mistakes by Paul Downton behind the stumps in the first Test of the 1981 Ashes series saw a press campaign to get Bob back behind the stumps. The selectors bowed to the pressure and Bob was back for the second Test at Lord's, Ian Botham's last as captain.

"It was great to be back in the side. Downton had missed a few chances and people were calling for me to return. I always loved playing at Lord's. I can tell you, walking through those Grace Gates on the first morning of an Ashes Test is something very, very special, quite nerve wracking actually. We drew the match; Botham bagged a pair and the press got on his back. Beefy's batting and bowling had suffered as captain and he resigned. Mike Brearley took over and we headed to Headingly 1-0 down. We were heading for an innings defeat until Beefy ended up with his famous 140 odd. Graham Dilley supported him so well. Their heroics saw us set them 130 or so to win, which in Test terms is not a big score."

I asked Bob, if the side felt the momentum had shifted and as a team, they felt they could win the game? "We had to believe we could do it. But we knew someone had to do something incredible. Bob Willis started bowling from the football stand end but he wasn't getting any rhythm. Mike Brearley, Ian Botham, David Gower and I got together and we decided to give Bob a try at the other end. He got rhythm, pace and bounce and the game suddenly started to change. When Dennis Lillee chipped one up to Mike Gatting who dived full length at mid-on, we knew we had a chance as the last two batters to come in were Ray Bright and Terry Alderman. I remember when they were eight down, and we were waiting for Ray Bright to come in, I turned around and saw the Ladbrokes marquee. When we were batting, we all saw the digital scoreboard put up the Ladbrokes odds. We were 500/1 against. I was genuinely going to put £2 on. The trouble was the marquee was on the other side of the ground. I started making my way over to it during a lunch break, but I had a ton of children coming up to me asking for autographs, who I couldn't say no to. By the time I finished signing, I had no time to get to the marquee. When I looked at the marquee at eight   wickets down, I realised I could have won a thousand pounds if I hadn't of done those autographs, which was a lot of money in those days – it still is now of course, but it was a huge amount then! As is well documented Dennis Lillee and Rod Marsh did put some money on - at least I was going to back my own team! Of course, it was different in those days, you would never get away with that now!"

England got the last two wickets and the game went down in history. Botham's Ashes was alive.

"We went to Edgbaston after that and we were in a similar situation again, albeit on a much flatter wicket. Australia only needed a low hundred score to win and at tea were 80 odd for 5. Mike Brearley told us we had to get stuck in. Just before heading out, Brearley had spotted that Beefy was putting his Nike tennis shoes on and asked him what he was doing and Botham, the strong personality that he was, replied that he wasn't expecting to be bowling. Brearley told him to get his bowling boots on. Beefy tried to call his bluff but the tone of Brearley's voice got a lot firmer and just told him to get his bowling boots on and get out to the middle, the umpires were all waiting for us. Brearley did make Beefy bowl and he went out and got five wickets for one run and won us the game!"

The result put England 2-1 up in the series – a remarkable turnaround. However, sadly for Bob, Alan Knott having returned from the Packer series was available for selection again and with England's poor batting in the series, he replaced Bob behind the stumps. A kick in the teeth for Bob after his great work behind the stumps in those two outstanding wins.

"It was very disappointing have gone from 1-0 down to 2-1 up and then get left out. I didn't get many runs but I caught quite a few catches and kept wicket well throughout. But the selectors just said I wasn't getting enough runs. I was naturally very disappointed but the team went on to Old Trafford and Ian Botham got another magnificent hundred as England beat Australia again to go 3-1 up."

I asked Bob about Brearley's captaincy. What made him such an astute captain? "He just knew how people's minds ticked. He knew how to get the best results from his players. He knew who needed a kick up the backside and who needed some comforting words. And importantly he knew the game of cricket inside, out. He always confided in his senior players and he just gave you confidence that he knew what he was doing. And above all, he was a lovely man."

Bob toured India and Sri Lanka over the Winter of 1981/82, playing in seven Test matches, his keeping accounted for another 19 dismissals. A home series against India followed and he was back down under in 1982 where he scored his 11,000th first class run in a match against Queensland. He kept in all five Tests of that Ashes tour.

His final appearance for his country came in 1984 in Lahore and he retired from first class cricket later that year.

"It was an easy decision to retire. I'd been playing for 23 years and the time was right."

But what a career; a world record number of dismissals and, for someone who was often left out for his batting, still scored over 12,000 first class runs by the time he hung up his gloves – an amazing record.

I asked Bob, reflecting on all of those dismissals, which was his favourite; but for him it was a dismissal that was never given! A decision not given by the famous umpire Shakoor Rana – think Mike Gatting's wagging finger, a few years later.

"As wicket-keepers we love making stumpings. I remember in Pakistan I was keeping to John Lever. We'd got their opening batsman out and Javed Miandad walked out to the middle. We were going to bat last on this turning wicket and they had a good leg spinner called Abdul Qadir. John Lever bowled to Javed and he played the ball back down the wicket. Next ball, I stood up to the stumps, as the batsmen were roughing up the pitch for the likes of Qadir. John bowled this ball, swung it, Javed danced down the wicket and tried to nip it through mid-wicket, he played and missed and I took the ball down the leg side and removed the bails all in one movement. It was a dream dismissal for a wicket-keeper. I turned around to the square leg umpire to appeal and there was Shakoor Rana looking up into the stands. He totally missed it and it was given not out. That would have been my finest stumping without doubt."

Bob kept to many fine bowlers during his career so I asked him who was the most difficult to keep to. "It was always the left handers. When I coach now, I always tell young wicket-keepers to practice and practice in the nets against left handers, because if you nail that everything else will become easier. One player I would love to have kept to though was Shane Warne. He was without doubt, the best spinner there has ever been."

Bob also talked at length about the importance of concentration and focus. "As a keeper, you have to concentrate from ball one through to the last ball of the day."

He recalled keeping in the sub-continent as a typical example. "There is nothing harder for a keeper than keeping in places like India, Pakistan and Sri Lanka. You're playing against some of the greatest batsmen on flat wickets, in 90-degree temperatures with searing humidity. At the end of a six-hour day you're hot and sweaty; you've hardly touched the ball as batsmen are scoring off most of them and if you're not concentrating on that last ball of the day, you'll drop that chance. There is nothing more deflating, because you know that batsman will go on and on. You have to concentrate all the time. It can be tough."

Cricket has changed a lot since Bob played. T20 cricket is now at the fore, batsmen are playing more expansive shots, I asked him how he felt he would fare. "They'd be no problem at all with my keeping. The shots have evolved but I'd have adapted; who knows my batting might have improved as well!"

Bob is still involved in cricket. He continues to coach young wicket-keepers at coaching clinics at Marlborough and Harrow schools - passing on his huge experience to talented youngsters. He also does some consultancy work for Dukes cricket balls. It's great to see him still involved in the sport he loves so dearly.

Bob is an icon in English cricket, one of the finest wicket-keepers this country has produced. People use the word 'great' quite loosely these days, but Bob Taylor was a great player for England, one of the best wicket-keepers to have ever played the game. In any other era, he would have played well over 100 Test matches for his count

2

CLIVE RADLEY
FORMER MIDDLESEX & ENGLAND BATSMAN

Clive Radley is a Middlesex legend. His first-class career spanned 23 years (representing just one county), and he scored over 26,000 first class runs, with a Test batting average of 48.10.

A late starter in Test cricket, Clive's average is up there with some of the greats of the game. However the fact it came from just eight Test matches is more to do with poor selection and of course a horrible injury when Clive was hit on the head by a bouncer (there was no helmet) which brought a premature end to what had become a promising start to international cricket. But we'll come on to Clive's international career later on.

Let's begin with Middlesex and how the start of his long career with the county began. "I came from Norfolk where there wasn't much first-class cricket," remarked Clive. "I was playing cricket at school when I got selected for Norfolk in the minor counties. Bill Edrich a former player for Middlesex and England had retired and came back to live in the area and signed for Norfolk and became their captain. He recommended me to Middlesex, where he was still on the committee – I guess I was just fortunate to be in the right place at the right time."

On the strength of that recommendation, in 1961 Clive was offered a three-year contract. "To get offered a three-year contact to play at Lord's, you jump at it. But it would never be heard of these days. Now you would have trials; play second eleven games. They must have thought Bill Edrich was a pretty good judge!"

The first year of the contract saw Clive play for Middlesex's 'club and ground' side, which was an XI that played local club sides and some county second XI's. "I did well in that first year and in my second year I progressed to being a regular in the second XI."

Clive broke into the first XI in his third year and from there didn't look back. It was rapid progress for the talented batsman. And his position in the first XI was cemented following an outstanding hundred against the touring South Africans in 1965. "I didn't look back after that. It was the last South African team to tour England before apartheid. They were captained by Peter van der Merwe and had players like the two Pollocks, Eddie Barlow and Dennis Lindsay. They were a top side. They had just come off a Test match win at Trent Bridge and

came to play us at Lord's. I scored 138 and that was the start for me. Fred Titmus and I put on 230 odd for the 6th wicket, which was a club record until recently."

"To get a good hundred that early in my career did make a few headlines. If I'm honest I always had a pretty ugly technique – but it was effective!"

In his early days in the Middlesex first XI, Clive would often find himself batting as low as number 7. "A couple of the old pros, Titmus and Murray batted at five and six and didn't like to be separated so I just slipped in at number 7. I knew I'd have to wait my turn to bat higher up, so I just had to wait for my opportunity to arise and make sure I took it when it did come. I batted at number seven for a while. In fact, in my first Gillette Cup game I went in at number 9, which was probably the lowest I batted!"

In Clive's early years as a first-class cricketer, the game was going through a lot of change. Limited overs cricket was introduced for the first time. I asked Clive how the players in that era adapted to the short format of the game being introduced. "The Gillette Cup was first launched in 1963 as a straight knock-out competition; so, if you got knocked out in the first round, that was it until the following season. You could play just one game a season. Cricket was all based around the 3-day County Championship. You'd play on Wednesday, Thursday and Friday and then Saturday, Monday and Tuesday with Sundays off. Regular 40-over cricket came in in 1969 and it meant you had to work out a new way to play, a way to score quickly. The shapes of bats have changed massively in recent years, but in those days, there were no huge edges, all of the bats were lightweight, so you had to take a few more risks with your batting in order to score quicker. But similar to T20 cricket now, limited overs cricket changed the County Championship. In those days you were setting a team a target of 250 after lunch, depending on the wickets. Now some teams knock that off in the last session! It has made the game better to watch."

"A lot of the older players weren't too enthused about limited overs cricket. We'd have team meetings and the older guys would say we'd need an anchor to bat all the way through, so somebody was employed to do that role. Look at the game now, you go all out from both ends."

Clive enjoyed a 27-year career at Middlesex and his list of honours is remarkable: four County Championships (plus one Championship that was shared) and six one-day trophies – a truly decorated career. What was the catalyst for such success? What made Middlesex so successful?

"We always had a good side, but when Mike Brearley came in as captain we really started winning. We typically had five internationals in our team at any one time. We also had a very good overseas player in Wayne Daniel. Wayne was a 100 percenter and because of the strength of the West Indian bowling attack at the time, we were fortunate that we didn't lose him to international commitments and we'd get a full season from him, year after year: he was a trier. He just gave 100 percent for 10 years. We also had a couple of very good spinners in Titmus and Emburey and after that Edmonds and Emburey. It was a strong side."

But what made players want to play for Brearley, where did his magic as a captain come from?

"You all felt you were included under Mike. He wasn't a massive up-and-at-them kind of a captain in a team talk situation. But tactically he would work different people out and was just outstanding. He'd also never be afraid to ask his players for advice. Yes, he'd have the final decision, but he made you feel that you were contributing to decisions. In my opinion, he is the best captain of all time. That said I'm not sure he always used his resources too well at Middlesex. My eight wickets from throughout my career came at exactly 20, I was a top-drawer bowler and he wouldn't bloody bowl me! He'd only bring me on if he was looking for a declaration! Who knows if he'd used his resources better he could have been an even stronger captain!"

Clive scored 53 first class and List A hundreds and 196 half centuries in his magnificent career, but what was his most memorable from all of these walks to the wicket?

"We had a one-day final at Lord's against Essex where we only scored 180 odd runs, but I scored 87 of them and was given man of the match. To be honest it wasn't my innings that made the game so memorable, but just the game itself. The ball was doing a bit and Brears was out first ball. We struggled to get 187 and when they went out to bat the sun came out and the pitch got flatter. Gooch was batting with them at 120 odd for 1 and the Middlesex supporters were beginning to head home. We then got a wicket and our only chance of winning was to put everyone around the bat. Remarkably they collapsed like a pack of cards and we ended up winning by six or seven runs. Through the years

there were lots of close encounters but this is the one game that always stood out for me. It's funny, for me it was never the hundreds that stood out, but more the matches. For example, I remember batting at Bradford, when I got the one injury I suffered in my whole career. I dropped a catch and dislocated my finger; Brearley told me to go home as it was unlikely I'd take any further part in the game. He just told me to keep an eye on the game, and if it did look like getting close then come back up. By Tuesday the game was close. I couldn't drive because my arm was in a sling, so I got the train up and the game reached a state where we needed four to win, when the 9th wicket fell. I went out to bat with my arm in a sling and because it was my left hand that hurt, I batted with just my right hand. It worked in the shower when people were chucking a ball at me, but out in the middle, I couldn't get my hand down in time. Anyway, I was kicking the ball away, but I was getting closer and closer to an LBW so I decided to take the sling off and just bat normally. The bloke bowled me a short one which I cut for three which made the scores level and kept me on strike for the next over. Next ball I got stumped by Bairstow and we drew the game! It was the first and only time I got a standing ovation from a Yorkshire crowd for batting so bravely!"

Clive's outstanding form for Middlesex was often overlooked by the national selectors, I asked Clive how frustrating was that? "It was frustrating. I felt I was pretty consistent over the years, but I knew I wasn't a flair player. I didn't really come into the reckoning until 1977, when in my benefit year I had a very good season. I thought that year was my final chance, if I wasn't going to get picked after that year then I'd never get picked."

At the end of that season Clive did finally receive a letter from the selectors. Sadly, it wasn't selection, but it was a notification asking if he could keep himself fit for the Winter tour to Pakistan and New Zealand, if injuries were to arise. Clive was finally in the selectors' thoughts.

"A letter dropped on the doormat from Alec Bedser, the chairman of selectors, asking me if I would be prepared to stay fit for the Winter for the princely sum of £50 in case a batsman went bust during the series. I honestly thought that was as close as I'd ever get as batsmen rarely get injured on tour – it's always the bowlers. Anyway, I said yes and I headed to Australia to do some coaching for Kerry Packer. I left my phone number with the selectors in case of any eventualities; at 2am the phone rang and it was Donald Carr at Lord's informing me that Mike Brearley had broken his arm in Karachi. I was to be on a flight at 8am so I thought I'd better getting packing! My Mrs woke up and asked what I was doing, I'd forgotten about her! I told her I had to go to Karachi! I was booked on a Thai International flight. I made the flight and we stopped off at Bangkok to refuel. When we took off, the captain announced that we had to go back because the wheels wouldn't go up. So, we turned back. 24 hours in Bangkok meant I missed the Test match, they selected Mike Gatting instead. I was angry with Thai International and I thought they had cocked my chance up of ever playing for England. Thankfully Gatt only scored 4 and 0, which meant when I flew on to New Zealand for that leg of the tour there might still be a chance of getting picked. We lost the first Test in

Wellington and I got picked for the second Test in Christchurch. I nearly didn't play though! Geoffrey Boycott had taken over from Brearley as captain and it

wasn't until 15 minutes before the start of the game, that he made the decision to pick me. I found out when he came back from doing the toss!"

Clive scored 15 on his Test debut, but in the second Test at Auckland, he made history. His 158 was the slowest Test century ever scored! In total Clive faced 524 balls during his 648-minute stay at the crease! "It was a bloody boring innings! It was a flat low wicket and there was a rugby match being played the following week so they kept the grass a bit longer – you couldn't hit the ball off the square! I just kept receiving messages in the middle from Boycs telling us just to keep batting and batting. So, we did. I returned to New Zealand 15 years later, when I was coaching and as I was walking around the ground to the commentary box, some guy in the crowd shouted: 'there goes that bastard who bored me to death'!"

Clive followed that hundred up with another century in his next Test match the following Summer in the first match of the series against Pakistan at Edgbaston – a century that was a lot quicker!

"I played in all of the Test matches that Summer and did OK." He certainly did do OK, with back to back half centuries in the second series of the Summer against New Zealand, Clive had cemented his place at number three and was selected for the Winter Ashes tour to Australia. It was a dream come true.

Sadly, for Clive, he never added to his Test caps following a horrific injury in a warm-up game in Adelaide. "I got hit on the head by Rodney Hogg and players didn't wear helmets in Test cricket in those days. I thought it was meant to be a flat wicket but this kid had just come on the scene and was pretty quick and I ended up with a nasty bump! Adelaide Hospital did a good job, stitched me up and I was back in the dressing room. Both (Ian Botham) of course asked me what all the fuss was about! When we flew up to New South Wales, Brears asked me to go and have a net with Botham and Willis with a new ball and have them bowling bouncers at me to see if I had lost my confidence. I had one of the first batting helmets that they were using in the World Series in my kit bag – a big white crash hat that looked like a motorbike helmet! I wore that into the nets when some guy came up to me and said why didn't I try one of these new helmets. He gave me one and said he made them in his backyard. It was a helmet with flaps on the side and didn't look as bad as the motorbike helmets. I wore it and then took it back to the dressing room and the likes of Gower and Randall were saying it didn't look so bad. By the end of that series, all the players on both sides were wearing them. That's when helmets started. They took off like wild fire after that."

Clive's confidence had taken a knock though and he never played for England again after that blow to the head. "With the likes of Jeff Thompson around my confidence did take a knock and you know what: injury was the reason I got into the England side and injury was the reason I had to stop. But I played eight times for my country. If I'm honest, I probably wouldn't have got into the England side if it wasn't for World Series and England losing a few players. So, I have to be happy with eight caps and a Test match average of 48."

But Clive's confidence wasn't totally shot as he still played another 10 years for his county. "I'm not sure if the blow did affect my batting, but helmets did make you play a bit differently. I certainly felt safer."

Clive went on to play until he was 43 and was a one-club player having represented only Middlesex. "In those days, no one ever really moved to other counties. I don't know if that was because of loyalty or because of wanting a benefit. With the financial rewards in the game today, benefits don't mean as much, but they certainly did back then. But for me, Lord's wasn't a bad place to be playing your cricket and secondly, we were successful – that makes a big difference. It's far better playing for a winning side."

I had to ask Clive when he looked back throughout his long career who were the most difficult bowlers (and batters) he faced? "Derek Underwood was always difficult on a wet pitch, but Sylvester Clarke was lethal. Batting wise Barry Richards was a class act as was Graham Pollock. I remember when Barry Richards scored 77 against us and Emburey and Edmonds on a turner; in his book, he said that was the best knock he played. It's very sad he never got the opportunity to play many Test matches."

When Clive finished playing, he did a 2-year stint coaching Middlesex's 2nd XI before taking over as head coach of the MCC. "Timing again was everything for me. I did a couple of years at Middlesex and they were looking for me to take over from Don Bennett, but then I could see Gatt was coming towards the end of his career and so I felt they would be lining something up for him. As it happened, at that time the MCC head coach role became available. I was asked to apply and I got the job. You know what? It was the best thing that could have happened to me. I felt it was a prestigious role and I enjoyed developing youngsters. We'd have 18 to 22 young cricketers typically on the staff who were trying to get a deal with a county. A lot of good players went through that MCC system. For me it was a fairly secure job, compared to the pressures of a county coach, where a few bad results would put you under pressure."

Clive remained in that role until he was 65, when he then took another role, in the MCC Universities programme. "Coaching was always the next best thing to playing. I got a great satisfaction when players went on to have good careers. 25

percent of professionals came through that system."

Clive did so much for the sport of cricket; so much so, that his efforts were rightly rewarded with a trip to Buckingham Palace after he was awarded an MBE in 2008. "What a lovely day that was. Brilliant. The Queen though I think thought I was the groundsman! She said to me that I must know every blade of grass on that Lord's outfield; I didn't know how to respond. The only words that came out were 'yes, and I'm going back to cut it!'. She honestly must have thought I was the groundsman! She did laugh though!"

This wasn't the last honour to come Clive's way. In 2013, he was named President of his beloved Middlesex. "What another great honour. It was a little bit different sitting in committee rooms rather than dressing rooms, but you always got looked after at away games!"

Clive may now well be trimming the grass in his garden and picking up leaves, but he has left cricket with a real legacy. Cricketers and cricket fans throughout the country should be forever grateful for what he has done for the game we love so much.

Clive – thank you.

3

JOHN LEVER
FORMER ENGLAND & ESSEX SWING BOWLER

John Lever was one of the finest left arm seamers to have pulled on the Three Lions. A bowler who took over 1,700 first class wickets in a career that brought 21 Test appearances, 22 one-day internationals, four county championships, three Sunday League titles, a NatWest Trophy and a B&H Cup.

I caught up with John, just a few weeks after the 2017/18 Ashes series finished in a comprehensive win for the home side. With people questioning the depth of our fast bowling it seemed an appropriate place to start. Are our bowling stocks really so low? "Let's be honest we got blown away by three of the quickest bowlers around at the moment. I watched it and just thought we had no answer to that. To be successful you need to have that fast pace, especially on flat pitches, but you also need your 'technical' bowlers. We have the bowlers in England. We just have to encourage our quick bowlers with the pitches we prepare. Mark Wood has that x-factor and I honestly believe

Steven Finn can come good again. But we have to encourage them. They need to be playing on pitches which encourages the ball to really hit the gloves of the wicket-keeper." Wise words.

John was the one of the finest swing bowlers to play for England. Sadly, for various reasons (form, nerves, poor selection decisions, and of course a rebel tour to South Africa) he only played in 21 Tests – it should have been so many more.

But, let's start at the beginning: John Lever the schoolkid.

"When I look back, I was very lucky to have a headmaster at my junior school, who was very keen on cricket. Every lunchtime in the Summer I was bowling at stumps in the playground and it totally fired my interest in cricket. It was great bowling in front a crowd of kids!"

John's love, passion and talent saw him develop quickly and by his early teens he was invited to the Ilford Indoor cricket school which has been a breeding ground over the years for many Essex cricketers.

"A gentleman called Bill Morris took me under his wing and thought I could bowl. He really pushed me forward. I was invited to bowl at Essex pros on a Tuesday evening which really helped my development to be able to bowl at second eleven players at such a young age. It was special."

With no contract on the table from Essex, Middlesex were keen to offer John a professional contract, but in those days a county had to gain permission from the county the youngster was born in before they could sign him. Middlesex's approach pushed Essex into offering the young seam bowler a contract. He never looked back.

"There wasn't any money at Essex at the time. As a result, they used to use a few good local club cricketers in their squad to make up the numbers. In those days we were playing 24 or 25 games of cricket, so a big squad was important. I was also fortunate that in my first year, I knew it was going to be Trevor Bailey's last year and Barry Knight had decided to move to Leicestershire so there was space on the staff at Essex for a seamer. K.D. Boyce also joined at the same time, as an overseas quick bowler from Barbados, and it was the start of a new young side at Essex."

While it took a number of years before the first trophy was secured, the foundations were being laid for a period of sustained success. "We were a young side that were always happy to learn. We were the best fielding side in the country and we were a team that really embraced the one-day game. Off the field we were also very disciplined. We stayed on the rails and it allowed Brian Taylor and Keith Fletcher to grow and flourish as captains. They turned us into a winning outfit."

To say that the Essex side of the late 70s and early 80s were like the Manchester United of the 1990s and 2000s is not far off the mark. The Benson & Hedges was won in 1979 – Essex's first silverware in over a hundred years and this was quickly followed by County Championship wins in 1979, 1983, 1984 and 1986, the Sunday League in 1981, 1984 and 1985 and the NatWest Trophy in 1985: nine trophies in seven years, a phenomenal achievement.

"To be honest we were knocking on the door from 1975 onwards. We were getting to semi-finals and quarter-finals and we were creeping up the county championship every season, but everything snowballed after we beat Surrey in the final of the Benson & Hedges Cup at Lord's. We hadn't won anything for so long, but we got over the line in that final and then the floodgates opened. We suddenly had a self-belief that we knew would win when we took to the field. Later that year we won the championship with a month to go, we were that far in front. It was a nice feeling. We all knew each other's games. Whoever ran up to bowl we had belief they would take a wicket. None of us wanted to play anywhere else. Essex was such a friendly club, the players, committee and supporters all played their part in that successful period."

John success at Essex brought its reward, internationally, in 1976, when he was selected for England's Winter tour of India.

"It was fantastic to get a call up. Its everyone's dream to play for their country. I was fortunate on that first tour that I knew most of the squad. I was very close to Geoff Miler and having Fletch on the trip really helped. I also think it's easier to make your debut away from home; away from the scrutiny that you can get at home with the media. To be honest the realisation that I was playing for England didn't really sink in until after we had won that first Test match and I received the press cuttings from back home saying how well I had done."

To say John had done 'well' is a bit of an understatement. His debut Test saw him make, what was, at the time, the best debut figures (10-70, including a 7-46) by any bowler to play for England, not to mention a first innings half century with the bat!

"It was fantastic to win in India, because winning out there is hard, and it was obviously nice to take all of those wickets. What made it special for me was that four of the wickets were LBW's, which with local umpires at the time was unheard of."

It was a proud record that stood for nearly twenty years until Dominic Cork bettered it against the West Indies.

"It was funny because we always used Duke balls in India. But in the warm up games, the Indian board were trying these new cricket balls, which were swinging around corners, so our team manager Kenny Barrington approached the Indian board and said how we'd be happy to use the Indian balls in the Test series and that we were impressed with the quality and it was important to give them a chance. This made the Indian board happy, not realising that we were only happy because of the amount of swing they generated!"

England won the series convincingly, and it had been a dream debut series for John. But controversy followed. John and the team were accused of doctoring the ball with Vaseline. "I was gutted. I worked so hard on that tour and for people to say I cheated to take those wickets really hurt."

With the heat in Madras at ridiculous temperatures, a number of England's players applied Vaseline above their eyes to stop sweat going into them. "It was an old trick which footballers used to do but we never rubbed Vaseline into ball."

Once the allegations came to light the authorities took the match balls away for independent testing. The results proved nothing was untoward. There was the usual sweat, saliva and sunscreen but no traces of Vaseline whatsoever.

"I felt vindicated, but some people still said I cheated, which was the downside of that tour for me."

Following that tour, England headed to Australia for the centenary Test match at the MCG. "I thought I was going to get a lot of stick from the Australian crowd while I was fielding on the boundary, but I didn't receive any at all."

John took four wickets in that centenary Test match, a one-off Test that the Aussies won by 45 runs. "I was never one for sitting in the opposition dressing room, but that Test match gave me the opportunity to meet Dennis Lillee. I was determined to go and meet one of my heroes after the game. He was such a great competitor and had the best bowling action of any bowler that I have seen. He just had such a superb attitude."

John went on to play 20 Test matches for his country before taking the difficult decision to go on a rebel tour to South Africa.

"I wish I had played more Test matches for England but there were a lot of quality seamers around at that time. There was Bob Willis and not long after my debut Ian Botham hit the scene. Then there was Chris Old, Mike Hendrick and me fighting for one place. I kind of missed out playing Test matches at home but would get selected for the overseas trips. I think it was because I was consistent on overseas pitches. I was happy to bowl the long spells and didn't really ever break down. I could be relied upon. I was desperate to play more Test matches at home; it just wasn't to be. I'm not sure why, however I'll admit I did get nervous at home and felt the pressure a lot more than when I played away."

So, with a passion for Test match cricket, why did he take the decision to go to South Africa? "I had just come back from the worst series I'd played in, in India. They went 1-0 up in that series and from then on, the pitches were the flattest pitches I'd ever seen. Add to that they were bowling their spinners at 12 overs an hour, and we matched that. It was boring. Absolutely boring cricket. I came to the end of that series and I felt blunted as a bowler. Nothing carried through to the keeper it was just awful cricket and I wasn't enjoying it. The main reason I played cricket until I was nearly 40 was because I enjoyed it. But this period was horrible. Keith Fletcher was removed as captain and I wasn't sure it was an environment that I wanted to be involved in. Then somebody said that there was a trip happening to South Africa with a few pounds in it and if I fancied going. I said yes straight away. I thought there might be a bit of come-back, but no way did I think I would be banned for three years. I thought that was way over the top, but anything around apartheid at that time brought a knee jerk reaction from the administrators. When we arrived in South Africa there were no cricket writers, it was all the news teams of the mainstream media. We voted Graham

Gooch in as our captain. The interesting thing for me was there were two big advertising boards in the ground, one was a well-known UK bank and the other a well-known UK petroleum company. So, it seemed a bit wrong that this team of cricketers were being punished when it was OK for big UK companies to carry on doing their business out there with no issues."

While John admits money was a factor in the tour, there was also a sense among the players that South Africa needed these tours to help with the development of cricket and to overcome apartheid. "They were trying very hard in the cricket to be multi-racial. Bacher was desperate to get South Africa back competing internationally and saw these games as part of their way back. The rest of the world I'm sure didn't see it that way. But after we got back a West Indian side went out, followed by a Sri Lankan side and an Australian side."

The squad lost the series. "They were really hard games. Some of the hardest games that I played in. They had some fabulous players. Richards, Pollock, Rice, Kirsten, Jennings. It was hard fought stuff."

Following that tour John and other members of the squad spent the Winter months while banned from playing for England, playing again in South Africa. "I went to Natal with Les Taylor where we played with Richards, Proctor and Chris and Robin Smith. Robin and I got close after that. He was a top bloke and an extremely dedicated cricketer. Goochy went to Western Province and Wayne Larkins to Eastern Province."

I asked John if looking back he regretted the decision to go?

"Honestly? No. I never sat down and thought I shouldn't have gone. There were times as I was taking 100 wickets each year with Essex that I thought if I hadn't been banned, perhaps I would have played more Test matches. But I wasn't enjoying my cricket. I can't tell you just how deflated I was after that India series and when I made that decision about South Africa. I think it also helped me during that period that Essex were winning. It filled the void. All of the games we played meant something and had to be won."

A 21st Test cap did eventually follow though; in 1986 John was recalled for a Test match against India at Headingley. "I was very proud to win another cap, but I probably didn't do myself justice. Headingley is a hard place to bowl. People talk about the overhead conditions but there is a horrible slope which means you are either bowling up or downhill."

Conditions aside, John did perform well. He took wickets, including Kapil Dev for a golden duck, but it was to be the only appearance of a brief recall. "I think Goochy helped get me back when Gatt was looking for a swing bowler for that match. It was a horses for courses selection, really."

That final appearance at Headingley meant John's Test career finished with 73 wickets from his 21 Tests at an average of under 27. The impressive thing about John's international career was his ability to bowl so well in all conditions as a seam bowler. I asked John how easy or difficult he found it, as a swing bowler, to bowl in such different conditions around the world. How much did he have to adapt his game?

"The hardest thing was adapting to the Kookaburra ball. Any bowler should be able to work out what length to bowl after an over or two, but it was never easy with a Kookaburra ball once it stopped swinging. That said I was always impressed with what Glenn McGrath achieved with that ball. It was a lesson to many. He had the ability to nip the ball back and bowled an unbelievable line. But I think if you're a swing bowler you can perform on all surfaces, in all conditions. I remember not getting picked for the West Indies, because apparently it wouldn't swing out there. Geoff Arnold went out there instead, swung the ball and got wickets. The only time it doesn't swing is if you have a wet ball. Otherwise you should be able to swing or get reverse swing."

John eventually retired from first class cricket in 1989 and he knew his time was up. "My arm had gone so I knew it was time. I made my mind up halfway through that last season. My final game was a one-day game, so I knew what my final ball would be. There was no fairy-tail – I was hit for four!!"

The following year, John was awarded an MBE for his services to cricket. "That was huge and a very proud moment. It came totally out of the blue. But I'd done my share of playing in charity games and it was given to me for my services to cricket. It was fantastic to go to the palace and receive an MBE from her majesty."

With John's cricket career over he moved into coaching at Bancroft School. A role he has remained in to this day. "I had a few opportunities once I finished playing. I was offered coaching roles at Northants and Hampshire, but I didn't want to stay on the circuit. I wanted to get out of my comfort zone and the role at the school gave me that opportunity. I also thought it was a cheap way to give my two youngsters a good education at a good school!"

Over the years John did keep some involvement in the county scene. He supported John Emburey at Middlesex and took several sessions with Essex, but the counties always wanted a full-time coach and John's heart has always been with Bancroft School.

Reflecting on his career I asked John who were some of the most difficult batsmen he bowled to?

"The West Indies boys. Greenidge, Haynes, Richards. They could intimidate bowlers; Graham Gooch was our equivalent. The difficult thing with these batters was you couldn't give them an inch, or they'd punish you."

And what about some of the best bowlers he played with or against? "Beefy was up there with Willis. Beefy could bowl quite quickly. He swung the ball and had a great belief in his own ability. Bob was genuinely quick. There was no better sight though for me than seeing Michael Holding run in and bowl. He was in the Lillee mould. You'd pay money to go and watch him bowl."

And finally, what about the best captain?

"Keith Fletcher. No question. I was always fascinated by his memory and how quickly he could sum up a new player. Within a couple of overs of seeing a new batsman, he had a plan and knew exactly how to get him out."

John was a fantastic cricketer and it was such a shame he didn't play more Tests for his country, however his 1,700 first class wickets brought special memories for supporters the world over and for that we say thank you.

4

ALAN BUTCHER
FORMER ZIMBABWE & SURREY COACH

If you're looking for a cricket book for your reading list, apart from this one of course, you will do no worse than logging on to Amazon and searching for 'The Good Murungu?: A Cricket Tale of the Unexpected'. The book chronicles former county cricketer and one-time England Test batsman Alan Butcher's three years in charge of the Zimbabwe national team. Amazon describes it as an 'insight into the, at times, schizophrenic nature of cricket in this intriguing country.' Part cricket memoir, part travelogue, part ode to Zimbabwe, part lament for a beautiful-but-troubled country, Alan describes the process of moulding a team out of a dispirited and disillusioned group of players.

And if that's not yet enough to tempt you to part with your cash, I spoke to Alan about his journey from a youngster, playing cricket for Beckenham CC, all the way through to his African adventure.

So what made Alan put pen to paper and write a book? "I woke up at 2.30am one morning and I just had this lightbulb moment that I wanted to tell the story," remarked Alan. "I opened up the laptop and started writing. At no stage did I have any thoughts about a plan to get it published. It was just fun writing it and getting all the thoughts off my chest."

But the book did get published and it's already on its second print run and has been put forward for consideration for this year's William Hill sports book of the year award.

So where did it all start for this former opening batsman. "I started playing cricket at Beckenham Cricket Club, but I really learnt my cricket in Australia."

At the age of 10, Alan and his family moved to South Australia. During his five years down under Alan played for South Australia at two sports, cricket and football. But cricket was always the first love. "My local club was South Road and I then played a bit for Brighton before playing youth cricket at Glenelg." Alan success at Glenelg saw him get selected for a B Grade district side called Junior Colts, which to use Alan's words were a "bit like the MCC young pros."

After five years in Australia, the Butcher family returned home to the UK. "We came back from Australia for family reasons. Personally, I would have been more than happy to have stayed. It was a great place to grow up, especially for lads who played sport."

On his return to the UK, Alan signed for Surrey, to the frustration of his mother! "My mother had dreams for me to come back and play for Kent! But we lived in Surrey and in those days you had to play for the county that you lived in. I trialled at the Oval and they offered me a contract near enough straight away. However, it was decided that I should carry on a school and get some O-levels. If I'm honest, I got an English A-level but never really did benefit from the O-levels - although they did always help with the Telegraph crosswords!"

Alan eventually made his debut for Surrey in a John Player League encounter away at Leicestershire, in 1971. "I made my debut as an opening bowler, rather than a batsman. Both Bob Willis and Geoff Arnold were injured and we had a shoestring staff at that stage. The debut went alright. I didn't have a lot of pace but I was accurate with the ball and bowled a good length which was accurate enough to trouble batsmen."

Figures of six overs for just 10 runs was an excellent return. However, with Surrey bowled out for just 116, his first experience with the bat was a painful one. "I got hit on the inside thigh by Australian opening bowler Graham MacKenzie. I'd never been hit that hard in all my life. The next day I played club cricket and was nearly run out trying to take a single to third man, my leg seized up!"

And that was the challenge for Alan - the increased skill of the bowlers. But his upbringing in Australia had given him good preparation. Remember, this was an era which included the likes of Holding, Garner, Marshall, Lillee, Thompson et al. "From 1976, there was more and more pace. But I found my time in Australia helped me. Playing B grade and district cricket against strong Australians - who also played Aussie Rules in the Winter - meant they bowled with some tremendous gas. They didn't mind bouncing a 13 or 14-year-old. I handled that well and I actually quite enjoyed it. It was fun. So I didn't find pace that much of a problem. The difficult aspect was the accuracy and you get less balls to score from. I had to learn to be more patient."

And learn he did. During Alan's time at Surrey, he enjoyed a successful opening partnership with Graham Clinton. The pair enjoyed 19 century stands as openers, including a 277 against Yorkshire in 1984. "Having a reliable opening partnership makes such a difference to the middle order of a team, because if you have stroke players coming in, and you've seen off the new ball and got the bowlers tired, they can benefit. It makes a huge difference to a team's ability to post a big total and put the opposition under pressure."

One amusing story Alan shared, was about an agreement he and Clinton had when facing the quick bowlers. "We had an agreement that we would always share out the batting against the quicks so one of us wouldn't get stuck up one end. We'd try and get the other off strike to share the load."

Sounds fair. Until one game at Old Trafford, when Surrey faced a Lancashire team, which included the hostile Michael Holding. "I remember we won the toss and put Lancashire into bat. We had a great day and bowled them out cheaply. The downside for me and Clint was we had to see out six overs at the end of the day. So Michael Holding had three overs to throw at us. He kicked off his run up from pretty much at the sightscreen and there was nobody fielding in front of me, apart from someone fielding at short-leg who was wishing me good luck. His first delivery bounced over the keeper's head into the sightscreen for four byes! The rest were length balls that came through at about throat height, at pace! A couple hit me on the bat handle, one went down the leg side, and I swayed away from another. I could see Clint's eyes getting wider and wider as the over went on. I walked down to him at the end of that first over, as you do, expecting him to meet me half way; I carried on walking and he turned his back on me. I said, 'here Clint, what's up? he replied: 'you know that agreement we've got; you can f&ck off'. I spent the rest of that session fending off Holding!"

I asked Alan, what it was like facing those bowlers without a helmet. "I faced Holding, Roberts and Daniel without a helmet. You never thought about it. I remember at Lord's, walking out to face Wayne Daniel. I put the cap on and walked out and honestly didn't think about it."

Not long after though, helmets were introduced for the players and after a while Alan knew the time had come to put safety first. "There eventually came a time, when I did think about wearing a helmet and I reasoned that if I was thinking about it, I probably should start wearing it. So I did from that point on. It wasn't comfortable at all to begin with, but I had seen the consequences of people not wearing them."

In 1979, Alan was picked to play for England against India in a Test match at The Oval. It was to be his only Test appearance and he was never selected to play for England again, despite the opinion of the then England captain Mike Brearley, who rated him one of the top players of fast bowling in the county game. A player who averaged between 1,300 and 1,700 runs each season during his time at Surrey.

"It was disappointing. Very disappointing. It was the usual thing, I got picked for the last Test match of the series at the Oval because of an injury to Wayne Larkins. Wayne had been earmarked for the tour that Winter to Australia. He broke his finger so I was in for him and I knew I had to do something special, as he would have recovered for the tour."

Scores of 14 and 20 meant Alan didn't cement his place. "I enjoyed the experience. It was a good Test match. But there were certain things that did disappoint me. For example, I can't remember being told where I was actually going to be batting in the order. I eventually found out 15 minutes before the start of play. As I put my pads on, I was pretty calm but as I walked out, Alec Bedser, who was chairman of selectors, called me into a corner and said, 'don't do anything bloody stupid out there will you?' Very encouraging words – I hope they don't do that now."

Understandably, that didn't put Alan in the greatest frame of mind to go and face his first ball in Test match cricket. "India bowled a good length. A few deliveries were wide outside off stump and in a county game I probably would have had a waft at a few, but in my first Test match and with those 'encouraging' words ringing in my ears, I kept leaving the ball. I only got to 14 by lunch, but I was feeling more comfortable; then I nicked one and got out. These things happen. At the end of the day, I didn't do enough to get on that plane ahead of Wayne Larkins."

Although Alan's international career was short-lived, his county career was far from so. Over 22,000 first class runs were scored during his time at both Surrey and Glamorgan at an average of 36.32, together with just shy of 150 first class wickets. Impressive statistics.

"We were a good side at Surrey. It was great to win the Gillette Cup in 1982, after being on the losing side for the last three. Those finals were big days in the cricket calendar. You always got big crowds and there was always a great atmosphere at Lord's. We were close a couple of times in the County Championship too. I was proud to have played in that era, with so many fine bowlers. It was really tough cricket. Teams were allowed two overseas players, so all of the best players in the world played over here. It was hard work, but good fun and enjoyable."

In 1986, Alan made the decision to move on from Surrey after 15 years to head west, to the Welsh county of Glamorgan. "I should probably have left a bit earlier. I was fed up with the way things were going at the club and how I was playing. It wasn't a difficult decision. If I'm honest, I was a little unsure of Glamorgan. At the time they weren't a very good side and moving from a big Test match ground to Sophia Gardens (as it was then) was a big adjustment. It was two totally different set-ups. But I quickly got used to that and it was good for me as I began to think that I was the best player there and that made me take responsibility and that brought the best out of me. I played really well and it was possibly the best period of my career. We had a lot of good players at Surrey, but I felt that if I nicked off, someone else would score runs and you might not always be 100 percent focused. Not deliberately, but maybe just as a consequence of having so many more, good players. At Glamorgan, I knew I had to get runs. I had to concentrate, work hard and score runs."

As mentioned in our interview with Hugh Morris, Alan took over as captain, after Hugh had stepped down from the position. "Hugh was young and captaincy was affecting his game. He had big ambitions of playing for England and felt captaincy was holding him back. Tony Lewis, the chairman, asked me if I would take over and I really enjoyed it. When I first arrived at Glamorgan it wasn't such a young side. The players had been there a while and were just chugging along. There wasn't the competition for places. Tony Lewis and I made the decision to get rid of some players and promote some of the youngsters. I found that brought the best way out of me as captain to bring players through. I felt we managed to change their mindset and, in some ways, the club and its members to. Previously we'd get beaten by a side like Middlesex and the reaction would be that it's Middlesex so it's expected. And we did change. Eventually (after I left) the team ended up winning the title."

One of the proudest games for Alan during his time at Glamorgan came in 1991, when he played against his son Mark, who was making his debut for Surrey, in a Sunday League match at The Oval. I asked Alan if it was an interesting week in the Butcher household, in the lead up to the game? "We didn't actually know! Glamorgan were playing at the Oval for a championship game. In those days, the championship game would start on a Saturday, then continue on Monday, with a Sunday League game sandwiched in between. I had a long-standing knee problem and decided I wasn't going to play on the Sunday to ensure I got through the Championship match OK. However, in the Surrey tavern on the Saturday night, Ian Greig told me that Mark was playing tomorrow. That was it, my knee was suddenly better! I just thought I can't miss this so I went to

Matt Maynard, who was going to captain the side and explained the situation. He said I had to play. Mark was 17 at the time and I remember we were winning the game quite easily, when Mark came into bat at number 7. He played well and in the end, he needed to hit the last ball for six to win the game. He said to me afterwards he had a plan. He knew he was going to receive a ball in the block hole, so thought he would step down the wicket so the bowler would drop his length, and then go back into his crease to then get underneath it and hit it on the up and out of the ground. As it turned out, I took my time to set the field and found myself at long on, thinking he'd have to hit it over my head to win the match. The bowler ran up, bowled the ball into the block hole and Mark just stood still and hit it into the ground. I asked him afterwards what happened, and he just replied that I took so long to set the field, he forgot his plan. Tough game son! But it was a proud moment."

Mark of course went on to a good career with England and is now impressing people with his media work on Sky Sports. "He's quite good isn't he? I enjoyed that 90s documentary he did for Sky. I'm getting a lot of people coming up to me, unsolicited and saying good things."

Back to the cricket, and in 1992 injury struck Alan, and he was forced into retirement. "It was a massive disappointment as I felt I was still playing really well and I knew that I was still capable of scoring enough runs. But I just couldn't shake the injury off. Even now it still affects me so I can't look back and think if I just gave it another six months."

And Alan shouldn't have any regrets. He had a great career during an era when some of the game's greatest players played the game. "Barry Richards and Viv Richards were the top batsmen I played against. John Edrich and Geoff Arnold were outstanding players and then there was the West Indian influx. It was unfortunate that I didn't play against them for England, but it was always a great challenge playing against them in county cricket. Holding was definitely the quickest, but I found the others gave me different problems. Croft had his funny action. Garner had the height and bounce. It was a tough era of county cricket."

After Alan's retirement, the former batsmen took on coaching roles at Surrey and Essex. "I initially took over at Essex after Keith Fletcher got the job with England. Goochie had retired as captain and Paul Prichard had taken over and we were building a good relationship. Then Keith got relieved of the England job and came back to Essex. I had been looking forward to the season, because I felt Pritch would need a bit more guidance from the coach than someone like Goochie would, so I was looking forward to a slightly enhanced coaching role, but then Keith coming back put paid to that. At just about the same time, Graham Dilley had given up his role at Surrey running the second team."

Surrey were a strong team in county cricket. "The team had won championships, one day trophies and had a good side, full of England players. So for me, being in charge of the second XI was important, as I was having to produce players to replace those that were away playing for England. It worked well, with the guys who stepped up from the second team, all performing."

Then in 2003, first team coach Keith Medlycott moved on and Alan thought his chance had come to take over the reigns of coaching the first eleven. "I felt I might have a chance to succeed him but the club went for Steve Rixon."

It was disappointing for Alan, given the way he found out, especially having applied for the position. "I was in the Surrey mail room one evening when one of the Surrey media guys came in and started talking about needing to get a press release out. I asked what it was about and he replied it was about Steve Rixon's appointment. I hadn't been told. I had been walking about the Oval for a week not knowing someone else had been offered the job and they were awaiting his reply. I was pi$$ed off. The reason I was given was that if they'd told me and he'd not accepted, I'd have known that I would have been second choice. My point was that if I'd have known, at least I could have been adult enough to make a decision with that knowledge, rather than be made to look like an idiot for a week." Alan remained as coach of the second eleven.

"I enjoyed the role so I carried on. But Steve Rixon and the first team squad didn't really hit it off and after a couple of seasons he was relieved of his duties and I eventually took over after we got relegated."

In Alan's first season as first team coach, Surrey secured promotion back to the top flight. "We got promoted the very next season. To be honest, the team were in a shocking state in terms of discipline. There had been a lot of problems with the coach, Ben Hollioake's death had, had a big effect and a few cliques were breaking out between the players. It wasn't a great atmosphere. I felt I worked hard to try and heal that and I believed I did so. Players were talking to each other again and we were walking in the right direction. We played some good cricket and won the division two title."

Sadly things got tougher for Alan after that successful first season. "A lot of the team I inherited were getting older and were creaking by the wayside. Guys like Mark (Butcher), who was captain, kept getting injured. His knee problems meant he missed a lot of the following season. Jimmy Ormond got injured, Ian Salisbury got injured, the list went on. A lot of people in the game thought we would win the division one title in that first season. We certainly prepared well, but with so many players injured at the same time, at the start of the season it was never going to happen. We had to bring young players in who weren't quite ready. Towards the end of the season we brought in

Harbhajan Singh and he helped us win games, as did Chris Jordan, and we ended up with quite a lot of youngsters coming in and doing well. We finished 4th which was credible. I remember we had a fantastic last game against Lancashire who needed to win to win the championship but we clung on and stopped them from doing so. Nothing against Lancashire but I just wanted the pride."

The third year was even tougher and Alan's side got relegated back to division 2. "We entered that following season thinking if could get those injured players fit, we could have a very good campaign. But Mark broke down again, Jordan got injured and we couldn't repeat what we did at the end of the previous Summer. We went the whole year without a win. But you know what? I couldn't have asked any more from the players. Everything we tried didn't work. We dropped an unbelievable amount of catches. I remember in one game we dropped 11. We got relegated and that was the end of me."

It was a frustrating end for Alan, especially as he had been tasked with guiding the team through the difficult transitional period. "I did feel it was a little harsh because the committee all season, and the season before, had said it was going to be a period of re-building. Mark had retired, Martin Bicknell had gone, Ian Salisbury had gone, literally everyone from our good side of the late 90s and early 2000s had left or retired. Having been told it would take four or five years by the committee, I was given six months."

It was a big learning experience for Alan. "One of the things I always found hard was what they call 'managing upwards'. Sometimes my relationships with my bosses were not as good as they could have been. I have to accept blame for some of that but if I'm honest, the reason for that was because I didn't have the respect for them. I didn't find it easy to have a good relationship with some of those people."

I asked Alan if it was easy or difficult to coach or captain his sons: both of Alan's sons, Mark and Gary played under him at various stages during Alan's captaincy and coaching career.

His response was that at times it could be difficult, but he recalls one father/son moment he was particularly proud of. "There was one time when Mark came to me after being left out of the England side. I stripped down his technique and put it back together again. He went on to score 500 runs against the Aussies in 2001. If you ask anyone who has worked in a father/son relationship, it can be difficult. You try and tell your son something and they never listen. But the fact Mark came to me made it easier. He took on board what I suggested and things worked out well."

Alan also has fond words for Gary. "Until recently, Gary was the last bowler to take four wickets in four balls. Alfonso Thomas did it again last season."

Interestingly, when Gary Butcher took those four wickets for Surrey against Derbyshire at the Oval, Alan had his first sighting of a young Kevin Pietersen. "I was at Leamington Spa, when news came through about Gary's wickets. We were playing Warwickshire 2's who had KP trialling for them. You could see his confidence. I remembered how commanding he was at the crease. Our opening bowler tried to rough him up, but KP hit him rows back into the stand. I remember calling my lads together in the dressing room and said that more of them needed that confidence and arrogance. Most of my players would go out to bat almost apologetically, whereas KP would stride out with a 'look at me' attitude. So even before he got a contract in county cricket, I'd always used him as an example for others."

Following his spell at Surrey, Alan tried to get back into the game quickly, but the right opportunity didn't come up. "I'd been out of work for a while when I went for an interview at

Lancashire, who were looking for a head coach. But they went for Peter Moores. In truth, I shouldn't have applied. It was still too soon after getting sacked from Surrey. That experience was too raw. I shouldn't have applied. I know a job is right for me because I get a mental picture for it inside. When I thought about that Lancashire job, I got nothing. I should have listened to myself. I didn't do a very good interview, so I wasn't surprised I didn't get it. I wasn't ready for it."

Instead, Alan spent some time working for the ECB. "I went to Pretoria with a group of youngsters, which included the likes of Hales, Willey and Bairstow. They were a group at the time, who were a tier below the Lions. I was a batting coach and quite a few of that group went on to good things."

Not long after this stint, Alan received a call out of the blue from former Zimbabwe batsman Dave Houghton.

"I had known Dave for a long time. During my time at Glamorgan we would often go on pre-season tours to Zimbabwe, when he was captain of the Zimbabwe national team. He also coached for a period, the second team at Worcester, so our paths often crossed and we shared similar philosophies on the game. Dave phoned me and said the Zimbabwe job was available and that he thought I'd be perfect for it. I said let me have a chat to my wife and daughters. We felt it'd be a good opportunity. I made my application and I went for an interview."

This time Alan had an excellent interview and the job was his. His first international assignment.

But it was going to be an interesting challenge. For a number of years Zimbabwe cricket had gone through a number of well publicised issues. England and other teams had refused to tour the African nation and they had not played Test cricket for many years.

"When I took over, they had been playing one day internationals, but there had been no Test cricket. Part of my job spec was to oversee the country's reintroduction to Test match cricket."

What followed was a project of trying to mould a team out of a dispirited and disillusioned group of players.

"Straight away they were due to go on tour to the West Indies, prior to the 2010 T20 World Cup. I went out there to observe. When I was appointed, Zimbabwe cricket was at the back end of their domestic season, so I went along to some matches and had some one-to-one chats with the tour party."

I asked Alan about the state of the domestic game in Zimbabwe and if he had a big pool of players to choose from?

"It's not a great domestic competition in Zimbabwe. If I'm honest, I've played for, and I've coached, county second teams that were as good as the franchise teams there. That wasn't to say there wasn't any talent, it's just if there are fewer talented players, it takes longer for them to develop and to get them ready for international cricket. The biggest problem was players didn't get continuous exposure to high quality opponents. I found that when we made some gains, there would then be no cricket for six months, and we were soon back to square one."

And then there were the off-the-field challenges. "I found out through various conversations I had that players were not being paid. They weren't receiving their bonuses. When I first arrived, there was a really good bonus structure in place. I don't think they expected us to win as many games as we did. It took me two years to get my bonus. It wasn't as much of an issue for me, but for some of the players not being paid bonuses or match fees was very serious, because of their personal situations. I was still getting my salary paid, so for me it was a minor irritation not getting my bonus and deep down I always thought I would get my money, eventually. But for some of the players it was the difference between feeding their family and paying their rent. It was that serious."

Alan recalls one occasion, prior to a tour to New Zealand, when one player who was selected had to ask Alan if he could borrow money. "This player hadn't featured for 18 months and wasn't expecting to be selected. He came to me and asked to borrow $300 to give to his wife so she could feed herself and the kids while he was away. It's not cheap in Zimbabwe to live. That player was not selected until three days before the tour, it was shambolic at times."

Alan had great help during his time in Zimbabwe from his coaching team. "They were very helpful at trying to understand and get information from the black Zimbabwe players, as they spoke the language and it meant I could get information on how they were feeling."

I asked Alan if there was ever a quota system in place, similar to that employed by South Africa. "There wasn't officially. There may have been in the past, but there were situations when selection was a definite issue."

So much so, it led to Alan resigning from his position on the selection committee – he later retracted the resignation. "On my last tour to the West Indies, we had a selection meeting to select the squad. The convenor of selectors had been in post for 18 months and we had had a running battle for all of that time. I remember he started off picking a team for a Test match against Pakistan and announced it to the press - before we had even had a selection meeting - and left out our two dead cert players, one a wicket-keeper and one a bowler. When I was handed the team sheet, I screwed it up and threw it on the floor. That was the start of our bad relationship. Anyway, for this West Indies tour we each had to write down what we thought the squad should be. There were three of us on the selection panel. Two of us had exactly the same names. The convenor of selectors came up with a different squad. He wanted to replace three white players, with three black players. The black players were good cricketers, but with different skills to what we needed on that tour. Our picks included two spinners and a batsman who could bowl left arm spin. My thinking was that in the West Indies, on flat, slow wickets, against a team who didn't play spin well, we should select a squad with as many spin options who could also bat. These three were replaced with a seaming all-rounder, and two leg spinners who couldn't bat. So, whichever team we picked we were either a batsman light or a bowler light. We wouldn't be able to balance the team. We each presented our squad, but we were told the convenor of selectors had the casting vote, despite two out of three of us having the same squads. We were told that's it, that's the team that is going and to write these names down on the sheet. We said we disagreed with the squad and explained why. To no avail. I got back home and fired off an email to tell people what had happened and I resigned from the selection panel. I never did receive a reply, so I assume they were happy with the situation. In the end though I withdrew my resignation, on the basis that when we were on tour, I needed to be able to argue to get the best side on the field."

Zimbabwe lost the series 2-0.

This was just one of the many challenges Alan had to endure. You can read many more in his book.

In the first couple of years, results were mixed. Zimbabwe pulled off some encouraging results in Africa but struggled in games outside of Africa. "We struggled outside of Africa, but to be fair most international teams around the world, struggle away from home."

But Alan did take Zimbabwe back into Test cricket. Their first Test match back was a one-off Test against Bangladesh and they got off to a great start, winning the Test by 130 runs and two years later they pulled off excellent drawn series against Bangladesh and Pakistan. In ODI cricket, a memorable home performance against Bangladesh saw the hosts win a five-match series 3-2.

"The team were excited to be back playing Test cricket. Confidence from our early Test matches helped us win that ODI series 3-2. We were actually 3-0 up. Not many had us down to do that. A year later we won a T20 competition that wasn't in the record books. It was an unofficial tri-nations series, between South Africa, Bangladesh and us. It wasn't ratified as South Africa had already played their allotted number of 'official' T20s that year and weren't allowed to play more. We beat South Africa twice and Bangladesh. It was the first time Zimbabwe had won a tournament involving more than two sides."

Despite all of the off the field issues, Alan enjoyed his time in Zimbabwe and has a soft spot for the country in which he lived for three years. "I love Zimbabwe as a country and would go back tomorrow. Its natural beauty will never go away. In the three years that I was there it became a much more vibrant place. Restaurants and new businesses were popping up. There's plenty of places to eat and bars are always open. It really is a good place, with friendly people. I had no problems at all there. It feels a pretty free society to me if you have enough income to overcome the almost daily frustrations of water and power cuts. But it's the people in the rural areas who struggle the most, especially after recent droughts. It's tougher for those people."

I asked Alan if he thinks England will return to Zimbabwe for international cricket any time soon? "England won't go until Mugabe goes. But others are touring. Australia have been, India go regularly, so do South Africa, New Zealand, Bangladesh and Pakistan. It's only really England."

I know from supporters who have been previously, it's a tour we all want back on the schedule sooner, rather than later.

I recommend Alan's book for a full account of cricket in Zimbabwe.

And where does Alan see Zimbabwe cricket right now? "I gather the administration hasn't got much better and they are losing their better players. I hope it improves but it's hard to see how until their political and economic situation changes. That will determine the future of cricket. If it gets better, cricket will get better. People are definitely passionate about it. White and black Zimbabweans love it - there is a following. But you hear stories of coaching clinics running with 50 kids and one ball. All that said, I'd go back tomorrow!"

And the future for Alan? "If I go back into coaching it has to be a job I really feel I want to do. It has to excite me."

5

ALLAN LAMB
FORMER ENGLAND & NORTHANTS BATSMAN

We often hear about the famous West Indian bowlers of the 1980s and 90s, and this former England batsman had an incredible record against them. While many players would have been delighted to have scored a ton against that great quartet of quicks, Allan Lamb scored six, including three successive tons in the Summer of 1984, a magical year for this England great.

"I grew up playing against quick bowling in South Africa and that grounding definitely helped me," said Allan. "But, not facing four at a time! You had to work out how to play them and one thing you had to do was alternate the strike. The last thing you wanted to do was face six successive balls. My plan was always to rotate the strike, score ones and twos and then hit the few bad balls for four. You always had to believe you could have success. I think that West Indies team always had the upper hand because they had four genuine quicks and batsmen were not confident on how to score runs. It was tough, but you had to have self-belief. I was just fortunate that I found a way to play against them and I was able to score runs."

We'll talk more about some of those innings later. But I wanted to learn a bit about Allan's life as a youngster in South Africa and how the move to England came about.

Born in South Africa, to British parents, it was a difficult time for cricketers in the country. South Africa were banned from international cricket indefinitely because of apartheid, an issue that prevented Allan and other aspiring youngsters to represent the country on the world stage.

"It was my dream to play for South Africa. As a youngster I admired South African players such as Jackie McGlew and Trevor Goddard, and later on the Proctors and Pollocks. However, what apartheid did do, was make every game you played very tough. With none of the top South African players able to play international cricket it meant they all played in domestic games, so it was tough cricket. Every game you played in provincial cricket was like playing in a Test match: you had to survive; there were no prisoners. If you weren't successful, you wouldn't be selected."

Allan represented Western Province, making his debut at just 18 years of age. Aside from a two-year absence when he undertook National Service in the South African Air Force and a year playing for Orange Free State, Allan spent all of his domestic career in South Africa at Western Province.

But in 1977 and with no sign of apartheid ending, Allan decided to make the move over to England. "My dream of playing for South Africa ended in 1977. For me to further my career, I had to make the move to England and play county cricket and to see what the future would hold and maybe to play internationally for England, if I was good enough."

Allan made the move over with two other cricketers, Peter Kirsten and Garth Le Roux. "Northants put an offer to Peter Kirsten, but he ended up signing for Derbyshire, so they put that contract offer to me instead, I was their second choice!"

I asked Allan what he found was the biggest difference, at that time, between cricket in South Africa and England. "It was the fact that we were playing on uncovered pitches in England. But, as a result, I became a better player of spin."

It was a great move for Allan as he went on to become a fixture in that Northants side for 17 years. However, despite being born to British parents, Allan had to undertake a four year qualifying period to be eligible to play for England on the international stage.

In 1982, with eligibility confirmed, Allan received a call from the England sectors and his dream of playing international cricket was realised. "I received a call on a Sunday while I was at a friend's farm having lunch. I was advised not to change the way I played, and to just go out there and play your normal way and that is what I always tried to do playing for England."

Allan made his debut against India at Lord's. He scored nine and 37 not out in that debut Test and what followed were 78 more Test matches and a permanent place in England's middle order.

And it wasn't long before his first significant innings. In just his third Test match for England, Allan hit his first Test match century at the Oval, an outstanding 107. "In those days you didn't get a long run in the side, so it was important to get a score. We won that first Test match; I scored a few runs and I think people could see that I could play a bit. But it was great to get that first hundred so soon after at the Oval. The only unfortunate thing was Ian Botham ran me out, I could have got 200!"

In the Winter of 1982, Allan got his first taste of Ashes cricket as England side travelled down under attempting to retain the urn they had won so memorably in 1981. "The Ashes was great. It was fantastic to play again Lillee, Thompson, Chappell and those guys. They were serious players and it was brilliant to get to know them and play against them. We lost the series 2-1, but unfortunately some very bad umpiring cost us. We should have drawn that series."

For Allan individually, it was a great first tour, scoring 414 runs at 41.4. He was firmly cementing his position as the backbone of England's middle order.

Allan's form continued the following Summer with two excellent centuries again New Zealand at the Oval and Trent Bridge.

But it was the Summer of 1984, that was Allan's golden year. As mentioned earlier, it was the year he scored three centuries against that great West Indian bowling line-up. What I didn't mention earlier though was immediately after that series, England played a one-off Test against Sri Lanka and no surprise there was another Lamb century. If Carlsberg did Summers this was most definitely it for Allan.

"It was one of those seasons where everything just went right for me. Everyone prays for a season like that and I was fortunate to have one. It was a great year personally. The only thing was as a team we didn't win a Test match! That was the poor thing of the Summer of 1984."

England 'righted' that West Indian whitewash with two memorable Ashes wins home and away. "It's one of the best feelings to beat Australia home and away." The away series was famed for a journalist who after the warmup games wrote that there were only three things wrong with this England team, they can't bat, they can't bowl and they can't field. "That definitely fired up the players. We went on to win all of the tournaments we played, the Tests and the one dayers. It was a great year for us. It was a brilliant team effort to win those series. We had some good players, but we also had players who weren't batting in the positions that they should have been, teamwork got us the success."

One of the most memorable performances for Allan on that tour was in a one day international against Australia at the Sydney Cricket Ground. Chasing a modest 233, England had a shaky start losing openers Bill Athey and Chris Broad quite quickly. David Gower and Allan put on 86 runs for the third wicket before Gower was dismissed by Simon O'Donnell with England's score at 137. Allan brought up his half century but was left stranded as England lost Gatting, Embury and Jack Richards quite quickly, reducing the team to 201 for 7. Allan was joined by Phil DeFreitas in the middle with the team needing 33 runs to register their second win of the series. The equation came down to 18 runs from the final six balls. What followed was something on a par with Carlos Braithwaite's savage hitting of Ben Stokes in last year's World T20 final as Allan hit Bruce Reid for 18 off of five balls to win the game. You can watch the video here.

"The funny thing was I hadn't scored a boundary until that last over - I thought there was something wrong with my bat! I just said to myself that I've got to win this and hit these runs or I will feel such a plonker because I batted so badly - I couldn't let my team mates down and I did it."

It was a stunning performance and that over became the subject of a cheeky banner in the crowd during the next match between the two sides which read "Can Bruce Reid please call Allan Lamb on 24624"!

Sadly, England relinquished those Ashes two years later. "We didn't play well in 1989. The Aussies played exceptionally well. We'd gone through a period of having so many captains, there were some bad selections, we had a few injuries, it was all very disappointing."

England headed to the Caribbean after that series in the Winter of 1989/90 to once again face the West Indies. To put into perspective how daunting this tour was: England had not beaten them in 23 Test matches. What followed was a moment of history and a first Test match victory, as the side pulled off a brilliant win in the opening Test of the series in Jamaica, with Allan scoring a memorable 132.

"That was my favourite hundred."

England should have won the second Test of the series, which would have put them 2-0 up in the series but ended up with a draw. However, there was another big highlight for Allan on that tour. In the 4th Test match in Barbados an injury to captain Graham Gooch saw Allan, who was vice captain of the side, stepping up to captain England for the first time. He marked the occasion with another a century. "Captaining England and scoring a hundred in Barbados was great. It's a great feeling to captain your country. But we didn't win the series and that was tough."

I asked Allan, what was the major difference on that tour, compared to the previous series against the West Indies. "Having a lot of young guys on that tour was a big thing. It wasn't the old heads there. It was tough for them competing, but that tour started the careers of the Hussains and Stewarts. It was a good learning curve for all of us. Just a pity we didn't win the series."

One of England's other big highlights (and disappointments) of that era was of course the 1992 World Cup, where England went all the way to final, before losing to Pakistan in the final. "We had a very, very good side and we should have won it. Some poor decisions in the final definitely cost us. I had a calf strain, but the selectors brought me back in for the semi-final and final. We were very disappointed. I remember we had Javed Miandad absolutely plumb off the bowling of Derek Pringle, but it wasn't given."

I asked Allan, why he felt England in the one-day game, were not able to build upon that tournament. "A few people dropped out, but we should have done better. Unfortunately, for whatever reason, it didn't happen."

Allan himself retired from international cricket, not long after. "I was bringing a book out and Northants said I had to put it through the ECB, but they thought I might get banned for the book, so I just thought bugger me, that's it, I call it a day. I probably had a couple of years left in me and I probably should have kept playing."

Allan did continue playing for his beloved Northants until 1995, when he retired from all cricket.

I asked Allan for his reflections of his time at Northants. "We won the Gillette Cup in my early years and I became cricketer of the year in 1979. We had quite a lot of success over the years but we were never up there for the championship, apart from in 1995; which was a shame as that was always one of my aims to win the county championship. Warwickshire just pipped us in 95, but we should have won it. Anil Kumble got a hundred plus wickets that year. But we did well over the years in one day cricket. It was my success at Northants which got me selected for England."

Throughout Allan's career he faced some of the best bowlers to play the game and he lists Malcolm Marshall as the stand out bowler.

"Malcolm Marshall was the best. The most awkward would have been Joel Garner and Curtly Ambrose because of the bounce they got."

The best batsmen? "Viv Richards and Barry Richards."

And the best players he played with? "Ian Botham, Graham Gooch and David Gower."

I also asked Allan how he thinks he would have fared in today's game? "Players in our day would have competed absolutely fine. To be honest I would have liked to have seen some of them playing against the four West Indian quicks! But England have some very good players, some great youngsters and the future is bright. We just lack spinners."

Allan now runs his own corporate hospitality event and travel company, Allan Lamb Associates and is a regular on Twitter.

Allan played a total of 201 international matches for England (79 Tests, 122 One-Day Internationals), and became, without doubt, one of our finest players of fast bowlers.

Allan Lamb – thank you.

6

IAN GOULD
FORMER ENGLAND, MIDDLESEX & SUSSEX WICKET-KEEPER AND INTERNATIONAL UMPIRE

July 2019 saw the sad international retirement of one of the games characters, elite umpire Ian 'Gunner' Gould. Gouldy has been a good friend of mine for a number of years, so I was delighted when he kept his word and gave me his first full post-retirement interview.

We started our conversation with the game at Headingly where he officiated for the last time in the final World Cup group match between India and Sri Lanka.

"A very emotional day," reflected Gouldy, or Gunner (or however you best wish to refer to him!) "Until the last minute I didn't realise that the ICC had organised for my wife and family to come and watch. That, of course, made it a bit more nervous and a bit more emotional, but it was a really nice gesture. My wife and kids had a wonderful time and that was important because they have made many, many massive sacrifices for me throughout the years."

The only downside of this wonderful surprise, however, was a family birthday party that was planned the following day! "I had to be back in a place called Holyport, near Maidenhead, at 10 am the following day, which meant I had to drive these drunks back home!"

We'll talk a lot more about Gouldy's umpiring stories later, but first I wanted to roll back the years.

As a player, Gouldy kept wicket for England in 18 ODI's (including at the 1983 World Cup) as well as playing in more than 600 combined first class and list A games for both Middlesex and Sussex. Yet, his career could have panned out very differently. Growing up, football stole his passion, so much so that he played youth football as a goalkeeper for Arsenal, hence his nickname of 'Gunner'.

"I didn't really study cricket that hard growing up. My ambitions were very much with football. My brother had been a professional footballer with Chelsea, Arsenal and Peterborough - and god knows how many other clubs - so cricket wasn't really on my radar. If I'm honest, it didn't excite me. As a 15-year-old kid, my dream was to be a professional footballer. I did play cricket, but I didn't have any cricket heroes. My Mum and Dad lived in a council house in Cippenham: we didn't have a television; we didn't have that much. So, I didn't really watch too much cricket but played it because it was a summer sport. My brother loved it, so if anything, that's where I got it from."

So, at what point did the realisation come that cricket would be a better career than football?

"I'd moved from Cippenham to Slough colts and a brilliant bloke called Dave Collins set me up for a course at Lords, when I was 13 or 14. I was getting bowled at by a kid who was a similar age to me when, suddenly, a group of adults appeared and started bowling at me. I was spanking them and it went from there, really. But even then, it still didn't excite me. Football did. I'd be at home and my brother would be knocking about in the front room with Peter Osgood who was waiting to go off to training at Stamford Bridge. That did excite me."

For a period Gouldy was balancing both sports. His cricket was running parallel to his football career at Arsenal.

"I didn't really twig it until I was about 16, when cricket took over. I left school and I was going to go and join Kent. I played a few games for their seconds but my parents weren't willing to let me leave home. I went to the MCC ground staff instead and once I was at Lords, Don Bennett and Harry Sharp - my original coach - recommended me to Middlesex and off I went."

It was the start of a long journey as a wicket-keeper, a coach and latterly an umpire. However, it wasn't always a smooth ride, particularly in those early years at Lords.

"At Middlesex we had an amazing side; an incredible side. But I don't think they really understood me, and I didn't really understand them. Mike Brearley is one of the nicest people I have ever met, but I don't think he really understood where I was coming from. I didn't 'get' the nostalgia of Lords. There were public school boys there and I resented that. My happiest memories were probably the lunches! So, aside from meeting Gatt and Mick Hunt (the recently retired head groundsman at Lords) I just didn't really have fun memories of my time at Middlesex."

In 1980 the county signed Kent's wicket-keeper Paul Downton. "I knew at that moment I didn't fit and needed to move on. Mike Sturt of Sussex, an absolute treasure of a man offered me a three year contract, but I looked him in the eye and I just said I've got to go."

What followed were ten of the happiest years of Gouldy's playing career. "John Barclay was captain and we had a really good team. We had a great crack and we played proper cricket without the feeling of people looking over your shoulder. You didn't feel insecure. It was a wonderful time."

His time in Hove saw the county win the Sunday League and the NatWest Trophy. "We should have won a lot more. Things went horribly wrong financially with certain players having to be let go. That stopped us achieving what we probably should have. But, even in those terrible times, it was a hilariously funny place to play cricket. We had a lot of fun on and off the pitch. Brighton's footballers were a decent side at the time - they got to the FA Cup final against Manchester United and should have won - and we were out all the time with those guys. It was just a fun place to be and also a beautiful part of the country."

Anyone who has read Derek Pringle's recent book knows that cricket at that period was fun. Players played hard and fair on the pitch but enjoyed it to its limits off it. That fun continued in international cricket. Gouldy first represented his country at the age of 17 when he was selected for a youth tour to the West Indies. Knowing him as I do, I felt I had to ask what was a tour of the West Indies like for a 17-year-old Ian Gould? "Chaotic," he laughs. "Seriously though, we had Gower, Gatting, Athey and Paul Allott on that tour. It was proper team. I'd just been released from Arsenal, so I was at a bit of a low ebb and I also didn't want to leave Middlesex at that point in the season as they were about to win the title, which they did. It wasn't easy, yet it turned out to be a great experience."

Full England recognition came in 1982 when Gouldy was selected as a back-up keeper on an Ashes tour to Australia and one of his fond memories was when he found out he'd be rooming with Robin Jackman. "I hated playing against him. I loathed him as a person with a passion. When I arrived in Australia, I was told my roommate was going to be Robin Jackman, all I thought was 'wow' this is going to be hard work! But he's become one of my greatest friends!"

And what was an Ashes tour like in the 1980s? "For me it was outrageous, because I knew I was never going to play. Bob

Taylor was the best wicket-keeper around, aside from Alan Knott. If I was to get past Bob Taylor, there would have to be a bomb scare somewhere. The only way I was ever going to play was if I could score a few runs. But I never got a game, apart from the third ODI That was in late January and I hadn't held a bat since the first week of December; suddenly I was opening the batting against Dennis Lillee and Jeff Thompson; it was like a Stevie Wonder day out!"

I asked Gouldy how difficult is it for a back-up keeper on those long tours when you know it's unlikely, you'll play. "It's about mentality. I had the mentality of having a bit of a crack and a laugh, so it was not difficult at all. For me, it was a great trip; 5 months of absolute paradise."

The following year, Gouldy was named in England's World Cup squad. "It was a bit of blur because we were all over the place. We should have won it. We lost to India at Old Trafford in the semi-final. I don't know who the groundsman was, but he produced a pitch that resembled Madras more than Manchester, and Mohinder Amarnath who's one of the nicest people you'll ever meet in your life, rocked up and went for about 12 runs from 11 overs. It was quite staggering, we got beaten and they went on to win it."

I asked Gouldy if he was frustrated at not playing more for England? "No. I didn't deserve to play more. I wasn't performing as well, consistently, as I should have been."

So, he went back to county cricket. "There were some hugely talented players who played the game in that era. Everyone got on with each other. I reckon I probably fell out with just two people over 20 years of playing. Everyone stayed in the same hotels, you just had a crack with the opposition, shared a drink and had fun. I'm not sure modern players have that. There was so much humour about. I remember a game against Essex; John Lever rocked up the night before the game and told me he could bowl me out with an orange. The next day the first ball he bowled to me was an orange! The place erupted. If you did that now you'd probably be sanctioned for disrespecting the game."

Throughout Gouldy's playing days he kept to some of the game's great players, but who was the most difficult? "Wayne Daniel. He bowled like the speed of light. The first two years you had no idea where it was going to go. I was diving around like I was playing in goal again. But when he got it right, he was terrifyingly quick."

Post playing, Gouldy went into coaching at Middlesex. "I wasn't keen on going into coaching at all. It was very much a chance opportunity. I was coming to the end of my playing career at Sussex and wasn't really happy. I received an offer from Middlesex through Don Bennett and Gatt. Clive Radley who was the second team coach left to take a role with the MCC, so I kind of fell into it. I would have loved to stay living in Sussex but there wasn't a job opportunity there. I moved back to Windsor. I probably enjoyed the first five to six years at Middlesex and did quite a good job; the final four years I did quite an average job. But I have to thank Middlesex for doing me two pretty big favours; letting me go twice. The first time allowed me to move to Sussex and the second to go off and umpire. Both releases were wrong but I'm very happy they did them."

So, why umpiring? "Well, I did a couple of games while I was a coach when the umpires turned up late. I went on to the field and thought to myself 'I actually really enjoy this.' When I got released from Middlesex, I had to stay on to see the season out and there was a game at Ealing, where one of the umpires didn't turn up, so I thought to myself I'll go and do this. The late David Shepherd was at the other end and he told me that he thought I had the personality to do it. I laughed at him. But afterwards I thought about it and I spoke to my wife. I was loving running my own business at that time, but she said to me 'You love this game and they love you; go and do it.' As it turned out someone was ill, and I got placed on the reserve list straight way and that's how it all started. And you know what, it's been the happiest period of my life. I wake up every morning looking forward to going to umpire."

Gouldy's first international appointment as an umpire came in a one day international between England and Sri Lanka at the Oval in 2006; Darrell Hair was at the other end. He's someone Gouldy holds in the highest esteem. "I was so lucky to have Darrell Hair at the other end. No matter what people think of Darrell he is the most outstanding character that I have ever met in my life because he tells you the truth. I did a series with him in India and bearing in mind they were burning effigies of him and all sorts of nonsense, he was able to just go out there and do his job. He was fantastic. And if I did anything he didn't like, he'd come and tell me, and I loved that. He was the first person who would always be brutally honest with me and I can't thank him enough. I wouldn't have achieved what I did as an umpire if it wasn't for him."

I asked Gouldy how much both umpires in the middle have to work in partnership. "When you walk onto the field of play you have to feel safe with your fellow umpire. I guess it's like your business partner, you have to be able to trust him. If you don't things can go horribly wrong."

Gouldy made his Test debut as an umpire with Steve Davis in South Africa and he openly admits he didn't feel the pressure of the step up from county cricket. "For me, no. I was all over it because it's where I wanted to be."

Gouldy has umpired in some of the most highly charged atmospheres during his Test career. He regularly umpired contests between India and Pakistan, he gave Sachin Tendulkar out on 99 and umpired numerous Boxing Day Tests in Melbourne and, of course, there was the recent infamous ball tampering scandal involving the Australians. What were those games/atmospheres like to officiate in? "Do you know what, there was never any issues with India and Pakistan; players on both sides got on famously well. It was always a myth to me that they didn't. The only issue in those games was the crowd. The noise could be crazy. But the players were outstanding."

I asked him how difficult was it to hear nicks, with such noise from the stands. "You could hear everything. When the ball is released it will always go dead quiet, the volume goes up when they smash it. But you hear the nicks. The only time it's a

nightmare is when the Mexican waves start as it's constant noise." And how difficult was that ball tampering incident to officiate? "It wasn't difficult at all. It was cut and dried and everyone could see it on the television, in black and white. Australia were probably out of control and they got caught. I was with two other English umpires, Richard Illingworth and Nigel Llong and we dealt with it. The Cape Town Test was followed by a Test in Johannesburg and it was like umpiring a Windsor 3rd XI game. Nothing was said. What people have to remember is nobody died, and it was a cricket ball. Move on."

When you listen to players, former players and commentators they always refer to Gouldy as a 'players' umpire'. I was keen to know how important it is for umpires to have that rapport with players? "Massive. If someone says hello to you in life, you don't turn your back on the them, you say hello; so, if a player speaks to you, you speak back to them. I always wanted to umpire how I wanted to be umpired as a player. When I played, I enjoyed having a laugh and a crack, but I felt it was harsh when as a result people would come down with a ton of bricks on me for being like that. I didn't want to be like that as an umpire. And when I finished the game at Headingley and heard the nice things people were saying about me, I cried . The only other time I cry is when I lose a family member. I umpired some magnificent people. Virat Kohli and Ricky Ponting were lovely people and if you treated them properly, they would treat you properly. And they knew the line with me and not to cross it."

So, what about sledging? "I never heard it because I wouldn't listen to it. The only time I would ever step in is if it got personal about someone's family. If people bring in a family member, I'd nail them, but otherwise just get on with the game."

Gouldy's time as an international umpire coincided with the introduction of DRS, he admits it was initially poorly received by umpires. "It's a bit like football now with VAR, the reason being you don't necessarily understand it or trust it. Previously a guy bowling round the wicket could never get an LBW; modern day science now says he can. The next generation of umpires will accept DRS, football will accept VAR, but as an umpire, as a referee, it's not the greatest thing you've seen! The important thing for officials in cricket and football now is to leave your ego behind in the dressing room and crack on. Mistakes will happen but just get on with it."

I was also keen to get Gouldy's thoughts on umpires being allowed to officiate in their own countries, thus allowing the ICC to appoint the very best umpires for each series. "I'll be gobsmacked if by the next Ashes an Englishman and an Australian are not umpiring. It's an absolute must. But it has to be everywhere. They need full blown DRS in every country and then it can happen. In football you have the best referees officiating the best matches, regardless of where they are from. It has to happen in cricket."

Finally, with all the games he umpired, what was the toughest? "Good question. I'd say South Africa versus India last year in Johannesburg. We should have abandoned the game. The pitch was not good enough. Someone could have got hurt; thankfully they didn't, so in the end the ICC got it right by continuing."

And what's next? Domestic umpiring? "I've still got a contract with the ECB. I have to sit back and see what my family want me to do as it's their time now. It might be back to cutting grass!"

Or, a well-earned pint down the pub – it's your round.

7

GEOFF LAWSON
FORMER AUSTRALIA FAST BOWLER

Throughout this book there are many Ashes stories and battles with formers players and coaches but for this interview I stepped into enemy territory and interviewed an Australian! A former fast bowler who during his career took an impressive 97 Ashes wickets. And that man is Geoff Lawson.

Geoff and I caught up immediately prior to the 2018 one-day series between the two sides, so while we couldn't comment on that series, I had to begin by getting his views on Sandpaper gate and where Australian cricket is right now.

"Well, the national team lost its way a bit and they have been forced to look at what they've been doing, which has not been good," commented Geoff. "But, it's not just the team, it's the management, the administrators and the board. They all need to look at where they are taking the game. It's definitely a transitional period at the moment. Australians love their Test cricket and so we will come back. We just need to find the acceptable way we want to play, both on and off the field. The positive thing for me is there is an underlying strength in State cricket where we have a few players beginning to make their mark. So, we'll get sorted."

Throughout the 1980s Geoff was one of the first names on Australia's team sheet and if it wasn't for injuries he would surely have added to the 180 Test wickets that he ultimately achieved. But where did the road to the baggy green begin for this tearaway fast bowler from the country.

"I was born in Wagga Wagga in New South Wales and as a youngster I used to love watching Dennis Lillee run in and bowl. He was definitely my role model in the playground where we used to play cricket every recess and lunchtime. In fact, I used to think I was Dennis Lillee just running in and bowling fast! Who would have thought then, that years later, I would be bowling alongside him!"

Geoff's playground cricket soon developed into more series games and his path to the New South Wales first team was a short one. "I played a lot of representative cricket when I was a kid, but I was lucky enough to play first grade cricket up in Sydney when I went to university. That was a good standard. Our captain was Chris Rogers' father and the father of Sam Robson, who went on to play for England – something I still don't get! – was also in the team. I then got selected for New South Wales' under 21 side. We played a lot of interstate carnivals which could be pretty taxing for a 19-year old. And then World Series cricket came along."

In 1977, media tycoon Kerry Packer formed a breakaway professional cricket competition, World Series Cricket. It was a tournament that tore apart the sport around the world as a number of the world's best players opted to play in this competition rather than represent their countries. For Geoff, it was an opportunity. With many of Australia's team banned, state sides around Australia were searching for new young talent to fulfil fixtures.

"World Series Cricket took away a number of top players and with the vacancies opening up, I managed to secure one. My club team mate Greg Watson also got a deal at New South Wales, so suddenly there were the two of us opening up the bowling for our State. If I'm honest I'm not sure I was ready to be playing first class cricket at that stage, but then we were all inexperienced. My captain was only playing his second game!"

I asked Geoff if this early introduction to first class cricket sped up his development. "Yes and no. I wasn't getting the opportunity to learn from experienced players. That happened in Test cricket when World Series ended. I bowled with Dennis Lillee and that was a great learning experience, but I didn't get that in my first years at New South Wales. That said it did test you out if you're good enough. But it would have been nice to have had some experience around the group."

Geoff got his first sight of England/Australia hostilities in a tour match for New South Wales in 1978. A match that saw Geoff appear in the following day's papers after a bouncer barrage at Geoffrey Boycott!

"That was me being a rat bag fast bowler rather than playing to the context of the game! The back story was I was batting at number ten and Bob Willis was sledging me. I'd played a few good shots and he then bowled a bouncer at me. I ducked it and then he pitched the next one up which I hit straight to mid-off and got caught. He mouthed me off which I thought was totally unnecessary to a young number 10 in a tour game. We were getting heavily beaten and England just had to come out and score two runs to win the game by 10 wickets. The captain said to me, not to worry about bowling he'd just get a batsman to bowl some balls so we can just get off the field. I looked at him angrily and said no, give me the ball. It was eight ball overs in those days. So, Boycott was facing up, the first ball was pitched up and the next three were all bumpers. The fourth one he gloved off his face and over second slip's head to win the game. The umpire warned me for intimidatory bowling, even though the game was over! I didn't expect it to make all the headlines the following day. But I was just a competitor and a competitor who was frustrated that we'd lost the game."

Geoff's competitive nature didn't go unnoticed by the selectors and in 1979 he was called up into Australia's squad that was touring India.

"I got pulled out of club cricket and went over for the last three weeks of the tour because of an injury. Kim Hughes had said he liked how I could bowl fast. I didn't have a clue - I just played the game. So, I went to India for three weeks. I almost made my debut at Eden Gardens but in the end, they went with the spinners which was fair enough."

The following year, despite the return of players from World Series Cricket, the selectors had seen enough of Geoff to select him for his Test debut against New Zealand.

I asked Geoff, what that was it like suddenly appearing alongside his boyhood hero Dennis Lillee? "It was quite surreal. But he gave me fantastic encouragement. I was out there, this kid from the country, playing with arguably the greatest fast bowler of all time. I didn't really learn technical stuff from the likes of Dennis and Thommo, but you more learnt the preparation that was needed to be successful at the top level, the attitude you need and game sense and game presence."

It wasn't long before Geoff's Ashes tales begun.

"1981 was my first Ashes Series."

Everyone in England knows about 1981, but what was that

series like from an Australia perspective?

"We actually played some pretty good cricket on that tour. People sum it up as Botham's Ashes, but we won that first Test a. We played pretty well for most parts of that Headingley Test! I also thought Willis should have been named man of the match because it was his bowling that blew us away. But I guess that's a bowler talking! When you break the series down, we won that first Test; they won a remarkable game at Headingley; we were close at Edgbaston and the series ended up being 3-1 yet it so easily could have been 2-2, but people judge you on the final result."

18 months later and Geoff took 34 wickets as a 'Lillee-less' Australia won back the Ashes. Was it good to exact revenge after that 81 series? "I hate it when people talk 'revenge'. Every time you walk on to a field you want to win. You don't think revenge. You just want to win a session, a day, a Test match and then the series. At the end of the series you might think, 'we've won back the Ashes'. But it'll never make up for losing the 81 series. The theory of revenge in any sport, doesn't sit that well with me."

Geoff's performances in that series were key to Australia retaining the urn. "Dennis Lillee was out injured, Terry Alderman had got hurt so we ended up with a very different attack. So, I guess to a degree I had to be the one to step up. But everyone bowled well. It was a good series. Both teams played some good cricket and it was close. I got given the new ball which gave me the chance to get some early wickets throughout."

And any stand out spells? "My favourite Test was probably Adelaide. Not the spell necessarily, but because I had to bowl really hard on a very flat wicket, in hot, dry conditions. Bob Willis won the toss and strangely sent us in. For a number of years, I was the only genuine all-rounder in Australia. So, I batted at number four in the first innings and number three in the second dig, as well as opening the bowling. A memorable Test. But from a bowling 'spell' perspective it was the Sydney Test and getting Tavare, Lamb and Randall out in an over. That was electrifying, and the crowd went berserk!"

England won back the Ashes in 1985 under David Gower, despite Geoff's 24 wickets, and retained the urn 18 months later when Mike Gatting and his team secured a famous 2-1 win down under in a series that Geoff admits England fully deserved. Although an umpiring mistake in the Oval Test of 85 still irks him to this day!

"In 1985 we had a depleted squad. 16 players went off to South Africa for a rebel tour, so nearly all our first-choice batsmen and bowlers were lost, but we still played some good cricket. The series was 1-1 at Edgbaston when a really poor umpiring decision went against us. That decision cost us the Test match. We batted really well and were on our way to saving the game when Wayne Phillips was given out, caught off David Gower's boot, but everyone could see it had bounced. The umpires had a discussion but gave it out and that was that; we were 2-1 down. Yet we still headed to the Oval knowing that if we won, we'd retain the Ashes." It wasn't to be, and Gower's men held the urn aloft.

"I only played the one Test match in Perth in that 86/87 series due to injury, but England played very, very well. Gatting captained well and they had a good team. We were inexperienced, and they fully deserved to win the series."

And then came 1989. England went into that series as firm favourites, but a different Australia turned up on our shores and Allan Border's men didn't just regain the Ashes they destroyed us – with Geoff taking another 29 wickets as he formed a formidable bowling attack with Merv Hughes and Terry Alderman.

"When we came to England in 1989 everyone wrote us off. You only had to read the English newspapers to get motivation. They were quite disparaging. We ended up playing some damn fine cricket. It was an interesting series because England had a good side. But they had off the field issues, and I think it was after the 4th Test that a number of their players announced they were going on a rebel tour, but we'd won the Ashes by then. England honestly did have a good side on paper, but we had Merv Hughes steaming in and Steve Waugh making his hundreds and our catching was great. To be honest it surprised us that we won like that, but if it wasn't for rain and thunderstorms at Edgbaston and the Oval we could have won 6-0. It was just good tough Test cricket and England couldn't cope with it."

Since that series both sides have experienced the highs and lows of Ashes cricket. Currently, neither side appears to be able to win away but as Geoff says, losing series doesn't make you a bad side.

"It doesn't take much to lose a Test match. You only need to be off the case mentally just a little bit and you can lose a Test. That's what happened with England recently against Pakistan at Lord's. They were off mentally, and they ended up getting hammered. It doesn't mean a team is a bad side, but you have to concentrate all the time in Test cricket. And momentum is a big thing especially now when series are so short, it can be hard to put an end to a losing run. It shows you what a tough mental challenge Test cricket really is. It's such a phenomenal sport. Is there a better game that tests everything you've got mentally and physically over five days and then over a series? The physical, mental and skill challenges are enormous. Test cricket really is an aptly named sport."

Speaking of tough Test cricket, I asked Geoff what it was like facing the might of the West Indies during that period. "That was brutal cricket. I remember we played them in 10 successive

Test matches; five in Australia, followed by five in the West Indies. I think we got beat 6-1 overall, which I thought was a pretty good effort! It was brutal. There were no bouncer limits in those days and they had unbelievable fast bowlers. We had some good cricketers, but we were made to look to ordinary against that attack. They bowled fast, caught everything and they had a world-class batting line-up. Yet, I loved competing against them. They were hard to beat and arguably one of the greatest sides of all time, but I had a pretty good record against them."

And what were some of Geoff's other Test match highlights during his career? "I bowled well in Pakistan in 1982 in what were pretty tough conditions. The conditions were alien to me and I think I lost eight kilos in that series. I didn't get ill but just bowled so much and didn't eat that much! We got beat by a very good Pakistan team, but I was happy with how I played. Half of my Test wickets were against England, but with the bat I did made 74 at Lord's with Steve Waugh. I threw away a Test hundred according to my team-mates. I was trying to get a hundred in a session and got out 26 runs shot with 20 minutes to go, caught on the boundary!"

Away from international cricket, Geoff enjoyed a successful domestic career with New South Wales and captained the side from 1988-1992, a period which culminated in a Sheffield Shield win in his final season. "I loved captaining New South Wales. I used to walk out as captain with Mark Taylor, Michael Slater, Steve Waugh, Mark Waugh, Michael Bevan, Mike Whitney and Greg Matthews behind me. It was a pretty good team that wasn't that hard to captain! We were all super competitive, pretty skilful, enjoyed each other's company and most importantly played some good cricket."

Geoff retired following that Sheffield Shield win; I asked him when he reflects back on his playing career who were some of the toughest batsmen he had to bowl to? "There were a few.

Javed Miandad in Pakistan, Viv Richards anywhere in the world, David Gower, Sunil Gavaskar, Gordon Greenidge and Desmond Haynes as an opening partnership; there were a number. Viv would be number one though, he was so destructive."

And the best players he played with? "Allan Border for his toughness and tenacity and ability to gets runs under pressure. I played a lot of cricket with AB. Steve Waugh was also irrepressible with the bat and Merv Hughes never gave in, he was a tough, tough bowler."

Best captain? "Difficult. I had time for them all. Kim Hughes was fantastic, and I learnt so much under Allan Border's tenure."

Following his retirement from playing, Geoff had a few coaching roles and went into the media writing for the Sydney Herald newspaper and commentated for ABC, but in 2007 came an opportunity to coach in international cricket and Geoff was named Pakistan head coach.

"I coached New South Wales in the mid 90s then move into the media. I did some private coaching, but I had no great desire to be a team coach. I was quite happy doing commentary for ABC and writing a column for the Sydney Herald, which I still do today. Then out of the blue I got an offer to coach Pakistan, I initially said no but then circumstances transpired and there I was. I had a great time. Pakistan is a fascinating country with some wonderful people. We had players like Misbah who was a great influence on the group and he helped me immeasurably. I look at them now and they are playing much more consistently and have lost that unpredictability. Micky Arthur is doing a great job and they are playing some really good cricket. When I was there we had some good young players coming through and enjoying their game. We just had to give them the right environment to play in. We reached the first T20 world final in my time there and I was also the coach when Pakistan last toured India."

Now that must have been an interesting tour? "It was great. The Indian crowds were fantastic; they had great respect for all of the Pakistan players. The cricket was intense but the way our players were treated by the Indian crowds was fantastic and a real eye-opener. I just hope more countries will get back touring Pakistan because it's such a hospitable country and the people love their cricket."

I know that's something a number of the Addis would concur with after they visited the country for England's 2005 tour.

Geoff's stint in charge of Pakistan didn't go unnoticed in India where he was named head coach of a new IPL franchise in 2011, the Kochi Tuskers Kerala. "It was a brand-new franchise but unfortunately we only had one season. We had to put a squad together from scratch and we had some useful players - Jayawardena, Murali, Jadeja, Srikanth, Brendan McCullum and Brad Hodge. It was a good side but owing to problems with the BCCI we only had one year, which was such a shame."

Cricket has changed a great deal since Geoff was running up to bowl to England's batsmen that I wanted to get his take on cricket today. "Obviously T20 is now on the scene and I was involved as a coach at the IPL and I'm currently on the coaching staff at the Sydney Sixers; it's a great circus and I mean that in a positive way. I think it's been wonderful for the game. The amount of families that come in school holidays for the Big Bash is huge. It's fabulous. And there's definitely a place in the game for T20 cricket. But Test cricket is still the ultimate and I believe it is still strong. It's strong in England, it's strong in Australia and strong in India. New Zealand has a good Test side and Pakistan are playing very well. The only people who predict the death of Test cricket are certain marketing people who think that it's a bit slow. It's a great game. I don't care about the pace. With Test cricket you have the chance to watch, to think, to decide. The fan can get involved with what happens next. You also have a fairer contest between bat and ball that you don't necessarily get in T20 cricket. When you get a true contest in Test cricket, it's absorbing you can't get that in other formats or sports. Test cricket can have you on the edge of your seat a lot over five days. 2005 is the proof of that; every day of that series was enthralling."

There has been a lot of talk recently about removing the toss from Test cricket, something that Geoff is passionately against. "Taking the toss away is just ridiculous. Players just have to learn how to play in different conditions. There are very few warm up games these days and that makes it hard for players. I keep hearing we have to do certain things like removing the toss to help the away side, but how about just going back to having a number of meaningful warm-up games? Pakistan came to England this year, played two proper warm up games and a Test match against Ireland and then they went into that first Test fully prepared and look how they performed. They'd adjusted to conditions. People talk about conditions, but that's the challenge of Test cricket. Home teams are allowed to prepare wickets to suit their sides. Lord's is very different to Perth - the overriding issue is lack of preparation in the lead up to series."

It's a valid point.Geoff enjoyed a terrific international career for Australia and was certainly a thorn in our side for many years throughout the 1980s. It's been fun getting some perspectives from the old enemy! Geoff – thank you!

8

HUGH MORRIS
FORMER MANAGING DIRECTOR, ENGLAND CRICKET

Throughout this book I spoke to a number of former players who played their part in the rebuilding of the England side in the 1990s and early 2000s; but this man played a leading role. He became managing director of England cricket following the 2006/07 Ashes whitewash and under his tenure, we became the world's number one ranked Test nation, won three successive Ashes series and, in 2010, our first global ICC tournament. It is of course Hugh Morris.

"Do you know what, when I took on the role I was always hopeful we could achieve something like that," remarked Hugh. "I honestly thought that after that Ashes defeat, we could get back playing good cricket. And, as in all sport, when you get on a roll, it's amazing how success begins to snowball."

But before we concentrate on Hugh's time at the ECB, we mustn't forget his own playing days. Throughout the 80s and 90s

Hugh was one of the most consistent and successful batsmen in county cricket. Yet as a youngster it was actually a close call between rugby and cricket for the young Welshman. "I come from a sports family. My dad, brother and sister all played different sports. For me, I always had a rugby ball in my hands in the Winter and a cricket ball in the Summer. My dream, from a young age, was to play for Wales at rugby, at the Cardiff Arms Park against England, and in the Summer to play cricket for England at Lord's!"

Hugh chose cricket. "I was inspired by a number of players at that time, most notably Viv Richards. I remember Viv came over to England with the West Indies in 1976 and scored over 800 runs in that series, scoring two double hundreds. It was at that stage that my focus switched more towards cricket."

It was a good decision, as the left hander was not only soon making his debut for Glamorgan (while still at school) but he was appointed first team captain at just 22 years of age, such was the high regard the county had for him. "I played for Glamorgan while at school. I then went to university for three years and halfway through my first full season, I was asked if I would like to captain the club, which was a huge honour."

Hugh took on the role on the back of successfully captaining his school and various England representative sides. "I captained my school side for three or four years and I captained the England schoolboys and the under 19s; so I had a lot of experience of junior cricket and managing and leading my peers, but it's a different kettle of fish when you're starting to manage professional cricketers and international cricketers. It was a significant step up."

A significant step up it was. "I was young and ambitious and I'd always wanted to captain the club but looking back, I probably should not have taken the captaincy at that age. It started to affect my form. I didn't really know my own game, let alone be experienced enough to manage a group of seasoned pros in the side."

After three years at the helm, Hugh stood down from the captaincy in 1989, to concentrate on his batting. "My coach at the time, Tom Cartwright, told me I was just not achieving what I should be achieving as a batsman and I should seriously consider whether it's the right thing to carry on. It's never an easy decision, but it was the absolute right one at the time to stand down."

It was a move which reaped its rewards, as 12 months later Hugh hit a club record 10 centuries and 2,276 runs, in the Summer of 1990.

"I spent a long hard Winter with Tom Cartwright working on my technique. 1990 was a pretty nice Summer. The weather was good, we spent a lot of the time playing on good pitches, and the season just went my way."

The form shown by Hugh caught the attention of the selectors, who called him up as batting cover, on the 1990/91 Ashes tour to Australia following an injury to Graham Gooch. "Graham Gooch got a very bad hand injury and I went down to join the tour party as cover for about seven weeks. It was a good experience that got me introduced to the England set-up."

Hugh remained in the selectors' thoughts the following Summer. First, he was first called up as cover for the injured Robin Smith for the third Test of the series against the West Indies at Trent Bridge and he was finally given his much-deserved Test debut in the fourth Test at Edgbaston.

"We'd been playing a game at Liverpool and I was driving back down the motorway when I heard of my inclusion on the radio."

As an opening batsman there were probably few greater

challenges at the time than facing the likes of Malcolm Marshall, Curtly Ambrose, Courtney Walsh and Patrick Patterson. "They were a fantastic quartet of fast bowlers, arguably the greatest fast bowlers to have ever played the game. It was a daunting challenge. Although I'd played against them all a lot in county cricket, handling all four at the same time was at a completely different level. You knew that in county cricket you'd be playing against one of them, maybe have five, six or seven overs, see him off and then life became a bit easier, but at Test level you know you're just going to get a battering from all four of them, all day."

Hugh scored 115 runs in three Test matches during that series at an average of 19.16. He never played Test cricket again. "Obviously I would have liked to have played more Test cricket, but it was era where we had some very good top order batsmen. Graham Gooch is one of the most successful batters that England have produced and as captain he was always going to play as an opener. Michael Atherton was coming through the ranks, along with Alec Stewart, so I was up against some pretty formidable opposition in terms of getting into the side."

Hugh did go on to captain the England A side on tours of South Africa, West Indies and Sri Lanka, but despite his form on those tours he remained on the fringe of further Test selection for a number of years, without ever being selected.

In 1993, Hugh returned to the captaincy at Glamorgan (following an injury to Alan Butcher) and in his first season back in charge led Glamorgan to the Sunday League title. "It was a much more appropriate time for me to captain. I was in my late 20s, I'd played for England and I knew my game a lot better. I felt I was better equipped to lead the side. We'd not won anything for 24 years, but we felt that we had the ingredients needed to become a successful team. We had a lot of players who had matured together and the Sunday League was a real target for us. Winning that trophy was a watershed moment."

A key member of that side was Hugh's boyhood hero Viv Richards. "Viv was a fantastic player. He threw himself into Glamorgan cricket. He's a proud man and a very proud Antiguan. With Antigua being a small island and Glamorgan a small county, there was a real connection. He was incredibly popular with our members and supporters and was a hugely influential member of the dressing room."

Under Hugh's captaincy second time around, Glamorgan became one of the strongest counties in domestic cricket. With their team built around the likes of Hugh, Steve James, Steve Watkin, Matthew Maynard and Robert Croft they went on to lift their first county championship for 28 years in 1997.

And that championship victory brought the curtain down on Hugh's excellent playing career. "In the Summer of 1997 I saw a job advert from the ECB, for the position of technical director. Micky Stewart was retiring and I looked at the job description and it really appealed to me, so I sent me CV in. Towards the end of that Summer, I was contacted by Micky, who sat me down and talked through the role. I actually had two ambitions at the start of that season, one was to try and get back into the England side, which was always going to be a long shot and then secondly to win the championship with Glamorgan. We won the championship on the last week of the season down at Taunton and the following week I had the formal interview at Lord's and was offered the technical director role. It was almost as if one door was closing and another was opening. I was fortunate the interview went my way; I accepted the position and started the role in November of that year."

The role meant Hugh was looking after all of the junior England men's teams through to the under 19s, coach education, coaching coaches, the ECB science and medical programme and he was tasked with looking at the feasibility of setting up a national cricket academy.

It was the start of a long career with the ECB. "I spent the initial few months shadowing Micky, which was invaluable as he was an extremely experienced cricket coach. I always thought Micky was 20 years ahead of others in his thinking. It was really useful to be able to learn from him."

Hugh spent a lot of his early years at the ECB looking to take the best from other sports into cricket. "I tried to pick up different ideas from different sporting organisations who had been successful over a long period of time. I spent time at Liverpool football club with their academy director Steve Heighway. I spent time with the RFU; with my rugby background I was always interested in what they did. I worked very closely with the guys there in setting up our academy and our general structure for England cricket. I also went down under to Australia and spent time with Rod Marsh to look at the Australian cricket academy."

The fruits of Hugh's hard work and research came in 2003 when Her Majesty the Queen officially opened the ECB's national academy at Loughborough University. The inauguration of this state-of-the-art facility marked a major step forward for cricket in England and Wales.

In December 2005, Hugh was promoted to deputy chief executive of the ECB, and then, following England's Ashes whitewash in 2006-07 and the subsequent Schofield Report, was named as the first managing director of the England cricket team. The Schofield Report recommended 19 changes to improve the state of English cricket, one of which was to have the selectors and coach report up into a Managing Director.

"It was a huge honour. I was very privileged and honoured to be appointed. But it was also a bit of a nervous time for me as well because at the time I was deputy chief executive of the ECB and that job as part of the re-structure of the ECB was made redundant so there was no guarantee I was going to get that role. Thankfully I did, and it was a role I really enjoyed and I look back at it with very fond memories, particularly the times spent with Andrew Strauss and Andy Flower."

Hugh presided over arguably one of England's most successful periods as a Test side, but it came with its challenges. Two of which, using Hugh's own words, were the most 'challenging of his professional career'. And both came within a dark six-week period.

This began on the 26th November 2008 when terrorists carried out a series of 12 coordinated shootings and bombing lasting four days across Mumbai. One of the locations targeted was the Taj Mahal Palace Hotel, where six explosions were reported, over 30 people killed and over 200 people were taken hostage.

England at the time were touring India and news of the attacks spread while England were on the bus back to their hotel, after a one day international in Cuttack. "We jumped on the bus at the end of that game and everyone's mobile phones were going off. We got back to our hotel about an hour later and just sat in front of the television, seeing the whole thing unfold. It was absolutely horrendous. We'd spent the first 10 days at the beginning of the tour staying at the Taj hotel. We knew the staff very, very well and they'd looked after us absolutely fantastically. We'd left a whole pile of our gear there as we were due to return later in the tour. We obviously then had to assess the situation and at times like that you have to have really good people around you and England's security manager Reg Dickinson was absolutely fantastic."

England immediately flew back home, while Reg Dickinson and his team assessed the situation.

"There was a lot of nervousness among the players and support staff, which was absolutely understandable. We knew we had to get the best possible intelligence. It was a very uncertain situation. We spent a lot of time with the foreign office and our security advisors. Once everything had settled down in India and we had the right levels of intelligence, we flew the players to a holding camp in Abu Dhabi and then myself and Sean Morris, who was the chief executive of the professional cricketers association, flew to India and we spent time with our security guys, the local authorities and the police and then we returned to Abu Dhabi and presented our findings to the players. Everyone was then in agreement that the right and proper thing to do was to go back to India."

And so the team returned to India for a two match Test series, which India won 1-0. But it wasn't about the result, it was about giving some joy back to the people of India.

"I take my hat off to the players. They were in a very difficult position, but they were absolutely persuaded by Reg and his team that it was safe to go back. If it wasn't safe there was no way we would have gone back. The local authorities in India did everything they could to get the tour back on track."

Weeks after the tour, England were scheduled to travel to the West Indies for the team's second Test series of the Winter. But in the lead up to that tour, Hugh had to endure the second most challenging time of his career, when coach Peter Moores and captain Kevin Pietersen were removed from their positions. But those changes brought together Andrew Strauss and Andy Flower, two figures who were to become the spearheads of England's revival. "The incident with Peter Moores and Kevin Pietersen, on the back of India, was extremely difficult to deal with. But the decisions were made and we moved forward with Andy Flower and Andrew Strauss. Those guys are two of the most impressive individuals I've had the pleasure of dealing with in 35 years of professional cricket and working with them was among the highlights of my time at the ECB."

I asked Hugh, what he saw in Andrew Strauss when he appointed him as captain, over other potential candidates for the role. "He had a very calm demeanour which I think is very important as a leader. He's not up and down as a situation is up and down; he's very calm about things. He was someone who had a very clear vision of what he wanted, and would keep things as simple as he could, plus he's just a bloody good bloke and he takes people with him."

Flower and Strauss took charge of the team for that tour to the West Indies, a tour which couldn't have got off to a worse start when England were bowled out for 51 in the 1st Test in Jamaica. "We had a nightmare start, losing that first Test in Jamaica, but it actually gave the two Andy's the opportunity to really set their stall out on what they wanted to achieve over a period of time. They were very impressive and it became clear pretty quickly that, that partnership would help England become successful."

Clear goals for the team were set: To become the number one ranked country in Test cricket and to win a global ICC tournament. Both came quickly.

"Those goals were a real driver for Andy Flower and Andrew Strauss. To be ranked number one in the world inspired the players and having that goal galvanised them as a team. They had a clear vision of what they wanted to do. For me that was the most important thing, that the players really, really got excited by those goals and truly believed they could do it."

And the success certainly did follow. Three successive Ashes series were won (including a win down under for the first time since 1986/87) and a 4-0 home series win over India secured the coveted number one Test ranking. While in limited overs cricket the side lifted the ICC World T20 tournament in Barbados. "Six months after Mumbai and all the issues with Peter Moores and

Kevin Pietersen we won the Ashes in the Summer of 2009 and then that Winter we went on to win our first global tournament in Barbados in the T20 World Cup. Those two wins gave confidence to the management team that they were doing the right things and it gave confidence to the ECB that investing in the England team was important because success would raise the profile of cricket in the country."

I asked Hugh with all of the success that, that England team went on to achieve, what was his personal highlight. "It has to be beating Australia for the first time in 24 years in Australia. And plucking one day out of that tour, it would be Boxing Day, December 2010 in Melbourne. We bowled the Aussies out for 98 and then to be 150 for no wicket at the close was right up there with the best days I've seen in professional cricket. I remember when we arrived at the ground that morning the pitch looked decent, but Straussy had a look and wanted to bowl. David Saker was around at the time and knew the MCG strip well and said it was a bowl first wicket. It was a ballsy decision on their part, but it really paid off in spades. After Melbourne, I'd say winning away in India. That win was really important. Also the T20 win in Barbados was very satisfying. We'd never won a global tournament and we really wanted to break that mould."

We'll come to that India victory later. But, at the end of the South Africa series in 2012, Andrew Strauss stood down as Test captain and was replaced by his vice-captain Alastair Cook. It was a sad day after everything Strauss had achieved as captain. And Strauss's decision came as a surprise to Hugh, but he's been delighted in how Cook has since grown into the role. "I was a little bit surprised when Straussy called me. It'd been a really tough time off the field for him in particular that Summer, but he was pretty adamant he'd done what he wanted to do in the game and could do for the England team. Alastair was always the obvious choice. I'm really glad we made that appointment. For any England captain whose there for any length of time, will come under the spotlight. He had some challenges but it shows how resilient Alastair Cook is and I think he's been fantastic. When you think he's the first man to ten thousand runs, at an earlier age than Sachin Tendulkar, he's just remarkable and shows what a cricketer he is, to have scored that many runs in all parts of the world, in completing different conditions. Remarkable. We knew when we appointed Alastair that we had someone who is passionate about the England cricket team, who is passionate about taking us in the right direction and who is resilient to handle the pressure."

Cook's first tour in charge was the tour to India, that Hugh alluded to earlier. "When Cooky looks back, he will treasure that series win for a long time. We lost the first Test over there and usually if you lose the first Test you get rolled over. Whilst the Ashes win down under was memorable this series really was right up there alongside it. In my view it was our best performance to come back from one nil down on tracks that turned so much, it was an unbelievable achievement to win there."

After losing the first Test in Ahmedabad, England headed to Mumbai knowing a win was vital to remain in the four-match series. After India scored 327 batting first, Alastair Cook's 122 and Kevin Pietersen's outstanding 186 took England up to a total of 413. Then, with spin twins Monty Panesar and Graeme Swann combining to take all ten second innings wickets, India were bowled out for just 142, leaving Cook and Compton to take to the crease to knock off the 56 runs needed for victory. It was one of England's finest wins in recent years away from home. The side followed that win up by winning again in Kolkata and a draw in the fourth and final Test in Nagpur, secured a famous 2-1 Test victory, in Cook's first tour following his appointment.

"Kevin Pietersen's knock in Mumbai was just extraordinary. By day three there just wasn't a top on the pitch and the ball was spinning around corners. Even the Indian greats like Sachin Tendulkar really struggled against our spinners Monty Panesar and Graeme Swann. KP just played a remarkable innings. We levelled the series, then went on to win the next match. It was a great achievement for Cooky."

The following Summer England won their third successive Ashes series, with a 3-0 victory at home. It was to be the final series under Hugh's stewardship. "We won the Ashes three times in a row, for the first time in 60 odd years, which was a very satisfying moment, but I'd been thinking earlier in the year that, that would be a bit of a watershed moment for me and the time would be right to move on."

What a period of time it had been for Hugh at the ECB. England cricket had been transformed.

I asked Hugh what he was most proud of during his many years at the ECB. There were the obvious highs with all of the successes of the men's sides but right up there also was the growth in women's cricket.

"One of the things I was most proud of was definitely the growth in the women's game. They won a women's World Cup, the World T20 and a number of Ashes wins. The growth of the women's game in England and Wales has been remarkable. The profile is now so much more than it was 10/15 years ago, which is great. We were very keen at the ECB to get as many people playing the game as possible. Women's cricket is now professional, they have the Super League this Summer it's fantastic. Clare Connor and Charlotte Edwards have been great ambassadors and it's great to see the girls doing so well."

Following the Ashes wins for the men's and women's sides in 2013, Hugh's cricket career went full circle when he accepted the offer to return to his beloved Glamorgan as the county's new chief executive.

"Towards the end of that Summer I got a call from Glamorgan completely out of the blue, saying that there was an opportunity to come back and I jumped at it. It's been really enjoyable to be back. It's where my roots are. I've supported the club for over 50 years. We have a vision to make Wales proud, both on and off the pitch. It's been lots of hard work, stabilising the finances, increasing commercial income, improving success on the field and producing international quality players. It's been fun."

With the county hosting the first Test of the 2015 Ashes series, it also gave Hugh an insight into what it was like being on the other side of the fence. "I got to see first-hand, what goes into hosting an Ashes Test, rather than preparing a side to play in it. It was pretty much the perfect Test for us. It was the first Test of the series, we had a full house, England won and the feedback we got from people attending was great. It all turned out very well."

I asked Hugh, being back in county cricket, how did he see the strength of the domestic game in England. "The counties are producing some very good cricketers, as has been shown by how England is playing. On the field, it's very strong. It's very different though to back to in my day. With so much international cricket played in our season and the competing T20 tournaments around the world, getting the best overseas players is the one real challenge. Obviously we'd all like to produce more fast bowlers and spinners and that's something we're all trying to do."

And looking at the England side now, Hugh sees no reason why our success can't continue. "I think the team has shown over the last 6-9 months that they have stepped up to the plate, especially in white ball cricket where we got to the World T20 final. We came so close to winning. We have a lot of talented cricketers and the style of the play in Test and limited overs cricket is really engaging with the public. It's a very exciting time. There are some great opportunities for us over the coming years with the Champions Trophy next Summer and the World Cup in 2019. We're a difficult team to beat on our own soil, so it's going to be exciting."

It really is. And should we continue our recent success we should all raise a glass to remember the fine work Hugh and his team did over many years, which laid the foundations for team England to be thriving now.

9

JACK RUSSELL
FORMER ENGLAND AND
GLOUCESTERSHIRE WICKET-KEEPER

Jack Russell is another player who arguably has been one of the finest wicket-keepers to have played the game; a wicket-keeper who was known for his world-class skills behind the stumps, his unorthodox – but extremely effective batting and of course his tea-drinking, Weetabix-eating and ha- wearing eccentricities!

I spoke with Jack at his fantastic art gallery in the picturesque town of Chipping Sodbury. The Gallery houses Jack's amazing art collection, as well as some of his memorabilia from his many cricket tours around the world. We'll come on to Jack the artist later, but there was only one place to start the interview, tea and Weetabix!

"It's all true. Don't soak your Weetabix for less than 13 minutes; it must be soggy. And I'm still drinking tea!"

Now, for those of you who aren't aware of Jack's tea drinking:

during his playing days, he would often get through 20 cups a day. The tea bag would be dipped in once, plenty of milk added and the tea bag would then be hung on a nail for re-use. Apparently in the final Test of the 1989 Ashes series at the Oval, Derek Pringle counted that he used the same bag for all five days, which roughly equated to 100 cups! "There was logic to everything!"

We'll come on to the famous hat later. I wanted to get to know Jack the cricketer.

Born in Stroud, Gloucestershire, Jack was part of a sport-loving family. In the Winter, he loved nothing more than playing football (in goal), in the Summer it was cricket and all year round it was playing snooker on the dining room table and watching rugby on the TV. So why cricket?

"I'd seen a catch by Alan Knott. He caught Rick McCosker off Tony Greig, diving to his right-hand side, one-handed in front of first slip. It was brilliant. It was at that moment I decided I wanted to be a wicket-keeper. And at 13 or 14 I realised I wasn't bad at it."

Interestingly though Jack never got to keep wicket at school. "There was a kid called Pedro Jones, he was the hardest kid in the school, he wanted to wear the gloves. I wasn't going to mess with him!"

So Jack batted at three and bowled some "medium" pace. "All keepers think they can bowl! We had a good team. We only lost one game in four years. We were lucky that the two sports masters were cricket mad and they gave us a lot of encouragement and opportunity."

Thankfully for Jack's wicket-keeping ambitions, he began playing for his local side Stroud Cricket Club and it was there that his wicket-keeping took off.

Such was the promise of Jack's keeping, one of his sports masters, Ricky Rutter, guided him in the direction of Gloucestershire County Cricket Club. "By the time, I was 15 or 16 I'd played quite a few games for the 2's. We used to have a team called 'The Young Cricketers' where for two weeks in the Summer you'd sleep in the pavilion, a lady would come in in the morning and cook you breakfast, and you played against other counties during that period. It was basically like an under 17s or under 19s now. It was a great way for us to learn and gain experience."

But interestingly, if it wasn't for a rule that doesn't exist today, Jack could have made his professional debut for Worcestershire.

"Worcester had been watching me for some time playing club cricket and wanted to sign me, but in those days, you had to speak to the county you were born in to get permission to speak to another county. As soon as Gloucestershire found out all hell broke loose and I was in the secretary's office the next day with a contract on the table. I grabbed the pen out of his hand as quick as I could and signed it. I didn't even read it. My boyhood dream had come true."

Jack made his first-class debut against the touring Sri Lankans; interestingly a few years later Jack's Test debut would be against the same opposition. "It was a debut to remember. I managed to end up with a record seven catches and a stumping – I then had to return to school!"

Balancing cricket and education became a struggle for Jack, but thankfully his undoubted skills with the gloves meant a full-time career in cricket was always on the cards. "I was supposed to go to university but I failed my maths A-level – in fact the whole class failed, which was kind of a bonus! I ended up going to Bristol poly to study accountancy, as I was always quite good at numbers – the problem was the course was all about stuff I didn't understand so I quit after three months."

Not that we condone giving up education, but it was undoubtedly the right decision for Jack as it allowed him to "plug" away for Gloucestershire with the aim of getting himself into the England team.

Jack broke into the Gloucestershire first team halfway through his first season, when he took over the wicket-keeping duties from Andy Brassington. "Brassey always gave me one hundred percent support. For a man who had lost his job because of me, I can't speak highly enough of him. Right throughout my career he was always there for advice."

Jack's early performances, in his words, were 'inconsistent'. "It took me two full seasons before I finally got to grips with my keeping. I am forever thankful to David Graveney, who was my captain, who stuck by me."

And it was great that he did, because in 1987, Jack received his coveted international call-up. Jack was selected for the 1987 tour to Pakistan - think Shakoor Rana and Mike Gatting's finger wagging. "It all kicked off on that tour! Maggie Thatcher was involved, the Americans got involved, the squad were threatening to go on strike. I just kept thinking that here I was not having played a game yet and we were having a team meeting about going on strike. My international career was nearly over before it had started! Thankfully John Emburey came up with an idea that writing a letter was perhaps a more sensible approach."

Finger wagging aside, it was an interesting first international tour for Jack, especially given his need for home comforts. "I was the microwave monitor! I couldn't eat the local stuff so I guarded the microwave in my room at night and brought it to the dressing rooms on match days. We had food shipped in and my beans and stew were always lovely!"

It was a tour that also laid the foundations for Jack's career as an artist. "The first thing Mike Gatting said to me on that tour was to welcome me and then to tell me that I wouldn't be playing a game! So, I started sketching. Prior to going out to Pakistan, the Bristol Gallery had seen some of my stuff and offered me an exhibition the following Summer. They asked me if I'd do some sketches on tour so as I had eight weeks of practising and nothing else, I thought why not. I did 40 sketches and when I got back, they all sold in two days. That's how my art started. I was bombarded with commissions after that. That tour was so important to me, when I look back."

With Jack now on the verge of getting into England's first eleven, he returned to Gloucester knowing if he continued to develop his game his chance was not far away. The Gloucestershire team in that period had a formidable bowling attack with the likes of Courtney Walsh, Sid Lawrence, Kevin Curran, Phil Bainbridge and David Graveney. Keeping to bowlers of that calibre would only enhance Jack's chances of selection.

Eventually in the Summer of 1988, the call did come. A Lord's Test against Sri Lanka. "Micky Stewart phoned me up as I was practising for a Sunday League game the following day, to tell me I was in the team and that he'd see me at lunchtime on Wednesday at Lord's. It wasn't like now where you meet up two or three days before. It was meet up Wednesday lunchtime, a bit of practice, team meal in the evening and play the game the following day. There were four of us making our debuts, myself, Sid Lawrence, Kim Barnett and Phil Newport. It was the Summer the West Indies had just smashed us and as well as using 40 odd players, every Test match we'd had a different captain – it was chaos!"

Having bowled the Sri Lankans out for just 194 (Jack taking two catches), England replied with an excellent 429. Batting at three was night-watchman Jack who hit an outstanding 94. "I should have got a hundred. I would have been the first wicket-keeper to ever get a hundred on debut – Matt Prior eventually did it. I should have had patience. The thing was my highest first-class score before that was 71, so I'd never been in that position. But do you know what? To run out at Lord's with the three lions on the chest, it was magic, it really was."

And Lord's was a ground that when you mention it to Jack his smile gets wider and wider. "It was always a dream to play there. When you run out through the long room, all those stud marks in that floor - that hadn't been changed in a hundred odd years, all that history. It really was magical. Even when it's empty it's magical, but for a Test match, to run out second behind the captain Graham Gooch, it was a dream."

England went on to win the Test by seven wickets.

Jack did get his first Test match hundred a year later though in the 4th Test of the 1989 Ashes series at Old Trafford. "It was great to get a hundred, but it was a bittersweet hundred."

It was during this series that a rebel tour to South Africa was being mooted and everything came to a head during the 4th Test. "I got my hundred on the same day we'd lost the Ashes and the day it was announced there was going to be a Rebel tour. I didn't have an inkling, but apparently talks had been going on for months. Gower was captain and I don't think he knew either. It made me angry. I just kept thinking we're trying to beat the Aussies here and everyone was going on about a Rebel tour. After the Test I remember sitting there for about two hours just thinking I can't believe it. A couple of days later I played an England X1 game at Jesmond, up in the North East – we used to play a couple of games up there each year – and I got a standing ovation as I walked out to the wicket. That made me think my hundred must have been alright. So, I do look back at it with fond memories. To play Australia and score a hundred you can't buy that."

Earlier in the series though, Jack had a scored a valuable 64 not out as England were bowled out for just 286 in the first innings of the Second Test and it was this innings that Jack's credits as one of his most important. "For me it was probably a more important and significant innings in that series because in those days if you had two bad Tests you'd been gone and not seen again. We'd lost the first Test at Headingley and I didn't have a particularly good game. I was out fending one to gully, which looked rubbish. In the papers, Richie Benaud had written that I was frightened of the short ball. But that comment did me a favour at Lord's as I knew they were going to try and kill me with the short ball. Alan Knott (who was coaching at the time) and I spent hours in the nets the day before with ground staff bowling bouncers to me from half way down the pitch; we worked out a system for me to play it. That 64 kept my career going. Without it, that hundred would never have happened."

I asked Jack how difficult was it to play with the fear that one or two bad performances and you would be out of the side? "It's just the way it was and you worked with it. It made you harder. You had to deliver right now or see you later. How many one Test wonders have there been? It toughened you up."

That 1989 Australian team under the captaincy of Allan Border were famed for their aggressive approach, they made sledging an art form. And Jack himself was known to say a 'few words' so I asked him how much of an edge did it give to his game. "Keepers always get sledged because they can't bowl fast! All the big fast bowlers wanted to be like bullies to batsmen. Big Merv kept sledging me in that Test match at Lord's, but he then realised the more he sledged the better I did and the more it helped me. I decided to give Merv some words back so I told him "why don't you just f%ck off", Merv didn't say a word to me after that. You must pick your moments and players when you sledge; you'd never chirp Graham Thorpe, he loved it. You'd never say a word to Stuart Law - you had to pick your players. My chirping though came later really when playing for Gloucestershire rather than for England. The thing is you can only sledge if your bowlers are bowling well. And the team must back it up, it can't just be the keeper. It was fun though; you could say things 'legally' without getting arrested!"

Over the next five or six years Jack was a regular for England but at the same time would also be the player who'd get sacrificed if the team were looking to better balance the side. Thus, he often had to pass the gloves over to Alec Stewart. How frustrating was that?

"People always say I should have played more Test matches, but I played in 54 Tests which is more Tests than Bradman. I was lucky so I don't knock it. And at the end of the day if I'd have scored 50 runs or more every Test, they wouldn't have dropped me, so in a way I should have done better with the bat. I just had to live with it."

But it was a Test match performance with the bat, where he didn't score even a 50 that to this day is still regarded as one of the finest Test match innings and partnerships of all time: The famous 1995 Test match at Johannesburg.

With England trailing by 478 runs heading in to their second innings England had nearly five sessions to survive and with the score at 232 for five and over two sessions still to go Jack walked to the crease to greet his captain Mike Atherton. What followed could be summed up in one word, 'amazing'. Jack batted with his captain for four hours and 34 minutes, scored 29 runs (which he kicks himself for) and secured a famous draw.

"People mention that Test match to me more than anything else, other than the hat. Athers did most of it, he batted for two days I just batted the one! There used to be a tunnel with a tin roof that you had to walk down as you went out to bat. The South African fans would whack it and whack it as you walked out. They then used to make noises like dogs to try and intimidate you, but it was stuff like that, that got me going. I walked out and I could see in Athers' eyes that this guy is not going to get out, someone just had to stay there with him. Donald was trying to kill him for two days and I just thought someone had to pull their finger out and stay at the other end with him. So, all I wanted to do was be nought not out at the end of the day. Not give them a single chance. I still don't know how I got to 29 but nought not out was the target, just block, block, block. I just took it ball by ball and over by over. It was funny I used to tap his pad in between overs, it became a superstition. I remember after a few hours, I'd forgotten to whack it, so as the bowler was about to bowl I ran down the wicket, touched it and run back! At one point, I hit a four, it was a full toss mind you, but I gave myself the biggest rollicking. I shouldn't have been scoring runs. The South Africans knew if they'd got me, they were into our bowlers. At one point I was a minute or two away from it being the longest period for a batsman not to have scored a run in a Test match. But that was my job, don't get out. Such was the zone I was in, when Daryl Harper picked up the bails to mark the end of the game, I nearly had a go at him. I thought what are you doing!"

Jack faced 235 balls for that 29 not out; at the other end Atherton faced 492 in his 643-minute stay at the crease. It was legendary stuff. "When we got back to the dressing room, it was like we had won. People were phoning up; we were receiving faxes from all sorts of well-known people. It hit home that we had done something that was alright. But Athers really did do most of it."

I asked Jack if there was ever a moment out in the middle that he thought they were going to do this. "No, never. I never wanted to relax. I was OK at lunch, but at tea we felt we

COULD do this, but that made me concentrate more; complacency is the root of all evil to me. It was funny though looking back, at lunch-time there was me all pumped up and there was Athers just casually in his corner reading the paper!"

What some people tend to forget about this game is that Jack also broke the world record for the number of catches taken in a Test match. A catch off Clive Eksteen from the bowling of Dominic Cork was his 11th in the match – an unforgettable Test match.

After the close of play Jack bumped into Sir Ian Botham who warned him his life wouldn't be worth living if he didn't join him and the team for a celebratory drink. "I'd done so well to avoid Beefy's legendary nights out that I suppose the law of averages meant that I was to fall into that dangerous net at some point! So, we all rushed back to the team hotel when John Barclay, the team manager, stopped me in the reception area and asked if I could do a quick interview for the radio before going upstairs to my room. 'No problem' I said. He then made a phone call from reception to find out where the interviewer was. After a short conversation, he told that the interview was off, and I was free to go to my room. What I didn't know was that he had been on the phone to my own room. When I got there, I opened the door and was surprised to see the lights on. A little puzzled, I could also see a reflection in the window. Someone was on my bed and it was female!

I was just about to go ballistic with 'Who the hell are you?' when the lady jumped up with a camera and took my photo. Blinded by the flash I couldn't see for a second, it was my wife. I couldn't believe it! It was the best surprise ever and got me out of the drinks with Beefy!"

The following Summer Jack's form continued with an impressive 124 against India at Lord's but the joys of that century at Lord's were short-lived as the gloves were once again passed over to

Alec Stewart. "I hadn't had the greatest of series heading into that Lord's Test – I got nought in the Test before at Edgbaston. We were 80 odd for five when I went into bat with Graham Thorpe. I knew I had to do something as we were in the mire and there was starting to be a bit of build up about Stewie keeping. For some reason, I just knew I was going to get a hundred that day. I never said anything but I was just in that do or die moment. This one was an attacking hundred. I thought if I could counter attack from the situation we were in, Thorpey could take it a bit easier and play his natural game. I took them on, got a hundred and finally got on that honours board! Three Tests later though and I was dropped! They wanted to play another bowler or something to try and win the series, so Stewie kept for the last Test at the Oval."

It was to be Jack's last Test match hundred.

By the time, England finally realised that Stewart's best position was opening and not keeping in 1998, Jack was 35. But there was still one more tour in him, the West Indies tour of 1998. A tour where Jack's famous hat became even more famous!

Now, look at any photo of Jack playing cricket and he's wearing a sunhat that was given to him at Gloucestershire - he wore the hat his entire first-class playing career. Through the years, it had been through many battles; none more so than in the West Indies. In 1994 the hat ended up being burnt in an oven. "The floppy brim on my hat had begun to annoy me during matches, so I decided to starch the hat myself. Once I had sprayed it thick with starch, I realised I didn't have a suitable airing cupboard handy so I decided to put it in the oven. After a few minutes, Graeme Hick shouted and asked if I had anything cooking in the oven and pointed out that the kitchen was full of smoke. I flung the oven door open only to discover a dark mess that looked something like a half-eaten Christmas pudding. Holding back the tears I sat down beside it figuring out what to do. With a Test match, only a few days away I decided the best thing to do was to knock off the charred bits, cut up my spare 'painting' hat and rebuild my old faithful one! If you turn it upside down now you can still see inside it some of the Barbados burn marks!"

A much bigger battle was to follow though on the 1998 tour. Lord MacLaurin, the then head of the ECB introduced a ruling that all England players were to wear the same tour issued clothing, which for Jack meant he wasn't allowed to wear his famous hat that he'd worn throughout his entire career.

"Apparently, he wanted us all to look tidy."

Jack offered up an ultimatum, unless he could wear his hat, he wouldn't play. "I spent two days on the phone to solicitors, it cost me a fortune. I was genuinely going to be sent home from the West Indies if I didn't wear the tour issued hat. In the end, I backed down because in the contract it said they had the right to tell me to wear whatever they wanted. I couldn't get out of it. Athers and Bumble argued for me and there were honestly team meetings about my hat! But I couldn't get them into trouble. The thing is it wasn't superstition, it was vision and comfort. The tour issued hat was uncomfortable as anything. In the end, I got in writing that I could cut the tour hat down so it was comfortable, so I did and it ended up looking scruffier that my hat! People didn't always realise how important that hat was to me. I'd worn it in every single first-class game of cricket I played in. I felt I'd had my soul ripped out. It ended up being the worst tour of my life. Not because I was sulking; I tried hard throughout but it just didn't go well for me."

And that was to be Jack's final tour as a Test cricketer. However, in the ICC Trophy a year later, in what was Jack's final swansong as an England cricketer he did defy his bosses one last time with the hat! "I didn't tell anyone but I knew that was going to be my last tournament. You were meant to wear blue hats so I sowed a blue hat on top of my hat and wore it in those last internationals in that tournament. They couldn't stop me as it was blue on the outside!"

And with that tournament done Jack's England career came to an end. To many his record of nearly 2,000 Test runs, 153 catches and 12 stumping's should have been so much more.

I asked Jack, when he reflects on his England journey what was his favourite Test dismissal? "Stumping Dean Jones down the leg side at Sydney, stood up off Gladstone Small."

Following his England career, Jack went back and enjoyed many years at his beloved Gloucestershire, until he eventually retired from first class cricket in 2004. Jack ended his first-class career with nearly 17,000 runs under his belt an amazing 1,192 catches and 128 stumpings. Add on 6,500 List A runs, 465 catches and 98 stumpings, what a phenomenal player and what a phenomenal record.

I asked Jack who were some of the best bowlers he kept to. "Courtney Walsh was the most prolific, Tuffers was the best spinner, Devon was the quickest, although Craig White was super quick, but overall, Walshy."

And what about the best captain? "They were all different if I'm honest. David Graveney gave me my chance – he ended the career of one of his mates to allow me to play, I admire him for that; Graham Gooch lead from the front; I always got on well with Athers; but overall? I'd say Athers for me. Even when I wasn't playing, he would knock on my door and tell me his reasons face to face which you always appreciated."

I asked Jack about cricket today and how he thinks he would have fared. "I wouldn't play today; I couldn't hit enough sixes. Then there is fitness, plus with the England lads playing all year round, they never really get to play for their counties, I used to love that. I'm not sure it would be as enjoyable for me now. I loved playing for my county, at the out grounds, it's all changed so much. I was so lucky to have played in the era I did, I wouldn't have changed a thing."

Jack's efforts now are all concentrated on his gallery and making a continued success of his art. "I've painted for 30 years and I knew it was what I wanted to do when I finished playing. When I look back my artwork kept me sane at times on tours and allowed me to recharge my batteries. It has always been mentally good for me. These days all I can do is paint and sign something, but I absolutely love it!"

And we all love Jack Russell. As England fans, we owe him an incredible debt of gratitude. He brought us so many memories. I urge you all if you get a chance to visit Jack's gallery in Chipping Sodbury, do it, he'd love to see you. You can check out more of Jack's art on his website www.jackrussell.co.uk and if you've enjoyed reading the above as much as I did writing it, then you can read even more in Jack's book: The Art of Jack Russell http://www.jackrussell.co.uk/index.php/counties

10

JOHN MORRIS
FORMER ENGLAND, DERBYSHIRE & DURHAM BATSMAN

With the current England team struggling to nail down a consistent number three batsman; for this interview I spoke to a former player who was one of county cricket's finest number 3's for nearly 15 years. Sadly, this former Derbyshire and Durham player was only to play three Test matches for his country. At a time when our national team was struggling, for many it was a loss to English cricket. The player in question is John Morris.

We'll come on to the reasons behind John's non-selection later, but given John amassed over 21,000 first class runs it'd be wrong to focus this piece on a single prank which was hardly a crime of the century.

A late developer, John began his career playing in the North Staffordshire/South Cheshire league for Crewe Cricket Club. Despite being a football mad youngster, he didn't start playing cricket properly until he was 11 years old. By the time he was 12 he was playing second XI cricket; by 14 he was in the first Xl at Crewe; at 15 he was opening the batting and at 16 he was playing for the league representative side. It was a rapid rise for the youngster who by the age of 17 had been signed by Derbyshire.

"I'd been spotted playing for the North Staffordshire/South Cheshire league side by people from Derbyshire and consequently was asked to go on trial and they signed me for the following year," said John.

It was wise decision, especially given the transitional period that the county was going through at time. "One of the appeals of Derbyshire was that it was an aging side. John Wright and Peter Kirsten were the overseas players at the time, but they weren't going to stay. Mike Hendrick had left straight after their NatWest Trophy final; Bob Taylor, Geoff Miller and David Steele were close to retirement so Derbyshire fitted nicely as I knew there could be an opportunity to break into the 1st Xl."

He wasn't wrong. John made his county debut in 1982 against a touring Pakistan side. "The debut didn't go too well, I scored just six before being caught off the bowling of Mudassar Nazar in the first innings and out for 12 in the second innings. I was definitely nervous!"

Not a surprise given the youngster was just 18 years of age. But, despite two low scores it was a terrific learning experience. After all how could one not learn when taking the field against the likes of Javed Miandad, Abdul Qadir et al?

What followed was arguably one of the most successful periods of Derbyshire's history. A new young team developed under the captaincy of Kim Barnett; Lord's finals were reached and the Sunday League was won - it was a memorable time.

"From 1988 to 1993 we had an excellent time. We had a team that grew up together and it just felt the right place to play cricket."

As well as John, they had a formidable new ball bowling attack of Michael Holding and a young Devon Malcolm. "Can you imagine at the time what was going through the opposition's heads turning up to play us and having to face Michael Holding and Devon - it was fearful."

The side reached the Benson & Hedges Cup final in 1988 but lost to a strong Hampshire side. "They beat us quite comfortably. Stephen Jeffries an ex South African all-rounder bowled us out cheaply and the game was a non-event after that. But it was a special occasion for us. At the time, the Benson & Hedges Cup was regarded as the FA Cup of cricket. It was special to us that we got so close to winning it. Two years later we won the Sunday League and that was huge."

But 1990 was not just a huge year for Derbyshire, it was arguably one of the best years of John's career. His runs at Derbyshire had finally caught the attention of the national selectors and he was called into the England squad for the Summer's internationals against India. A series that was to break many records and be the introduction to international cricket of one of the all-time greats of the game.

"I played really well in 1990, obviously you have to, to get in the team. But I just came off the back off three successive hundreds in one weekend down at Taunton – a hundred in each innings of the championship game and a hundred in the Sunday League which was sandwiched in the middle. I got back home after the game and received a call from Graham Gooch, inviting me to join the squad at Trent Bridge for the one-day internationals against India. I didn't play in any of the ODI's but it was brilliant to be involved. During that ODI series Graham Gooch pulled me to one side and told me that I'd be playing in the three Test matches – it was brilliant news to hear."

John made his debut in the famous Test match at Lord's where Graham Gooch scored his incredible 333. "I batted at six and was sat on the balcony for a day and three quarters before I went out to bat! I always thought I was the right man for a crisis as I walked out at 648 for 4! I'm not sure my four not out changed the game!"

I asked John what the atmosphere was like in the dressing room as Gooch piled on the runs. "It's funny in cricket. Superstitions can be quite bizarre. Fortunately for me I didn't really have any so I was able to enjoy the innings. Personally though, I was nervous at the start of the game, but getting there on that first morning and not having to bat was a big bonus as I could get used to the atmosphere. For the first hour I just looked at the Lord's crowd. The Test match was going on but I was absorbed by the crowd and the atmosphere. Thankfully that became less and less

the longer we batted. I was also lucky that Devon was in the same team. We were good friends and it definitely helped having a friendly face around in a new dressing room."

It was an incredible series for John to be involved in. People always recall Gooch's innings, but as John recalled there were a number of magical moments. "Mohammad Azhaurddin scored some incredible hundreds in that series, which get forgotten. Kapil Dev hit four successive sixes off of Eddie Hemmings at nine wickets down, to save the follow on at Lord's and the series saw Sachin Tendulkar's first Test century. It was an unbelievable series."

For John personally, there was perhaps frustration that he wasn't able to go out and deliver a big score to firmly cement his place. "I had to retire hurt in the second Test match. I remember it went quite dark and we were looking to declare so Robin Smith and I stayed out to try and set up a declaration. Kapil Dev was bowling and Robin Smith whacked one down the ground and it hit me full on the elbow. I never saw it. My arm stiffened up over night and the following morning I just couldn't hold a bat. Jack Russell came in and scored a 50 – he definitely scored my runs there! In the final Test at the Ova I was moved up the order to number 4, but then Neil Williams came in for his Test debut and he came in to bat as a night-watchman and scored 50, so again I was left to wait and wait in the dressing room. When I did get out to the middle, I nicked one for 7, so I knew I was then under pressure in the second innings. The Oval was always seen as the match where you would secure a Winter tour spot. I managed to put on a partnership with David Gower, who scored 170, I got to 32 and I felt I was batting well. I remember getting bounced and hooked the ball for four and thought I was in the zone, but then next ball I got caught behind down the leg side. A horrible death!"

John returned to county cricket with Derbyshire and knew he would have to endure a nervous wait to see if his 32 was enough to secure an Ashes tour spot that Winter. Thankfully the call did come and he was on the plane down under for his first taste of Ashes cricket.

"The Ashes tour is always the one you want to go on. I was desperately disappointed four years earlier that I didn't get selected because I played really well in 1986. They took James Whitaker instead. In 1989 I felt I could have gone to the West Indies but they took Rob Bailey and Nasser Hussain. I guess those disappointments made me more determined in 1990. To finally get the call was great."

Sadly, the tour was a frustrating affair for John and ultimately brought an abrupt end to his international career.

"It was hugely disappointing. We were beaten in the first Test at Brisbane. I didn't get any significant scores in the warmup games and they brought Alec Stewart in to replace me from the team that finished the Summer Tests. Wayne Larkins opened the batting, replacing Goochy who had split his hand open in a warm up game. But I did get selected for the one-day side. There was an ODI World Series competition featuring us, Australia and New Zealand with the games scattered throughout the Ashes. I scored 67 not out in the first game which gave me confidence. We should have won that game but we got beat needing 18 off the last over. I was out there with big Dev, so that was never going to be realistic! I was then asked to open after that and I got 30 against New Zealand at the WACA. I remember when we then played Australia next up and Wayne Larkins and I put on 50 for the first wicket – he got 40 of them, hitting Terry Alderman all over the park, leaving me to get bombarded by Carl Rackemann at the other end! I was getting hit everywhere! Goochie returned after that and I was moved back down to number six but I didn't get the consistency back."

John's tour and international career then took a huge turn following a first-class game prior to the 4th Test of the series.

"I was asked to bat at number 3, my preferred position and scored 132. Then came the Tiger Moth incident."

For those of you not aware of this event; after John and David Gower were out, they both left the ground and flew a Tiger Moth plane over the ground, with the sole intention of creating bit of laughter, raising morale among a group of team-mates who had been struggling on tour. It was a decision that effectively ended John's international career.

"Everyone has had their say on it but I've never really been asked. I got out just before lunch for 132 in what was a rain affected match. Robin Smith was 90 not out and David Gower had got out not long after me for not that many. Later on, I was walking down the steps back to the dressing room, when I heard David Gower and Allan Lamb having a conversation in reference to the plane. I asked what he was planning and he said that these planes had been buzzing about, let's give the lads a bit of fun and a lift. So, I said I'd come and join him. We knew we were batting until tea and that would be it. We flew over the ground and once we landed, we returned to the ground. Graham Morris, a photographer asked us if we would go back in the evening to the airfield to get some photos. I think that was what really annoyed Graham Gooch as David had said he was going for a run. The following day the photos were all over the papers. It wasn't pleasant from that moment on. I was fined £1,000. Did the crime fit the punishment? No, it was only meant to be a bit of fun but they wanted to make a bigger issue out of it than was necessary. There was friction between Graham and David Gower although David was playing out of his skin; he got one of the best hundreds you'll ever see at Sydney and another one at Melbourne. He was playing fantastically well. Robin Smith had been struggling and I thought I might get in the team after that knock so I was buzzing. I honestly thought it was a fun way to lift morale in a side that had been struggling and not winning games. I honestly believe it was taken out of context by the management. There had been other crimes that had been far worse in that period, with people kicking over stumps in games. It just didn't feel right. I didn't get back in the team after that. My series and Test career were over from that moment onwards. I hoped it wasn't and I was positive enough to think that if I could get back into the runs with my County I could get back into contention, but I never got a mention after that tour."

John went on score a bucketful of runs in County Cricket. In 1993 he scored six hundreds and one double hundred against the likes of Courtney Walsh, Waqar Younis and Wasim Akram, as Derbyshire went on to win the Benson & Hedges Cup, but his name never got a mention.

"In the Winter of 1993 there was a tour to the West Indies. I'd scored all those hundreds against some of the best quick bowlers around and I didn't get a mention. I realised then that was it for me at international level."

In need of a fresh challenge, with no carrot of international cricket, John made the move from Derbyshire to Durham.

"I had been at Derbyshire a long time, but things were changing. There had been friction in the dressing room and after the door had been shut for me on England, I needed a new challenge."

Durham, two years earlier had become the 18th first class county in England. Despite finishing bottom of the Championship in their first few seasons, they had lofty ambitions. A new stadium was under development and it was the perfect challenge for John at this stage of his career.

"There were other options open to me. Warwickshire tried hard to sign me, as did Somerset and Hampshire. But Durham was the perfect fit. It was definitely a struggle in those first few years, especially with the pitches in the North East, but I loved it at Durham and made some great friends up there. When I first joined, we were still touring around the County playing at Darlington, Chester Le Street Cricket Club and the University Ground. I loved those out grounds but the new stadium was on its way and that was a big attraction – I wanted to be part of that."

John had the honour of becoming the first player to score a first class hundred at Chester Le Street and his presence at the club helped lay the foundations for a talented group of youngsters that were emerging in the North East, including the likes of Paul Collingwood and Steve Harmison.

"We had to set a standard that was needed around the club and although we struggled and weren't a top, top team when I was playing, we knew had to help put standards in place that would stick with young cricketers for years to come. David Boon came in as captain and brought some good stuff with him."

John stayed with Durham for six seasons before moving on to

Nottinghamshire in 2000 and retiring in 2001.

It had been a long and successful first-class career; over 21,000 first class runs and 52 first class centuries. It's just such a shame we, as England fans, never got to see the John Morris that members of Derbyshire and Durham saw week in, week out. At a time when England was struggling for a number three batsman it seems crazy looking back why John wasn't given that opportunity and what can be described as a mistake, with the best intentions, had been held against him.

But John is proud of what he did achieve in the game. I asked him when he looks back at his career what his best innings was. "I genuinely can't answer that! If pushed, I would probably have to say a hundred I got for Durham at Old Trafford. It was a quick, quick wicket and they had Wasim Akram roaring in so that is definitely right up there."

And the best bowler faced? "Without any shadow of doubt, Malcolm Marshall. There was nothing he couldn't do. He could bowl quick; he could swing it and he could seam it. His understanding of how to set up a batsman and then get them out was second to none. He was also a bloody good bloke. I always loved the challenge of playing against him as I knew it would be a challenge. I know a lot of players may have been like 'oh I hope Marshall isn't fit and not playing today, great'. But I was disappointed if that ever happened. I wanted the challenge of playing against the best players – it was part of the game."

Graham Gooch is the batsman that John ranks at number one of all those he played with. "Graham Gooch just had this sheer ability for big scores and destructiveness. It's why his record is up there with the best. I always looked at Gooch as the flagship batsman I played with – and I only played three Test matches with him! Aside from Gooch, I loved watching Viv Richards bat. He was my idol as a batsman. Playing against the likes of him, Joel Garner and Ian Botham was a big thing for me."

To be honest, John could have a list of 20+ players given the all-time greats that were around playing County cricket in that era. "We had a thing in the Derbyshire dressing room that if you weren't switched on you'd get your head knocked off because wherever you went apart from Yorkshire (who didn't have overseas players at that time- you had to be born in Yorkshire to play for them) every County had a top overseas batter and a top overseas bowler. It was great to play against Joel Garner, Patrick Patterson, Wasim Akram, Richard Hadlee etc but that list didn't include the England players who were also playing. County cricket was so strong then. I'd never belittle County cricket now, but in today's game England players rarely play and with all of the competitions around the world you don't get the best overseas players playing County cricket."

It's a very valid point.

John is now enjoying life after cricket. He runs an events business with former England, Newcastle United, Charlton Athletic, Derby County and West Ham footballer Rob Lee. And as well as this business, he is a Business Development Director of Vin-x, a fine wine investment company.

As England look to fill the problem number three position, let's hope somewhere there's another John Morris waiting for a chance.

11

PETER SUCH
FORMER ENGLAND & ESSEX SPINNER

The 1990s was an interesting decade for English cricket, as characterised by Mark Butcher's documentary on Sky Sports. It therefore seemed apt that, for this interview I spoke to a cricketer who experienced the highs and lows of playing for England in the 90s, former off-spinner Peter Such. "I loved the era I played in," remarked Peter, who is now the ECB's national spin coach. "I was fortunate I played with, and against, some really great players of the game."

And I think something we often forget when we refer back to the 1990s was just how strong that decade was - some of the greatest players ever were lining up to play England: the likes of Wasim Akram, Curtly Ambrose, Allan Border, Allan Donald, Anil Kumble, Brian Lara, Glenn McGrath, Viv Richards, Sachin Tendulkar, Courtney Walsh, Shane Warne and Waqar Younis. The list goes on and on.

Regular changes of the captain and coach throughout the decade meant Peter only played 11 Test matches for England (over a six year period), yet he was arguably one of England's most consistent off spin bowlers, picking up five wicket hauls both home and away against Australia, which in itself is no mean feat. "I've always appreciated the fact I was able to play for England and seven out of my 11 Test matches were against Australia home and away which are the iconic series to play in so I am incredibly pleased to have done that."

Interestingly, when growing up, Peter actually had ambitions of being an out and out fast bowler, in the mould of his childhood heroes John Snow, Dennis Lillee, Jeff Thompson and the great West Indian fast bowlers. "I quite fancied being a fast bowler when I started playing as a child. Then everyone else matured a little bit quicker than me and I got left behind a bit so I started bowling off spin in the nets one day and fortunately for my career, my sports master saw me bowling off spin and told me I was playing in a game that evening, bowling off spin and I bowled spin from then on!"

It was sound judgement from Peter's sports teacher, as a few years later, in 1982, he was making his debut in county cricket, bowling off spin for Nottinghamshire at Trent Bridge, playing alongside the likes of Eddie Hemmings. However, knowing he was behind an experienced campaigner such as Hemmings, Peter knew his first X1 opportunities would be limited and in 1987 made the move slightly south, to Leicestershire. "I wanted to play more and more cricket and that was never going to happen for me at Notts so I moved to Leicestershire."

Despite a good first year at Grace Road, Peter's stay at Leicestershire was a short one. "The move to Leicestershire worked out well for the first year I was there. I played the vast majority of all the championship cricket and was reasonably successful. But it was a period where there were a lot of green pitches and following that first year I didn't get much of a gig and was slowly squeezed out. Essex were looking to sign a spin bowler and I knew if I made the move to Essex there was a proper opportunity for me to play cricket."

It was a wise decision. Just three years later, Peter was making his Test debut, in the first Test of the 1993 Ashes series. "Playing for England is what you aspire to try and do. I was just fortunate, that my debut was in an Ashes Test".

However, such was the unprofessional manner in which the game was governed in those early days, Peter found out about his selection through a journalist, who had called him for his reaction. "It was disappointing to find out I was about to play for England that way. I received a call from a journalist who had obviously been a recipient of a leak somewhere and he told me I was playing and wanted my reaction. It was later that I then got a phone call from the England selectors, to tell me that I had been included in the Test squad for the first Test at Old Trafford against the Aussies."

It was a huge step up for Peter, but from a personal perspective his debut couldn't have gone better. "With the increased media presence, television cameras, big crowd, it was a nerve-wracking experience. Fortunately, I was given an early bowl and managed to bowl a maiden over first up, which helped settle me down."

And settle him down it did, as Peter followed up that maiden over with an impressive haul of six first innings wickets. "My wickets were split over two days. I remember the first day's play started late and so we lost some time. In the evening session on that first day, I managed to get David Boon caught at first slip by Chris Lewis. Then I caught and bowled Mark Taylor and finally I bowled an off-spinner's dream delivery, one that drifted one way and then spun back through the gate to bowl Steve Waugh's off stump."

Boon, Taylor and Waugh – not a bad first three Test wickets!

Despite not sleeping well that night, no doubt because of the inevitable high of taking those three wickets, Peter's early success continued the following morning. "There was still a little bit of damp in the pitch on that second morning and the ball continued to grip. I got Allan Border stumped, Brendon Julian caught at short leg and for my sixth wicket Merv Hughes had a slog and was caught at deep square. At the end of the innings I received a standing ovation which was absolutely brilliant and as I walked passed the Australian dressing room, both Allan Border and Mark Taylor were stood there to shake my hand and say well bowled, which I thought was a lovely touch."

It was dream debut. But, sadly, England went on to lose that opening Test, in part due to the exploits of Shane Warne, who of course bowled that ball to Mike Gatting. "I watched it live from the balcony. In those days the Old Trafford pitch was square on, so you saw the shot that Gatting had played, and just thought how did that get past the bat? We had to pop inside to watch the television replays. It was a wonderful delivery."

England's fortunes didn't improve in the second Test at Lord's, losing heavily by an innings. The selectors rang the changes for the third Test at Trent Bridge, with the likes of Graham Thorpe, Mark Lathwell, Martin McCague and Mark Ilott coming in for their Test debuts. Despite an improved performance by the side, who achieved a creditable draw, the selectors decided not to play with any spinners for the fourth Test at Headingley and so Peter missed out. The side suffered another heavy defeat and the Ashes were gone. "Graham Gooch resigned after that Test and Mike Atherton took over."

The fifth Test, Atherton's first, saw Peter restored to the line-up, alongside veteran John Emburey, as the selectors went from playing without any spinners to fielding two in the same side. But after another heavy defeat, the selectors made yet more changes for the final Test at the Oval, with Robin Smith, John

Emburey, Martin Bicknell and Mark Ilott all omitted. This time, the changes seemed to have the desired effect as England finished off their disappointing Ashes campaign with an excellent Oval victory.

Although it wasn't a successful first series for Peter from a team perspective, at an individual level, his consistency with the ball, led him to be the leading English wicket-taker with 16 wickets.

I asked Peter if he thought all of the constant changes during the series had an adverse effect on both the team and the players as individuals. "I can't say it really bothered me; it was just one of those things. The selectors pick a team and you go out and play. I was just focused on trying to perform as best as I could."

Following that series, England went on to tour that Winter to the West Indies, the first tour under the captaincy of Mike Atherton. It was said to be the beginning of a new dawn for English cricket. However, the surprise element of the squad was the non-selection of Peter, despite being the leading wicket taker in the Ashes, as the selectors favoured Phil Tufnell and Ian Salisbury as spinners for the tour.

"It was difficult to take from the fact that I had played five out of the six Test matches, was the leading wicket-taker and I bowled well throughout the series. But what really frustrated me and made me angry was again I wasn't informed by anyone in an official capacity. I just turned on the television, looked at Ceefax and saw that my name wasn't there."

Peter was recalled to the squad the following Summer, where he played three home Tests against New Zealand, but then didn't play another Test match for his country for four years. "I played those three Test matches against New Zealand in 1994 and although I started pretty well, my performances did fade a little bit and by the time I got left out, I probably deserved to be left out."

Peter went back to county cricket with Essex and regularly took in excess of 70 wickets as he bid to win back in his place. "It was a tough time, but all I could do was do the best I could. I had some big seasons taking 70/80 wickets in three successive seasons, but I just wasn't the kind of cricketer Raymond Illingworth was looking for. He was looking for a more all-round cricketer and I just didn't fit the bill. Everyone else was being given a go and it was frustrating knowing I was performing but wasn't getting an opportunity."

As luck would then have it, an "average" season, using Peter's own words in 1998, ended up with him being selected for the 1998 Ashes tour to Australia. "It was quite ironic that the years I was playing really well, I didn't get picked and then I have one average season, and I get selected for the tour. I often say to young cricketers now that you never know when your opportunity will come, so don't ever give up and try to be ready when it does." Wise advice.

England headed down under in the Winter of 1998 with a completely different set-up to when Peter last played for England in 1994. David 'Bumble' Lloyd was now England coach and Alec Stewart was captaining the side. "I really enjoyed that tour. We managed to draw the first Test in Brisbane but then lost the next two, so the Ashes were gone pretty quickly. But we fought back really well in Melbourne, Dean Headley bowled fantastically well in that final innings to help us win the Test."

Indeed it was a magnificent win, and if you speak to a lot of England supporters who were in Melbourne for that Test, it was one of the most memorable England Test wins overseas in recent times.

As a result of that win in the fourth Test, England went into the final Test match of the series in Sydney knowing that a win would level the series. A hat-trick by Darren Gough restricted the Aussies to 322 in their first innings, however a five-wicket haul from leg-spinner Stuart MacGill saw England succumb to 220 all out, a deficit of 102 runs. England however, scented victory and fought back, as thanks to five wickets from Peter and four from Dean Headley. The Aussies were all out for just 184 in their second innings, a lead of 286. 123 of those 184 runs came from the bat of Michael Slater, who scored an outstanding 123. But it was a brilliant England bowling performance. The only regret was the non run-out of Slater when he was only on 35. "The TV umpire couldn't see the bails get dislodged because some idiot called Such was in the way of the throw! Headley threw the stumps down from long on and I was stood in a place that obscured the view of the stumps being broken. The funny thing is, Slater had actually given up and started to walk off, when Mark Waugh shouted at him and told him not to give himself out and let the third umpire make the decision."

England lost that fifth Test but the performances in Melbourne and Sydney made the supporters proud and showed the Aussies that English cricket did have some fight. "It was a wonderful experience to get five wickets in Sydney and I really enjoyed that tour. David Lloyd was a good guy and a coach I really liked."

Sadly for Peter, he only went on to play one more Test for England, against New Zealand at Old Trafford the following Summer, the ground where it had all begun six years previously. Despite taking four wickets in that final appearance, his final Test will be more remembered for his batting. His first innings 51 ball duck was the longest duck in England Test history! "You have to appreciate I wasn't very good when it came to batting. I was always very nervous about batting and, in that innings, we were in a precarious situation at 152 for eight when I went out to bat. We'd had an absolute stinker, having won the toss and batted. It was a case of trying to block it and try and keep Mark Ramprakash company as long as I could, as he was batting very well at the other end. It was quite embarrassing to be honest, walking off to a standing ovation, having scored nought!"

And so Peter's Test career came to an end with a total haul of 37 wickets, at an average of 33.56 runs and at an economy rate of just 2.38 runs per over.

I asked Peter if he thought one of the unfair challenges for English spinners in the 1990s was the ongoing comparison to the likes of Shane Warne and Anil Kumble, who were all-time greats of the game. "You were always judged alongside them because they were playing in your era, but the fact of the matter was they were great bowlers. Shane Warne is the greatest spin bowler that I've ever seen. I wouldn't say it was unfair, but sometimes we were judged alongside them and people thought we should be as good them, but they were geniuses. We were as good we could be, but we were just not as good as them."

I also asked Peter of his favourite memories from those 11 Tests. "Nothing tops your Test debut, but the five for in Sydney was brilliant. Also on that same tour I was proud of how I held it together in the Test match at Adelaide, where it was played in sweltering conditions and we had to field for a day and a half. But overall, I was proud of the fact I was worth my place in the side pretty much every time I played in terms of the way I performed."

After that Test against New Zealand in 1999, Peter went back to play county cricket for his beloved Essex and it was obvious when speaking to him how much he enjoyed his time at Chelmsford. "We won back-to-back county championships in 1991 and 1992. To me, winning the championship is the one you want to win in county cricket. To win it you've got to play quality cricket over six months. But we also reached three one day cup finals at Lord's and in those days those final were proper massive events with packed houses, the FA Cup finals of cricket. We lost the NatWest trophy to Lancashire, but the following year we went back and beat Warwickshire convincingly and the year after that we beat Leicestershire in the Benson and Hedges final. It was great times and we had some fantastic players. Graham Gooch was the glue that held it all together and he was the outstanding individual and cricketer in the group. But we had some real quality performers in the likes of Neil Foster, Derek Pringle, John Childs, Mark Waugh, Salim Malik, Stuart Law and some quality youngsters who came through like Nasser Hussain, Nick Knight, John Stephenson and Mark Ilott. We had good players and I always believe good players make good teams. We were fortunate."

Peter finished playing in 2001 and a year later he was invited to apply for the position of academy director at Essex. He was successful in that interview and went on to hold that position for five years before moving out of cricket for three years. But, in September 2009, Peter was asked to lead the spin bowling department at the ECB, where he remains to this day. "I love this role. Spin bowling is my passion so it's a perfect role for me. Coaching is one of those things that is as close as you can get to playing. I really enjoy working with spin bowlers trying to help them become the best they can be and hopefully go on and fulfil their ambitions."

Peter works with spinners both collectively and on a one to one basis and is also responsible for coach education in the country.

I asked Peter what kind of challenges the three formats of the game bring to spin coaches. "The basics of the game will always remain the same, but the most important thing you can do as a spin bowler is to spin the ball as hard as you can. That will get you the drop and drift in the air you need to get the break and bounce off the pitch, so no matter what you're doing you need to spin the ball hard. It then comes down to the different sort of skills and attributes that you need to be effective in the three different formats. But, whatever the format, the basics are the same so with any young spin bowler you must encourage them to spin the ball hard and then if they can put that into a bowling action that is repeatable, they will get the consistency that they need and then you can build things from there."

The fruit of Peter's hard work was definitely visible in the recent under 19s World Cup where some of England's new breed of young spinners were on show and Peter is definitely excited about the future of spin bowling England and if he can produce spinners who, like himself, have the ability to take five wicket hauls both home and away against Australia and over 800 first class wickets in a career, we'll be in a very good place.

12

ANGUS FRASER
FORMER ENGLAND & MIDDLESEX SEAM BOWLER

Another influential player from the 1990s was a bowler who was consistent, hugely accurate, a wicket-taker and someone who, but for injury and strange selection decisions, should have played many, many more Test matches for his country, Angus Fraser.

And with the 2019 tour of the West Indies drawing to a close, it seemed a good place to start our discussion, particularly given Gus's success in the Caribbean. In 17 Test matches against the West Indies home and away, he took an incredible 70 wickets at an average of just 23.70 and at an economy rate of 2.69. So, what made him so successful, particularly on those Caribbean pitches and against arguably one of the strongest sides (and batting line-ups) to have ever played the game?

"It's a good question. I just love the Caribbean. When we played, every island was like a celebration of the sport. The West Indies had a damned good side and it was raw, tough cricket. The pitches definitely favoured my style of bowling. In somewhere like Australia where the pitches were quicker and bouncier, they probably favoured slightly quicker bowlers than me. In the West Indies, where the pitches were typically lower and slower, the balls would tend to hit the stumps more meaning batsmen had to play at every delivery. This brought more LBWs into play. And of course, the mentality of the West Indies' batsmen was always to be slightly more aggressive and they didn't necessarily respect bowlers as they perhaps should. All of which helped bowlers like me and Glenn McGrath, at our paces, to be so effective in those conditions."

Many more West Indies stories to come, including that 46 all out "in which I was the not out batsman, remember!" but, as with all of our interviewees let's rewind to those early days. What was Gus's cricketing upbringing?

"Well, I was actually born in Lancashire and though we moved to London when I was two, I grew up as a Lancashire supporter. My brother was born in Edgware, so when we played cricket as kids in the garden, I'd be Lancashire and he'd be Middlesex!"

"My father played a lot of club cricket for Stanmore. He was never a great cricketer - I think he might have played one game for the 1st eleven - but captained their 3rd team. So, my brother (Alastair) and I would spend many Saturday's and Sunday's at Stanmore in the nets while Dad was playing. You obviously play all sports as a kid, but the fact your father played a lot of cricket meant you spent more time in a cricketing environment than others."

And who were some of those early cricketing heroes?

"1981 and Botham's Ashes was obviously a big memory and had a huge influence on me. It was always fast bowlers that I enjoyed watching more so than batsmen. Dennis Lillee was another."

Gus and his brother followed in his father's footsteps and both pulled on the Stanmore sweaters. Yet, it was his brother who made the bigger initial impression.

"My brother was a better athlete than me and still is! We were two decent youth cricketers. He played in all of the Middlesex youth team sides and was picked for all of the England age group sides and was seen as the Fraser that was going to make it. I didn't really play any representative cricket until I was 17."

"Luck played a huge part in my development. I was fortunate that cricket was a big sport at my school. I had a brother rather than a sister, so that pushed me in my cricket. I lived in a street where there were two or three other lads of similar ages who all enjoyed playing cricket, so I'd always be playing on the street and on the grass verges etc. I suddenly shot up in size and caught Middlesex's eye."

Gus made his debut for Stanmore's 1st XI at the age of 16 his performances in the Middlesex League soon got noticed by Don Bennett, the Middlesex coach.

"Suddenly you hear than Don had been at a Stanmore game to watch you bowl and then all of a sudden at the age of 17 I was getting picked for Middlesex Schools and Middlesex Young Cricketers and by 18 I was offered a first-class contract. So, for me everything happened very late and very quickly."

And what was it like walking into a successful Middlesex environment that contained famous names such as Gatting, Butcher, Radley, Downton, Emburey, Edmonds, Cowan, Williams and Daniel?

"It was a wonderful side. But, in those days there used to be a real hierarchy around the dressing room in that there were two groups: capped players and uncapped players. The uncapped players didn't get certain privileges and your job as an uncapped player was to look after the capped players. But slowly those attitudes started to change. The arrival of players like Phil Tufnell probably helped with that!"

The success and strength of that Middlesex side also meant England regularly came calling, opening up opportunities for the younger players. "At times we were probably losing three or four players a Test match to England. Add injuries to that and opportunities opened up for players like myself and suddenly your thrust into the spotlight."

And what made Middlesex such as successful side in your early years?

"Success was expected. For a six or seven-year period there probably wasn't a season where we weren't either winning a trophy or competing for one and we were very serious about our work. We used to get together a week earlier than anyone else for pre-season to work on our fitness. OK, it wasn't as scientific as it is now but while other counties were probably easing back into their pre-season routine, we were in a dusty gym in Ealing having an intensive week of fitness training. It wasn't breath-taking but it showed how serious we all were about our cricket and how far ahead of other counties we were at that moment in time."

In Gus's time as a player at Middlesex, the side won numerous one-day titles and cups but the icing on the cake were three county championships. One of the keys to success was the side's ability to evolve, quickly.

"In a relatively short time we lost the likes of Barlow, Radley, Downton, Edmonds and Daniel. In their place came the likes of Desmond Haynes, Mark Ramprakash, John Carr, Philip Tufnell, Keith Brown and me. We became a very different team. We still had a core of that older side with the likes of Gatting, Emburey and Cowan etc, but we became a 'mate's together' team. We all socialised a lot and, in a way, it was a very chalk and cheese environment to what there had been before."

And with all the success that the side achieved, what were some of Gus's early Middlesex highlights?

"Being awarded my county cap on the balcony at Lord's was a big thing for me. Getting a wicket on my debut, in my 3rd over, knocking Jeff Hopkins' middle stump out of the ground was brilliant – although I did end up with match figures of 1/120! Winning all of those titles was obviously big, but a particular high was the NatWest final in 1988 when we beat Worcestershire in the Final at Lord's. In those days the NatWest Final was the biggest domestic occasion. The lead up to the game was all about Graeme Hick coming in and being the great white hope of English cricket. I bowled well and got him out in my opening spell. We won the game and playing on that stage in front of the TV cameras and performing, showed me I could handle the occasion. The two-county championship wins in 1990 and 1993 were brilliant but fast forward to today and where I am now (Managing Director of Middlesex), winning the county championship in 2016 surpasses those title wins in my playing days, as far as satisfaction goes. As a player you can be quite selfish; it's about you and you don't always see the bigger picture. In the position I'm in now, you see what a title means to a lot more people: to the board, to the members and to the supporters. Seeing young players come through and achieve their dreams and goals is something very difficult to put a price on."

Gus's performances for Middlesex saw early international recognition when he was selected in the squad for the second Test of the 1989 Ashes series at Lord's. Gus wasn't picked in the final eleven, but finally did get his chance, one Test later at Edgbaston.

"Without trying to sound arrogant, throughout my career I always felt I was ready to move up a level before I actually moved up. I always thought I was ready to play for Middlesex before I was selected, and it was the same with England. I took 80 odd wickets in the 1988 season and bowled well in that NatWest Final. I thought I was ready to tour in the Winter with England. The tour to India got cancelled, but the following Summer I felt I was ready, but I had to wait. I was picked in the squad for the 2nd Test at Lord's. I was given my kit and then because I wasn't picked in the final eleven, I had to give it all back. That was heart-breaking. Everything you strive for is to own that cap and jersey, so to be given it and then have to give it back wasn't a nice feeling. In those days you weren't allowed to keep any of your kit, until you played for England. I eventually made my debut in the next Test match at Edgbaston."

England drew the Test and Gus made an immediate impact taking 4/63 from 33 overs. "I remember it was a very hot and humid day and I refused to take off my England sweater all day! I was so proud to wear it. My first over was a maiden to Mark Taylor but that first day was curtailed by thunderstorms. On the second day I got my first wicket, Steve Waugh, and went on to take 4/63."

I asked Gus how important is to get early success when you make a debut?

"Very. It proves to yourself you can do it. You look at some players like Hick and Ramprakash and they unfortunately had to wait a while to put in a performance which showed people that they were capable to deliver as that level. But the confidence you get from putting that performance in early is much stronger. So, for me to get 4/63 in that first innings was acknowledgment that I could perform at this level and that I wasn't out of my depth. I was playing against good players and making them work hard."

Gus ended up with nine wickets from his three Tests in that series and was one of England's bright lights in what was a heavy Ashes series defeat.

"It ended up being a pretty miserable Summer for English cricket. Everyone had England as favourites after Mike Gatting's win down under in 86/87, but the side was heavily beaten. Added to the Ashes, there was the announcement of the Rebel tour to South Africa. I wouldn't say it disillusioned me, but it definitely punctured the balloon. From getting picked to play for your country, the pride and the honour you take in that and then to see that, halfway through a Summer a number of players had had enough and would rather go and earn a few extra quid in South Africa on a rebel tour than play for England, brought a bit of reality to the situation."

Towards the end of that 1989 Ashes series, David Gower stood down as England captain and was replaced by Graham Gooch in what many hoped would a new dawn for English cricket.

"In many ways despite the Summer of 1989, it became an exciting little time and when I look back at the 1990s, I see it as a period where players did become more valued by the ECB. The decade started with players choosing to go on a Rebel tour to earn extra money but yet it finished with central contracts being introduced."

Gooch's first task as captain was to lead England on a tour to the Caribbean and a series against the formidable West Indies.

"We went to the West Indies with a young, exciting side. There was Alec Stewart, Nasser Hussain, Mike Atherton, Robin Smith was young at the time, Devon Malcolm, me, Philip Tufnell came through. There was a shift in direction that should have been a bright new dawn. We never really got that going for whatever reason. I guess those reasons could have been that domestic cricket in England didn't lend itself to England performing brilliantly because of the volume of cricket you had to play. You could play a Test match one day and then the next day would be driving to the other side of the country to play for your county."

England famously won the 1st Test in Jamaica, with Gus's 5/28 from 20 overs in the 1st innings playing a huge part in bowling the West Indies out for just 164; a side that contained so many great West Indian batsmen.

England lost the series 2-1 but had restored pride after the heavy Ashes defeat and, in Gus and Devon Malcolm, England had found an opening partnership that SHOULD have gone on to become one of England's best opening partnerships.

"Devon and I built up a really strong partnership on that tour. We complemented each other because he bowled bloody quick. When he got it right, he could be lethal. He made batsmen uncomfortable with his pace and I may be covered the fact that he might concede a few because I tended to be pretty tight. So, I felt I could feed off him and he could just concentrate on bowling fast."

I asked Gus if he felt that, if central contracts were around for that group of players, how much a difference that would have made.

"A huge difference. I played 46 Tests and took 180 wickets, averaging around four wickets a Test. With central contracts I probably could have played another 40/50 Tests. I loved my time playing for Middlesex but if we had central contracts my best overs would have been kept for England. But not just bowlers, the batsmen as well. Someone like Mark Ramprakash could have been a different player with a central contract and the confidence and re-assurance it would have given him."

The Summer of 1990 saw England beat India at home. People always remember Graham Gooch's famous 333 at Lord's, but Gus's eight wickets in the match went a long way towards the side winning by such a big margin. A Winter tour to Australia followed and after Gus's 6/82 in the Boxing Day Test at Melbourne, many believed England had unearthed a truly world class opening bowler, someone who would go on and have a long career for his country.

"Everything was going well for me. I loved how well it was all going with England. I loved how well I was playing. Middlesex was going really well and then I had the hip injury."

It was an injury that was career-threatening.

"When you get an injury like that, you realise how fortunate you are. I had no idea what I would have done if I didn't recover. I questioned whether I would ever play competitive cricket again."

The injury kept Gus out of the England side for nearly three years. He returned to the side for the final Test of the Ashes at the Oval in 1993 and he carried on where he left off with eight wickets in the match (a 5-wicket haul in the 1st innings) in what was a man of the match display, as England went on to secure a consolation victory over the Australians.

"Any wicket gives you satisfaction but that first wicket getting Mark Waugh caught behind, was as happy a wicket as I have ever taken."

The Winter of 1993/94 saw England return to the West Indies, this time under the captaincy of Mike Atherton and once again Gus didn't disappoint with 16 wickets in four Tests. This was the series that was famous for the 46 all-out in Trinidad and the win in Barbados where the West Indies had not lost for decades. Let's start with the 46 all out!

"It was a game we should have won. We dropped a couple of catches and we went from a position of needing around a hundred to win to having to chase nearer 200. The pitch wasn't easy. My abiding memory of that Test was my failure to get a roti! In those days the food in the dressing room was OK but in Trinidad I loved the rotis! Now, while you're bowling you don't want to eat one because you don't digest it and it's like bowling with a stone in your bloody gut so I waited all day and decided that once we had bowled them out I'll make my way over to the roti tent, which was at the other end of the ground to the dressing rooms. Despite losing two wickets in the first over I still decided to make my way round to the roti tent. But honestly, by the time I got halfway round I had to turn back to get my pads on - it buggered up my food for the day! Missed rotis aside, when people talk about that 46 all out, people forget we were playing against some bloody good cricketers. Ambrose is one of the all-time greats and he just bowled brilliantly and exposed any vulnerabilities we had. He was magnificent and we weren't up to it. Sometimes you just have to accept that. Cricket is a funny game. In some games you'll see the ball beat the bat 35 times and there will be no edges; on other occasions everything gets exposed. There are days when sides could easily be 20/5 without actually having done a lot wrong. Embarrassingly for us in Trinidad, the game went into the following day with us eight wickets down. But it must be remembered that I never got out!"

And then there was Barbados…

"People were talking about a 5-0 drubbing. All of a sudden, all the families had arrived, all the British tourists had arrived. People were calling us a disgrace. I remember the applause from the England supporters when Mike Atherton punched the ball through mid-on to take us past 46! Alec Stewart played brilliantly with two hundreds, it was a famous win."

And not forgetting of course, Gus's own 8/75 in the first innings as England restricted the West Indies to 304 in reply to England's 355.

Gus's comeback was going from strength to strength, but less than 12 month's later, he was incredibly left out of the 1994 Ashes squad entirely. New 'supremo' Ray Illingworth thought Gus didn't have the pace needed to unsettle Australia's batsmen.

He instead preferred the raw pace of Kent seamer Martin McCague. It was kick in the teeth for Gus, whose previous tour down under showed just how effective he was in those conditions.

"Obviously my relationship with Ray Illingworth wasn't a particularly positive one. Why I don't know. He had his view of what a fast bowler should be, and I didn't fit that image. I played five tests in the Summer, then was dropped for the last Test at the Oval when Devon got his nine wickets. Joey Benjamin came in and Ray felt he wanted to fight fire with fire in Australia and I wasn't part of his plan. The disappointing thing for me was I found out I wasn't in the squad from watching Sky. So, I positioned myself in Australia and played grade cricket, as I was put on stand-by, in case there were any injuries and illnesses."

As fate would have it, there were injuries and Gus was called into the squad prior to the 1st Test in Brisbane.

Gus didn't play, but he was recalled for the Test match at Sydney and he proved a point to Illingworth in the best possible way, by taking wickets. As England battled for victory, Gus bowled an outstanding spell of 5/73. It wasn't quite enough to get England over the line, but it was the perfect response.

Gus continued this form the following Summer against the West Indies. His 5/66 at Lord's (which helped England to victory) and his 4/45 at Old Trafford (in a 6-wicket win), were just two of his important contributions.

However, the Illingworth curse struck again in South Africa, when despite taking three wickets in the second innings of the Johannesburg Test (remember Atherton and Jack Russell!), Gus was again left out of the side, this time for two years. Some would say, a harsh way to treat a bowler who had regularly proved his value.

It wasn't the and for Gus in an England shirt. With Illingworth gone, Gus was recalled, unsurprisingly, for the 1998 tour of the West Indies in what was to become a memorable year for the seamer.

"When the squad was initially picked, I wasn't sure I was going to be in the starting eleven but then Darren Gough withdrew through injury and I was given my chance. 1997 had been my benefit year and I'd had a good year at Middlesex. I'd got really fit so I was confident going into that series and the series was a good one. The first Test in Jamaica was abandoned, then we played back to backs in Trinidad with two low-scoring, nervy games where we won one and lost one. We lost in Guyana, were winning in Barbados until it rained which would have made it 2-2, then lost in Antigua."

And for Gus it was an outstanding tour with the ball, taking 27 wickets in the series, including 11 in the win in Trinidad.

The series finished on a low point however, as Gus's big mate Mike Atherton stood down as captain. "Athers was a big mate of mine and we knew what the captaincy meant to him. To see him give that up was very sad. It was an emotional moment in the dressing room when he addressed us and told us the news. There were a lot of tears."

Alec Stewart was appointed captain and the home Summer of 1998 saw England beat South Africa, our first win in a five Test series for many, many years. "We got stuffed at Lord's and then we went to Old Trafford where Robert Croft and I managed to survive some hostile overs from Donald to see us secure a draw. We then went to Trent Bridge where I thought I might get dropped as I'd only taken one for a hundred in the previous game, despite my batting efforts. I didn't and I got 10 wickets in the match, which we won."

When Gus talks of some of these spells, I can imagine how

frustrating it must have been knowing that a lot of his big performances for England would often get overshadowed by notable performances of others. For example, in this Test at Trent Bridge people remember it for Donald/Atherton rather than Gus's 10 wickets. People remember Lord's in 1990 against India for Graham Gooch's 333 rather than Gus's eight wickets or the win in Barbados in 1994 for Alec Stewart's two hundreds rather than Gus's eight wicket spell. But I guess, that's professional sport.

Following the win at Trent Bridge, England moved on to Headingley and a famous win to clinch the series. "It was to become the only five Test series I was to win during my career, and I remember in the one day series that followed against Sri Lanka (Ed: England played a one-off Test and an ODI series against Sri Lanka straight after that South Africa win), I was 12th man and took a drink around to Goughy. As I walked around the boundary, I got a standing ovation. The series win meant a lot, to a lot of people."

It was fair to say Gus was back and he headed down under to Australia that Winter full of confidence. What he didn't realise was it would be the final time he'd pull on an England jersey.

"That was a tough tour for me. I'd gone there having taken 50+ wickets in my last two series. I played in the first Test. I wouldn't say I bowled well in the practice games but came on 3rd change on the 1st morning in Brisbane and then was left out the second Test. I remember Alec Stewart, who was captain, coming to my room to tell me I was left out for Adelaide and us having a rather emotional conversation. Having bowled as well as I had done for those last two series, and then after one Test where I didn't bowl badly, it was pretty much the end of Test career. I did come back for one further Test match when Alex Tudor pulled out on the morning of the Test match in Melbourne ill but that was that. If I'm honest, I don't think they were far wrong. The things about tours to Australia is, if you're young, fit and performing, you'll thrive, but if there are any weaknesses or shortcomings in your game, they'll get exposed. The fact I did struggle in Australia showed I was nearing the end. Maybe I could have played the following Summer against New Zealand, but an Ashes defeat, then the World Cup shambles, a new coach, a new captain, it was a new start and on the back of that I was a casualty really."

I asked Gus, how difficult that was to accept. "One of the characteristics of being a top sportsman is to never give up and to always believe you're good enough. For a period of time after being left out I possibly did feel I could do a better job than some of those being picked. But, my last involvement with England came in the Summer of 1999 when I received a phone call on a Wednesday evening before the Lord's Test which was starting on the Thursday. I was told that there was an injury and a fitness test, and could I get back to Lord's as cover. Middlesex were playing in Taunton and the day's play had finished; I'd had a couple of pints so I couldn't exactly drive back to London that evening. I got up early the following morning and headed to the ground in Taunton to pick up my kit then got on the M4 and drove all the way back to London. I got to the Hogarth roundabout when I received a phone call from David Graveney telling me 'its OK the player is fit' so I just drove straight around the roundabout and back to Taunton and that was my last involvement with England – I also got 0/100 that day in Taunton, so it wasn't the best day!"

In 2000, with his England career behind him, Gus took over the captaincy at Middlesex.

"Middlesex weren't in great shape at the time, with coaches coming and going. Mark Ramprakash who was captain, decided to leave so it was a situation where I either left the club or got more involved. I chose to get more involved and took on the captaincy. I was captain for a couple of years and combined that with a bit of media work. Then in 2001/02 there was quite bit of movement in the media and a position at the Independent became available. Paul Newman, who was sports editor, phoned me up, asked me to lunch and offered me the job. It was difficult to turn down. I spoke to a few people at Middlesex who I had great respect for and they both said I had to do it. Middlesex would move on and these opportunities don't come along that often. So, I took it and announced my retirement. I played the first few weeks of the season to ease the transition, but my best parting gift to Middlesex was Andrew Strauss becoming captain, which helped launch his captaincy career."

And how was the world of the media?

"It was very tough to begin with. But I really enjoyed it. Every day you have fears. Every morning you wake up worried that someone else will have a story that you don't have. But travelling around the world watching cricket was great. Sometimes your relationships with certain cricketers could become strained if you write something they don't necessarily like. But my view was always I was never going to be critical for the sake of being critical. If I was critical it was because it was backed up by fact or from my own experiences. Maybe a couple of times when you have a deadline and you have a couple of minutes to write 300 more words down you might as a result overstep and get it wrong, but if I ever did, I apologised."

Sadly, Gus's media work came to an end after his son was diagnosed with a brain tumour, which thankfully he has now fully recovered from. "He's all healthy now, but at the time he was 13, and you start thinking about things. It's a lovely existence as a journalist, if you're single. You're away for 30 weeks of the year, you're in top hotels, visiting great countries etc, but it's not much comfort if you're not single, for your family with you being away so much and I took the view that my children were now in their teenage years and I wanted to be part of that."

Gus started to explore other opportunities, when fate would have it, a role as Director of Cricket at Middlesex came up. "Middlesex weren't in great shape when I came back, and the immediate goal was to try and get the club moving back in the right direction again. We had to make some difficult decisions to move some senior players on and give some youngsters a chance, the likes of Sam Robson, John Simpson, Dawid Malan, Steven Finn, Toby Roland-Jones etc. We made some signings, some good, some not so good, but everything culminated in the 2016 title win."

Gus combined his role at Middlesex with being on England's selection committee. A role he proudly held from 2014 until 2018.

"Being a selector was a huge source of pride. It was a great honour and a big responsibility. You are performing a role that is significant in that it's for the performance of the national side. You're also a dream maker and a dream breaker. Giving people their England debuts is a source of great joy but at the same time you can also be ending careers. It was challenging at times and you'd cop a lot of flak. When I started, it coincided with Kevin Pietersen not being picked, which was a pretty uncomfortable period. But you have to back and believe in the decisions you are making. For example, after the 2015 World Cup people were questioning Eoin Morgan and his place and his role as captain. We backed him, supported him, believed in him and seeing the one day move forward as it has is extremely satisfying."

And what about the Test side? "The Test side had some really good periods and but also some disappointing ones. When I look back, I'd say we probably weren't able to complete two or three things we were hoping to do. We weren't able to solve the problem at the top of the order where we still have issues, and we didn't find replacements for Broad and Anderson. It's brilliant they are still playing but they're not going to last forever. The final area is spinners, although they seem to be coming through a bit better now. So, overall with the Test side I'd say we've made some progress in my time as a selector, but it'd be wrong to say we made huge progress. However, in white ball cricket it was extremely positive."

I asked Gus if he could give supporters an insight into a typical selection meeting, maybe one for a tour squad.

"If we take the 2017 Ashes tour. There were four selectors and Joe Root. We all had to begin by writing our squads out and explain why we'd selected the players we had. All the squads were then put on the wall. The players that were in all five squads were then obvious choices and we then discussed the others. In the majority of selection meeting's, you're really only talking about one or two players and what the options might be. Sometimes the options are out there and sometimes they aren't. But sitting there trying to plan a way forward for the England cricket team was great fun."

In 2018, the ECB re-structured their selection panel and Gus decided not to apply for any of the new roles on offer. "I miss it. But I understood the ECB's stance. They didn't want selectors to be involved with counties anymore. They deemed it to be a conflict of interest. I chose not to apply because I wanted to carry on at Middlesex. I just prefer being on the development side rather than the cherry on the top which is picking the England team."

Back at Middlesex, the team were relegated a year after that title win, and last season they found themselves in division 2, so what are the aims with Middlesex this Summer? "After the disappointment of the last couple of years, we knew changes had to be made and with Stuart Law we're confident we can get everything back on track again. We've some good youngsters coming through."

We closed our conversation with Gus naming the best player he played with and against. "Brian Lara is the greatest player I had played against. He was absolute genius. I did hate bowling to Michael Slater though. He used to go after you from the very first over. Very aggressive and not much fun to bowl to. But Lara was the greatest. To see him at his best was a joy. Even though you were having to bowl at him, when you were fielding, you had the best seat in the house."

And played with? "Graham Gooch. He was the best English player I played with. A fantastic man and a great cricketer. The Middlesex team I walked into showed me how to be professional cricketer, but Graham Gooch showed me how to be an international cricketer."

And what a cricketer that was. Thanks for the memories Gus!

13

NEIL BURNS
FORMER ESSEX, SOMERSET & LEICESTERSHIRE WICKET-KEEPER

This former county cricketer, turned coach and Professional Mentor, was arguably one of the most talented wicket-keeper/batsmen not to play Test cricket for England.

And while the England selectors didn't give him the opportunity some thought he deserved. He was certainly a top professional that the members at Essex, Somerset and Leicestershire, firmly took to their hearts.

"I was very lucky to have played in the era that I did, with so many world-class players involved in county cricket" remarked Neil Burns. "From when I started in July 1982 after my GCSE's, through to the end of 2002, it was a period that was arguably one of the best for county cricket. Playing cricket professionally offers the individual a unique opportunity to experience a range of emotions and be part of spontaneity that you wouldn't normally experience in the workplace. The camaraderie at times can be hilarious."

"Over the period of a career, you have a full spectrum of experiences that offer opportunities for powerful learning about yourself and life. From a personal point of view, these days I try to recall only the best ones! When I think about some of my better days, I am proud to reflect on the fact that I scored first-class centuries against the some of the best fast bowlers such as Malcolm Marshall, Courtney Walsh, Franklyn Stephenson, and Simon Jones, and half-centuries against other bowling 'greats of the game' such as Shane Warne, Wasim Akram, Allan Donald, Shaun Pollock. And I look back with immense pride that I took the field and played against the likes of Ian Botham, Imran Khan, Jacques Kallis, Brian Lara, Sachin Tendulkar, Murali, Rahul Dravid, Richard Hadlee and Clive Rice, as well as my early cricketing heroes Sir Vivian Richards and David Gower. I feel fortunate to have played against some top teams including the brilliant Australian teams of 1989 and 1993, plus the all-conquering West Indies teams of the late 80's/early 90's too. I am proud to have kept wicket successfully to Anil Kumble and Mushtaq Ahmed and privileged to have played alongside the likes of Allan Border who was at the crease in each innings of my first-class debut, Steve Waugh, Michael Bevan, Jimmy Cook, Martin Crowe, and Graham Gooch. Taking the field for Essex under the captaincy of Graham who was also an influential role model when I was growing up in Essex was a big thrill. I have been very fortunate."

Was there ever just a tinge of disappointment about not representing his country? "Yes, of course. When you have a dream and it doesn't come true it is disappointing. I set out with a clear vision of what I wanted to do in my career, but as you grow older and wiser you realise that success is more about getting the best out of yourself in any given situation rather than purely the realisation of a childhood dream. As a professional person, you must be honest and with the likes of Jack Russell and Alec Stewart around, I wasn't good enough to present a strong challenge to either of them – Jack was a brilliant keeper and Alec was a superior batsmen to all of us 'keepers in the game at the time. However, despite my early promise and initial success at Somerset, I think I played my best cricket at the end of my career and became more consistent in every aspect of my cricket. At this time, there were some very promising young 'keepers around like James Foster and Chris Read so the opportunity to be a serious candidate for international selection, despite my record at the time, had passed me by. England were unlikely to replace a 38-year-old Alec Stewart with a 36-year-old Neil Burns! But I would have loved the chance to play at that time in my career because I felt I had developed the temperament to have a big impact on a team. I found comfort in some kind things that Jack Birkenshaw, Michael Bevan and Anil Kumble said about my cricket and went into retirement as a cricketer feeling I had given my best at all times. Because I gave it my very best shot in terms of dedication to excellence, I feel I succeeded on another level."

The disappointment aside, Neil was the kind of wicket-keeper that teams loved to have in their side – a keeper with an ability to score important middle-order runs as a genuine all-rounder before it became the norm for 'keepers to bat so well.

So, where did his journey begin?

On the playing fields of Chelmer Park, home to Chelmsford Cricket Club. "From the age of 7, our house backed on to Chelmer Park. As children, we had 30 acres of sports fields that we could play our own Test matches on." And these were competitive 'Test' matches! The 'Tests' comprised of seven youngsters from Neil's road, including his older brother Ian, and the now famous academic Professor Robert iliffe. "We'd play all day and into the evening. We only went in when we were called in for food – often timed to coincide with Peter West introducing the Test match coverage. This is where I first watched Rod Marsh and Alan Knott perform behind the stumps and I find it remarkable that I have come to know both men and have played cricket with each of their sons too! Our 'Test matches' were highly-competitive games, so much so, five of those seven lads ended up representing Essex County-Age Group teams, with four also progressing to play in the Essex 2nd XI eventually. I was the only one to turn professional, but looking back, those early days were very influential in my development."

Neil recalls these days with fond memories. "Playing all sports with others that were older than me gave me a head-start over others who were my age and I was able to dominate my own age group in school games."

And why wicket-keeping over batting or bowling? "I always admired Alan Knott and Rod Marsh as a schoolboy. I also liked the fact that as a wicket-keeper you were always centrally involved in the game. Plus, with our 'Test' matches on Chelmer Park, I worked out that if I kept wicket, with only seven of us playing, it meant I wouldn't have to go and chase the ball!"

Another of Neil's influences as a child was Kent captain Mike Denness through watching Kent appear regularly on BBC2's John Player League live coverage when Kent were a brilliant one-day team under Denness's captaincy. Soon after, in 1978 Denness made the move from Kent to Neil's home county of Essex. "This was quite big news at the time and in no time at all he added some experience to a developing team and helped to make them serial winners. A few years later, I was making my debut as a 16-year-old for the Essex 2nd XI under the captaincy of Mike Denness!"

But Neil's biggest influence was his father. "He has been an inspiration and incredible supporter of me."

Neil admits he was fortunate as a youngster that he often got to play in age groups above his own, which accelerated his own development. "Paul Prichard was a year older than me and was an outstanding young batsman who also kept wicket. Paul's ability and high-promise meant he was selected for many representative teams in both his own age group and above, which enabled me to play County Age-group Cricket up a year. So, I always played a year ahead of my age group, and when I look back things like that helped me further on in my career. You knew that if you could perform at a higher age group it would enhance your reputation, but it also added to my inner confidence that I could compete successfully against older and better players."

Someone who played a big part in Neil's early development was his coach Ray East. "When I was in junior and youth cricket Ray and former Essex cricketer Graham Saville took a great interest in coaching the highly promising youngsters. They took a real interest in my development.

Ray went on to become Essex's 2nd XI coach. "I was lucky that for three of my four years as a full-time professional at Essex CCC I had Ray in a position where he could guide my ongoing development. He had such a warm personality, cared deeply about the game, and was great fun to be around too."

Although his 1st XI appearances were limited at Essex, he learnt a huge amount from his spell at the county. "The club won the county championship for three out of the four years that I was deputy wicket-keeper. The whole culture of the club was about winning. Essex won championships, one-day titles and we had players in and around the England team, such as Graham Gooch, Neil Foster and Derek Pringle. It was a very significant time to be part of Essex Cricket – the culmination of hard graft and fostering a collective spirit that took them from being 'a Cinderella club' being transformed into serial Champions. The club's ambition was always high. I look at that time as serving an apprenticeship; the timing of me being there could not have been better for a young, ambitious, developing professional sportsman."

The biggest shift in Neil's development came when he was 18, when he spent the Winter months playing cricket in South Africa for Northerns in the Western Province. "It was terrific. I learnt quickly that as an overseas player/coach I had to prove my worth. There was a core of good young cricketers in the region, including the likes of Eric Simons, Dave Rundle, Brett and Craig Matthews John Commins and Daryll Cullinan. They became good friends. Plus, there was a core group of other English pros like Colin and Alan Wells from Sussex and David Turner from Hampshire, and a small group of 'Test' cricketers like Peter Kirsten Kenny McEwan, Garth Le Roux, Stephen Jefferies, Hylton Ackerman, and Bob Woolmer playing in the competition. Graham Gooch had previously played in it, and his influence was always in the back of my mind as I set off for South Africa because I knew he respected the cricket down there at that time. The cricket was highly competitive and the standard was strong. That boosted my confidence in my playing ability and made me realise that I was good enough for higher-level of cricket."

And prove it he did. He hit an impressive 150 on his debut, and in the following six weeks followed that up with a couple of other excellent tons.

But on his return to Essex, it was tough for Neil not being involved in the 1st XI due to David East's excellence behind the stumps. "It was frustrating that I couldn't break into the team, particularly as the standard of 2nd XI cricket wasn't as tough as what I had been playing in the Winter. But what it taught me was that I had to be patient and I had to keep my standards up. Ray was terrific for me and he kept telling me that I was good enough to play in the 1st XI, but I just had to bide my time. It fuelled my appetite to get better, to take the chance when it came and keep doing all I could to knock the door down."

Neil knocked hard on the door but came to realise that for his game to develop further he would have to make a move to another county, despite his long-held ambition to play for his home club.

And that new county was Somerset.

"I had the opportunity to go to Surrey, and I really liked Mickey Stewart and Geoff Arnold's vision for Surrey cricket and how they thought I could develop further. But Somerset were a very similar club to Essex. Their ground was situated in the centre of the town, they were very well supported and had some similar successes to Essex, albeit they had lost their way for a few years after being dominant in the late 70's/early 80's. I think the fact they were looking to re-build and develop another winning team was exciting. It was also a tantalising prospect for me to play with Viv Richards and keep wicket to Ian Botham and Joel Garner. Brian Rose made a strong impression on me around the same time. He was passionate about Somerset cricket and it was very clear they wanted to build a new, young team. They wanted runs from their wicket-keeper. It was all very persuasive."

However, it didn't quite turn out that way! "Not long after approaching me they announced publicly that things at the club were changing and they were not going to re-engage Viv and Joel and in their place, were going to sign Martin Crowe and were intending to sign other ambitious young players too. I felt quite uncertain about the move despite the opportunity to play regular first team cricket. I met Martin up in Scarborough when I was up there playing for Essex in the Asda Trophy and he was up there playing for New Zealand. He was very impressive – and shared a vision for Somerset County Cricket Club in a very articulate and helpful way."

It was the right move for Neil and what followed was eight years of enjoyable cricket for the young wicket-keeper. "I loved it. It was fun to keep wicket to someone like Vic Marks – a canny bowler, and delightful man. Steve Waugh came over from Australia and played for two seasons – we'd played together previously when he had a year for Essex 2nds so it was great to reconnect with him, and we just had a strong group of youngsters, all of whom were of similar ages. They were good times. We reached a couple of one day semi-finals and quarter-finals and on big match days at Taunton, the ground would be rocking. There was just always a big buzz around the town. At some clubs, there isn't the following for the game that there is in the west country, and I soon learnt that Somerset Cricket means a lot to so many people. I suppose it's similar to Essex, and in many ways to what people say about Yorkshire. It is always a great feeling to be part of a club that really mattered to both the local and also the broader community."

I asked Neil about some of his most memorable games at Taunton. "My debut in 1987 v Lancashire was memorable on a personal level for making 52 at a vital time on the first day, but another 4-day game against Lancashire stands out, and not just because it was all over on the second day. They needed 88 to win and we bowled them out for 72. A young Andrew Caddick got nine for 32 – and it was also the match in which Marcus Trescothick made his first-class debut."

"But my biggest personal highlight was my 166 against Gloucestershire in 1990. We were five down for 87 and I was 16 not out at tea. By the close of play I was 148 not out! Somerset v Gloucestershire were always big matches which meant a lot to the locals so to pull out a career-best performance in one of those matches was something pretty special."

"Another personal highlight was my first time back at Chelmsford against Essex in 1987, where I scored my maiden hundred. I got a lovely reception, and it was special to have family witnessing it at the ground too."

And the disappointments? "Losing in too many semi-finals! It wasn't until I left the club, they managed to win a final. "They beat us at Lord's when Keith Parsons played really well. It was fantastic to have enjoyed the experience of a final but no one really wants to remember playing in a Cup Final and not winning. But a small consolation was that for Somerset I knew what it meant to the club and their brilliant supporters."

In between those counties however, was a period where Neil thought his first-class cricket career was finished for good. "Somerset released me in 1993. It was a very tough period in my life. It was difficult and caused quite a lot of turmoil in my personal life. I wasn't sure whether to continue playing because full-time coaching was something I always wanted to eventually do. So I took the opportunity to be player/coach for Buckinghamshire in the Minor Counties Championship. I was then appointed Director of Cricket for the county and it gave me the chance to influence the whole system from top to bottom. We would go on to establish some proper structure with some clear principles. For example, we decided to only select people who either went to school in, lived in or played cricket in the county to represent the county. It was about putting down some foundations that would allow the county to focus on its emerging talent as opposed to hiring in players from outside the county to enhance the 1st XI's playing potential on a short-term basis ."

Many Minor Counties didn't have such criteria back then, while Neil wanted to ensure he had a genuine Buckinghamshire team of cricketers. One of the other processes that Neil introduced was to pick the best 10 cricketers and then make one place available for the most promising player from the county age group teams. It was an innovative idea that paid dividends. "I really wanted the age group teams to know that one spot was available to them. I really wanted to broaden their cricketing and social education by incentivising them to earn selection and be around more established cricketers. In a smaller way, I also hoped the coaching philosophy of inspiring greater opportunity for highly-promising young players would filter through to the clubs in the area too. I often felt that young players' development is stultified by lack of opportunity to perform in more dominant roles in league teams because established middle-aged cricketers refuse to give up their 'privileges'."

"I hoped we, as the peak of the county's cricketing pyramid would be an exemplar in this regard. The way it worked was this: a young player has one season to play in the team 'with grace' and then he has to make the spot his own the following year by gaining selection in 'the best 10 cricketers in the county'. The 'grace' position would then move to another player the following year and so on, year-on-year. We had three young players from that process who went on to become professional cricketers."

I asked Neil what the quality of minor counties cricket was like compared to the professional game. "It could be challenging as you had to play 120 overs in a day, which is a serious amount of cricket. It could be very demanding physically but it also encouraged plenty of overs from spin bowlers, especially young ones, which must be a good thing to achieve more variety in the game. The standard of quick bowling is obviously very different to first-class cricket but there were some very good, accurate seam bowlers as well as some highly-promising young bowlers like Alan Richardson emerging at the time. Obviously, the lack of pace and bounce in most of the pitches affects the type of cricket played and some teams could be quite defensive with ring-fields and medium-paced accurate seam bowlers bowling to effectively 'strangle' the opposition through run-starvation, as opposed to bowling a delivery that could dismiss a batsman purely on its own individual merit, which is what is needed at the highest level of the game. The competitive nature of many teams was a feature, and I believe more young county professionals would benefit from playing minor Counties cricket against established cricketers rather than just playing for the first-class county 2nd XI team on an exclusive basis. Today, 2nd XI Cricket looks like an under 19s match to me – with all players knowing each other since county-age group days. Sometimes, being in the mix with strangers who are very 'savvy' with their game can be transformative to an emerging player's development. If a possible future England player can dominate Minor County cricket at 18/19/20 then I think it says a great deal about their ability to adapt their game at such a young age, and augurs well for their future progress. Plus, there are some solid, experienced ex-pros in the competition who can be most helpful to an emerging cricketer's 'game intelligence', as well as offering independent encouragement of a player's potential. I liked the responsibility of being the Player/Coach and because of the experience I had and the responsibility of the role I had, I think the Minor Counties period of my career was invaluable to my overall development as a cricketer, and as a coach. There were some tough games, and none more so than the NatWest Trophy 1st Round matches against professional teams. I really enjoyed preparing my teams to play in these fixtures, and I am proud to recall how competitive we were on occasions against some very good teams like Essex, Surrey and Warwickshire.

After five years in the role and at the age of 35, Neil received a call from Leicestershire and so came his return to the first-class game. "I received a call from Jack Birkenshaw at Leicestershire saying that they wanted an experienced cricketer in their team. The call came completely out of the blue. It was wonderful."

I think playing with top batsmen like Jimmy Cook and Chris Tavare at Somerset was both a joy and also a hindrance. The hindrance came from playing 'second fiddle' to better players and how easily one can lose a sense of self as a front-line player in such circumstances: my serious pretensions to become a top player I envisaged becoming in my earliest days as a professional, for instance. But simultaneously, it was a joy because it enabled me to see 'up close and personal' how good each of these two outstanding players were, especially in one day cricket. On reflection, as a middle order batsman I had become accustomed to playing around others' contributions and had lost the sense of responsibility for being 'the main man' that had characterised much of my junior cricket and also my early days as an overseas pro in South Africa."

"Playing in the Minor Counties Championship demanded that my level of personal performance was key to my team's overall total in each and every innings – this level of responsibility enhanced my cricket no end. It was as if I returned to my youth, and it re-activated thinking patterns which had probably been laying dormant. I think the process really enhanced my accountability as a professional cricketer. I went back to having high expectations and took on the personal responsibility to win matches. I brought this attitude into my cricket at Leicestershire, even though I returned to life as a middle-order batsman again."

The move to Grace Road was a great move for Neil and he describes it as his most successful period as a cricketer. "I broke records for the number of one-day dismissals in a season, the number of first class dismissals by a Leicestershire wicket-keeper in an innings, I made my highest one-day score, I played in a Cup Final, topped the list of first-class dismissals among all the country's wicket-keepers in each of my last two seasons, I scored more first-class hundreds and played my part in some significant victories. There were a lot of highlights."

"Despite the 2001 C&G Trophy defeat to Somerset another highlight was the 'Road to Lord's'. We played some brilliant cricket along the way, especially the televised semi-final victory over Lancashire at Grace Road when Pakistan all-rounder

Shahid Afridi played a sensational innings, after Scott Boswell's in swingers had sliced through the all-powerful Lancashire top order of Atherton, Lloyd, Fairbrother and Flintoff. We'd played really good one-day cricket that year and we had a group of wonderful cricketers, led very well by Vince Wells and Jack Birkenshaw."

"Dan Marsh was our overseas player in 2001, and what a wonderful team man he was. He was also a very savvy cricketer, mature beyond his years. Unfortunately, he missed the second half of the season due to a fractured cheekbone but his contributions helped the team become consistent winners from all manner of positions. We developed a super-confidence that whatever they got, we could get, and if we batted first and 'under-scored' we felt that few opponents would be able to chase down a winning target against the competitive bowling and fielding unit we had developed into. Shahid Afridi came in and was such a game-changer of a cricketer for us. His scoring rates were ahead of his time and the violence of his play caused havoc in the minds of most opposition players. His incredible ability to score at 10 or 12 runs an over from the start of an innings was unheard of, and in those early days, suggested he would become a world sensation if he could harness his talent to perform at the highest level of the game. His leg-spinners were very fast-paced and his quicker ball was frightening pace to be stood up to. His throwing was remarkable too – what a gifted cricketer we had in our midst. Unfortunately, he was 'outfoxed' by Somerset in the Cup Final – their smart strategy of bowling hard into the pitch to hit the splice of his bat caused frustration and he played an injudicious shot which caused his dismissal and gave them a belief that the game could be won from that moment onwards. Despite our efforts to stay competitive, we fell away as the innings unfolded and left ourselves too much to do. Having said that, eight runs per over in the last 12 overs today would seem like a cakewalk to the modern cricketer!"

In Neil's time at Grace Road, he had an excellent bowling line-up to keep wicket to, including the likes of Philip DeFreitas, Devon Malcolm, Chris Lewis, James Ormond and Anil Kumble. I suspect the current Leicestershire faithful would like a return to those days.

I asked Neil what it was like to play in a Lord's final in a period when finals were truly like the FA Cup final of cricket. "It was everything I dreamt about. I remember in the final against Somerset, there was a moment in between the first and second overs when I looked up at the pavilion, as I waited for the slips fieldsmen to take their positions and just took it all in. It was beautiful Summer's day; the pavilion was packed and it remains a moment."

Neil retired from the game after the 2002 season, and as mentioned earlier, it was a 20-year career that spanned a golden era for the game so I asked him who was the toughest bowler he ever kept wicket to?

"There was a lovely Dutch lad at Somerset called Andre Van Troost, better known as 'Rooster'. He was very, very quick indeed. And his bowling was very challenging to keep to because he got incredible bounce, especially at places like Taunton, The Oval and Old Trafford. And, his radar wasn't always working as well as it did on his best days, which made 'keeping 'interesting' to say the least! The speed of footwork and the range of movement needed, added to the complexity of the challenge on some occasions. The hardest deliveries to take were his 'unintentional off-cutters' when he was unable to get his wrist properly behind the ball – he got excessive movement so with the distance you had to stand back, it meant that the angle of deviation got bigger and bigger by the time it reached me stood back. In fact there were other occasions when I had to stand MUCH too close for comfort, especially on slow, low-bouncing pitches which made the reaction time if the ball was nicked really short. So all in all, 'The Rooster' was a mix of difficulty and also real thrill. He offered an exciting dimension to the team and to my life as a 'keeper.

Richard Snell the South African paceman played for us in 1992, and used to make the ball wobble and dip horribly once it went past the bat, like no one else I had kept wicket to – so he presented a real challenge and the odd very difficult moment when the ball would 'aeroplane' from its initial height and climb towards your throat at pace! The contrasting opposite experience to this was 'keeping to Andrew Caddick, who was a dream to glove – you could see the ball so clearly from his hand with an immaculate wrist position and controlled outswing which made you feel you were likely to get an outside nick from almost every ball he delivered. Javagal Srinath was the best seam bowler I kept to, although I think he would have been a tougher proposition to glove earlier in his career when he was much quicker through the air. By the time we played together at Leicestershire in 2002, he was a master of swing and control – a really skilful and intelligent bowler. But, by some distance, my professional pride is reserved for the success I had 'keeping to the variety of leg-spinners from Nasser Hussain in the Essex county age-group teams through to Andy Clarke in the Minor Counties, and Mushtaq Ahmed, Anil Kumble and Shahid Afridi. Anil's pace combined with big bounce made his bowling very difficult to glove at times, but we struck a great partnership in 2001. It really boosted my confidence upon my return to the first-class game that a world-class bowler was so complimentary about our partnership. Next to Shane Warne, I rate Anil Kumble as one of the bowling greats of the game, and it was a genuine privilege to play with him and become good friends too."

I also asked Neil if he thought the art of wicket-keeping had changed much since his playing days. "Definitely. Nowadays it's not just runs from your wicket-keeper that are important but runs scored in a certain way. Keepers are now picked first because of their batting; Jonny Bairstow and Jos Buttler have reached the heights of Test cricket through their batting first. That's very different to the careers of Bob Taylor, Alan Knott and Jack Russell."

Neil is now involved in the game via London County Cricket Club, the club which was originally founded in 1899 by WG Grace. Despite its name, the club is much more than a cricket club. They are in fact a professional mentoring organisation and Neil is the Managing Director. "When I finished playing, I had thoughts about coaching full time, but I felt coaching was in danger of becoming 'role justification' in some ways. I felt it was becoming less about empowering players to find their own answers and, inadvertently, it was becoming increasingly a culture of near-dependency on support staff and shared responsibility for performance outcomes. I firmly believe that cricketers and captains should run the team and be accountable. The coach should act as a consultant asking incisive questions at relevant points in time to stimulate better quality reflection in players. I believe cricketers play their best cricket when they do so in their own particular way.

The mentoring process is about helping people to develop the trust and confidence in who they are and how they want to play and thus empowering them to get there through their own self-inspiration. If we don't empower people to find their own answers, then we are eating away at their ability to become self-learners and develop the all-important characteristic of self-confidence."

"Across various sports, not just cricket, London County - through its performance coaching programmes - has enjoyed a track-record of transforming the careers of professional athletes, and in business they have provide learning events to stimulate people's thinking around 'inner and outer leadership'. Their professional support is designed to offer leaders 'a safe place' to think so they can return to their normal working environment with more clarity about how to inspire better results from their own people which in turn will deliver better results for their company."

"Through our bespoke mentoring programmes, we intend to create greater opportunities for people to understand and realise their full potential."

The work that Neil and his colleagues have done is fascinating and you can read more here: www.londoncounty.co.uk

Neil's story is a wonderful one. A cricketer, who through sheer dedication and drive, made the most of his abilities and was rewarded with not only 7000+ first class runs and over 500 dismissals, but a career full of treasured memories. It's great that he continues to give so much back to so many people. But, as he says: 'when you give, you receive."

14

GRAHAM ROSE
FORMER SOMERSET & MIDDLESEX
ALL-ROUNDER

Graham Rose was one of county cricket's leading all-rounders in the 1990s. His close to 9,000 first class runs and 600+ wickets made him a folk hero at Somerset – and Graham holds the world record holder for the fastest List A limited overs hundred, off just 36 balls. More to come on that later.

Graham made over 250 first class appearances for Middlesex and Somerset in a career that spanned 19 years and included 11 first class centuries and 15 five wicket hauls. He finished his Somerset career with 588 wickets to his name.

So where did it all begin? "I was cricket mad as a kid," remarks Graham. "My dad played club cricket in and around London and I used to tag along with him on Saturdays and Sundays to play with the other kids and it all went from there, really. Cricket had always been in and around my life. The game was readily available on television in those days, which made a huge difference. I was just obsessed with the game."

Such was Graham's obsession as a child, there was no preference for being a batter or a bowler, he wanted to excel at everything! "I loved having two bites of the cherry, and that continued all the way up to when I became a professional. I always liked the fact that if I had a bad day with the ball, I could make it up with the bat, later on."

Graham is forever indebted to his mother who helped his cricket dream come true as she pushed teachers to give him an opportunity to play. "It all started at primary school. My mother knew the sports master and explained to him that she had this cricket obsessed younger one and could he come along and train with the bigger boys. He was more than happy to oblige, so I ended up playing for my primary school under-11 team when I was just eight years of age and everything went from there. I got picked to represent my borough, Haringey. We used to play inter-borough games in those days. A gentleman called Jack Robertson, who had played for Middlesex and England and was a junior scout; he went along to these games and that was how I got into the Middlesex system. Through Jack, I got selected for Middlesex under 11s when I was 9 or 10. I remember the first game, I turned up, Jack welcomed my Dad and me. I had no idea of his background, but my Dad was so excited 'you know who that is? It's Jack Robertson, he played for Middlesex and England!' I played in and around that system for a couple of years and it was a fantastic introduction into the game and the art of batting, in particular. It was also an education into being a gentleman. All of the lads adored Jack – when you went away and saw how he carried himself in the game, it made you want to be him."

Graham progressed quickly through the youth ranks at Middlesex all the way through to the 1st XI where he made his debut in a John Player league game in 1983 against Northants, at

Milton Keynes. "I wasn't officially on the staff then – I got taken on the following year – and because of my age, I didn't really feel any nerves heading into the game."

It was so nearly the dream debut, as with his first ball, he tempted Wayne Larkins into a mis-hit only for his captain, Clive Radley, to shell what Graham describes as a 'dolly'! "Running into bowl that ball, I just kept thinking to myself, keep it simple, just run up and bowl straight. It left the hand perfectly. Wayne Larkins very kindly chipped it to Rads at backward point and he shelled the biggest dolly! Thankfully it didn't cost us, as he was out not long after, but it was so close to being the dream debut!"

Graham broke into the first team at Middlesex at a time, when they were arguably one of the most successful counties in the country. As a result, his first team opportunities were limited. "We had a fantastically strong team. Half the team were the England Test team at the time, so I only really got an opportunity when the big guys were away with England or if someone was injured – it was the reason why I later had to move to Somerset to get a regular game in the first team."

Despite limited appearances at Lord's, Graham did enjoy some memorable highlights, including a 6fer on debut which went some way towards Middlesex winning the county championship in 1985.

"I made my county championship debut against Worcestershire and I got a 6fer to win the game. We had a really weakened side out due to international call ups. Gatting, Emburey, Downton etc were away and Wayne Daniels was away as well. So, it really was a second-string team we had out; but we managed to win the game and that turned out to be significant in terms of us winning the title. I was only 21 years old at the time, but lots of things fell into place for me and I was able to walk away from that game with a lot of confidence."

Unfortunately for Graham though, he knew deep down that if he wanted to develop his game and make the most out of his talent, he had to move on from his home county.

"I left Middlesex at the end of 1986 and signed for Somerset. They'd had a bit of a difficult 1986. Viv Richards and Joel Garner were released and Ian Botham moved on. So, suddenly there were some spaces available in the team, particularly for an all-rounder. And so, I felt it was the best place for me to be able to play first class cricket."

It was the start of an incredible 15-year career at the County Ground for Graham. While silverware escaped him, it was a wonderful adventure full of great games, semi-finals, finals and a period that Graham wouldn't change.

"When I first signed it felt a bit like treading on egg shells in the dressing room, following the Viv, Joel and Beefy situation. It was like a fantastic marriage that had gone horribly wrong. Wounds were definitely deep. If I'm honest some people still hold a grudge to this day, on both sides. But I had a terrific time at Somerset. My first game for them was against Lancashire and although we lost, I made 95 on my debut. I should have scored a hundred, but it was a poor shot. That said, walking off having scored 90+ was great. If I'm honest I didn't consistently back that up for a couple of years."

With Graham in the ranks, Somerset slowly re-built after the loss of the famous trio and were always a tough side to beat, especially in the cup competitions. "We always did well in the one-day competitions and towards the back end of my career we were arguably a better championship side than one-dayers. I played in five semi-finals for the club and lost the lot!"

In 1999, Graham and his team mates finally broke the semi-final curse and made a return to his old hunting ground for a NatWest Trophy final appearance against fierce rivals

Gloucestershire. "I was fortunate to be selected for the final as I'd missed the semi-final through injury and Stefan Jones had bowled really well. It was one of those difficult decisions that management teams have to make and thankfully it went in my favour."

Somerset lost the final by 50 runs. "It didn't help that my first four overs weren't great and they got off to flyer, although I should say it wasn't just my end that went for runs! I managed to claw it back in my second spell and got a couple of wickets, but we struggled to keep up with the rate with the bat and lost by 50 runs. They talk about Somerset being the nearly team, I'm afraid it's a legacy that has continued to this day with the current crop of players.

But what was Lord's like as an occasion for a cup final? "It was absolutely fantastic. I've never played cricket for the thrill of being in front of a crowd; I would happily play if there was one man and a dog watching. But this final was a derby and it just had the wow factor. Once you're in a game, either batting or bowling, you don't really notice the crowd, but in between overs, you kept getting the realisation that there were 30,000 people watching and it was quite something."

While silverware on the pitch eluded Graham and his team-mates, the personal milestones came thick and fast for the talented all-rounder. In a NatWest Trophy, first round match in 1990, Somerset were drawn away to Devon, a game in which a world record was set. "In 1987, we'd drawn Buckinghamshire in the 1st Round and we suffered a poor defeat. To draw another minor counties side three years later we were determined not to lose. Everything just came together. Jimmy Cook got a substantial hundred, Tav got a hundred and I came in with about 10/12 overs to go."

What followed was utter carnage.

"Jack Birkenshaw had been our coach for a while and he just gave me license to go for it. He was instrumental in taking the shackles off me. If I got out first ball, so be it. It didn't matter. I guess when I look back now, I played an innings which is similar to a standard T20 innings today. If I'm honest I don't talk about it too much, after all it was against a minor counties side, and as professionals we were expected to score big totals against those counties. We won the game by 300 odd runs. Everything just went our way."

Graham's hundred was brought up in just 36 balls – a world record, his first 50 had taken just 16 balls, the third fastest in the history of cricket. I asked Graham, what goes through a batsman's head which they are in such form, out in the middle.

"It was just important not to think too much about it. You have to trust your instincts. When you're at your best, you're just in a zone. You have to be relaxed enough to just go out and do it."

For youngsters reading, Graham also pointed out the importance of practice, practice, practice and don't over think things. "It's so important to practice like hell. Groove your shots. And importantly don't have too many preconceived shots. Too often you see batsmen get the mind-set of just having to stick around and don't get out; what happens? They nick off. It's the same with bowlers, too often they think too much about the ball and suddenly bowl a big half volley. Don't clutter your thoughts, just relax and trust your instincts."

Of course, that's easier said than done when you're in bad run of form, like we all experience. "It's much harder, but you have to back yourself. If you've done the right things in training and you keep on practising the right things, you'll get a bit of luck: a big shout for LBW, which isn't given, or you nick one and they shell it. Suddenly you then play a good shot, and you're away."

I guess it's that old adage, don't get too high when things are going well and don't get too down when things aren't going so well.

Did being an all-rounder help in terms of not getting too down on the game. "It really did. As an all-rounder, you have two bites of the cherry. If I got out for a nought, I could still run in and take a few wickets. If you're a top five batter and you nick one, you can have a lot of time to stew, while as an all-rounder you can get your anger out with the ball later on in the game."

So, finals and semi-finals aside, what were some of Graham's other favourite memories during his time in the game?

"You always remember you're first hundred. Mine was against Yorkshire. That was a pretty special day. Another favourite memory was when Tav and I batted out most of the last day to save the game against Lancashire at Old Trafford. I look back on that with great satisfaction. Tav just dropped the anchor. The funny thing with Tav was that everyone just saw him as a blocker, but I kid you not, when the mood took him, he could destroy attacks. One of his first knocks for Somerset was away to Hampshire and he smashed them for 130, an attack that included the great Malcolm Marshall - it was breath-taking. We thought we'd hired this really solid batsman, but he played an innings that was just jaw-dropping. Anyway, in this game at Old Trafford we hadn't batted particularly well and were behind on first innings. On the third evening, we lost four or five wickets and we were well sunk. I got in early on the last day and Tav was already there and it was just fantastic application. It was absolutely brilliant to save that game."

Graham also recalls the wonderful overseas players he was fortunate to play alongside. "Mushy was brilliant. He was a laugh a minute guy off the field. On the field, he was just magical and watching him bamboozle the opposition was amazing. It was a privilege to watch that. Jimmy Cook was just fantastic to watch. An interesting story here. He always reeled off hundreds for fun, but after one particular game we'd gone for something to eat in a restaurant. The waiter brought the menu over and told us that the specials were up on a board. Jimmy looked across at the board, puzzled and then turned to me and asked if I could read what was on the board to him. I asked him if he couldn't see it properly. He responded, 'no, I've never been able to see much out of my left eye.' To think he scored the best part of 8,000 runs in three years with us and yet he couldn't see that well out of his left eye!!"

And favourite memories with the ball? "I think I got better as I got older in that I understood my role better. I learnt control and discipline and how to swing the ball consistently. My best match figures were 13 in a match at Taunton, which was special. I suppose whenever you took five wickets it was nice. Bowling at the other end to Caddick was helpful, but I knew my role was to support him as he was our spearhead. I just had to control things and keep things tight. That made him more potent. If we both dried things up, you could get on top of teams. Bowling was always hard work, but it was enjoyable. I understood my role."

Throughout Graham's career he bowled to some of the best players to have graced the game. I asked him who were among the hardest to bowl to.

"One of my few games for Middlesex was against Somerset and I bowled against Viv at Lord's. I remember he got a hundred and at that age it was a real eye opener in terms of the step up in levels. You didn't feel like you could get him out and he could hit you for four whenever he wanted to. That was a pretty special experience. Graeme Hick always got runs against us at Somerset. His famous 405 was against us. He was someone special. I remember we had them 132 for 5. We'd just got Botham out and thought we were through them, but Hick was unbelievable. He just took the game away from us. Players like Steve Rhodes and Richard Illingworth just stayed with him as he hit the ball to all parts; you thought how is this guy not going to score runs at Test level? But he just never did. Some people would say he was too front foot oriented and we weren't quick enough to really push him back. He did play against the West Indies at their peak, but he'd played against these guys in county cricket, OK not collectively, but he still scored a bucket full of runs, it was real surprise he only managed to score two Test centuries in his career."

What about bowlers faced, with bat in hand? "Allan Donald was never easy. I don't think he knew how to bowl slow! Whenever you saw him bowl in practice before the start of play, he was bowling bloody quick. I just don't think it was in his DNA to bowl something slow. Every ball hit the bat hard or whistle past your nose. Wasim was pretty special. He was a frantic blur of arms and legs and suddenly this thing was past you and had hit you on the pad. He was something special. As of course was Waqar, although he never blew us away, we actually did OK against him. That said whenever you saw him take his sweater from the umpire, you were definitely relieved! Courtney was another one who was always at you. Looking back, I was just fortunate to play against some of the greats of the game and it was bloody hard work!

Despite a bucket full of runs and wickets, Graham didn't get the opportunities at international level. "It just never came my way. I'm not sure if I was frustrated or disappointed, it just didn't happen. And if that's the worst thing to happen life then so be it, it wasn't the be all or end all of life. It would have been nice but there's no point getting bitter and twisted about it. I was fortunate to play as long as I did and in the era that I did. And you know what there's a list of far better players than me who didn't get international recognition."

Graham spent 15 years in total at Somerset, was he ever tempted to look for a new challenge? "I really enjoyed it at Somerset. It was a different system back then, in that a benefit was a quite a significant thing in your career, so it did somewhat tie you to a club. You could move elsewhere, but you'd forego a benefit. I suppose I could have looked to go elsewhere, but we had a decent team and I really enjoyed it."

Graham retired from the game in 2002, a decision that was an easy one to make. "My contract had reached its end, but to be honest I'd reached the end of the road. My body couldn't do what it once could. Even bowling for the 2nd XI I felt in pain the following day. Everything hurt and it felt like I would break. I had just reached the end of my natural life as a cricketer. There was no way I could do one more year. I had got to 38 and it was time to say goodbye."

Life after cricket saw Graham working as a civil servant in the ministry of defence and he's now working in IT for Boeing. "I feel very lucky to have ended up in a job that I really enjoy."

Graham doesn't watch too much cricket these days. He doesn't subscribe to Sky Sports and catches up with international highlights on channel 5 but memories of those 9,000 first class runs and 600+ wickets will always remain with the members at Middlesex and Somerset.

It's players like Graham that make our county game so special.

15

ANDY MOLES
FORMER AFGHANISTAN COACH & WARWICKSHIRE BATSMAN

Andy Moles is a former opening batsman who scored over 13,000 runs for his beloved Warwickshire and went on to enjoy a coaching career that took him from Hong Kong to Kenya, New Zealand, South Africa and to war-torn Afghanistan.

Andy gave me an excellent insight into county cricket in the 80s and 90s, modern day international coaching, and the strength of the associate nations.

"The game has been very kind to me," says Andy. "I've travelled all around the world, which is remarkable."

And his story really is remarkable, as this this cricketer, who made the most of his abilities through hard work and determination, could so easily have been lost to the game.

"When I was 22/23, I wrote to all of the counties asking if I could get a trial. I didn't get a single reply, which was massively disappointing; but it's why I look back at my playing and coaching career now and say it's remarkable."

What a shame it would have been if this young cricketer would have been lost to the game.

Thankfully, one county gave Andy a break and that was Warwickshire and boy did he repay them - 12 years' service, 13,316 runs, two County Championships, and five one day trophies. I wonder if all those other counties regretted their decision not to reply to Andy's letters.

The journey that would eventually take Andy all over the world, had begun.

For those of you who remember the 90s, Warwickshire were the team to play for: the innovators of the game. But looking back at his time at Edgbaston, I asked Andy what was the trigger for the success the county enjoyed, especially as prior to making his debut in 1986, they had tasted little success. It appeared to come down to five main ingredients: mindset, simplicity, teamwork, culture and personnel.

"In the late 80s, Bob Cottam and Andy Lloyd came in and they changed the mindset of the players. Winning became something that was expected. We weren't there just to compete in games. When I first joined the club, a draw was often good enough. Bob and Andy changed our thinking. Then Bob Woolmer, Dermot Reeve and Tim Munton came in and continued to challenge us. We had the personnel with the likes of Allan Donald and Brian Lara, who played massive roles in us being successful, but there were also the home-grown players who really stepped up to the plate. As a unit we believed we could win things. We worked so hard off the pitch, that every time we took to the field, we thought we could win any game, from any situation."

And importantly, the players knew their roles. "Bob Woolmer would explain to us what each of our roles were and we just had to concentrate on those. My team mates knew my role and they trusted me to do it and I trusted them to do theirs. My role was to face the quick bowlers, see off the new ball and bat as long as possible and try to accelerate the score the longer I batted." It was simple advice.

And at the heart of Warwickshire's success was teamwork and culture.

"One thing we had that was pretty unique at the time was genuine enjoyment when your team mates did well. There was never any jealousy, no ulterior motives; if someone did well, players didn't think a person might take their place, there was genuine enjoyment and that was the real key to our success. It fostered a winning culture and when I think back, my personal highlights fade away and I remember what we achieved as a team."

Allan Donald, Brian Lara, Shaun Pollock, Tom Moody and Brian MacMillan were all overseas players but in Andy's mind it was the English players that really stood up to be counted.

"Gladstone Small and Tim Munton were exceptional. Roger Twose scored a mountain of runs with the bat. Dermot was an outstanding leader. But an unsung hero was Trevor Penney. Trevor used to bat at five or six for us and was an excellent fielder but he would score magnificent 20 or 30s, especially in one-day cricket, that would win us games. He would go in when the pressure was really on, when 9 runs an over was a lot of runs – not like now! He would give us that extra late flurry that would either give us a winning score or finish a game off. He didn't score many 50s, 60s or 70s, but he was identified as our 'finisher'. He never took the headlines, but in our dressing room we all knew he was a superstar in our team."

In truth, that Warwickshire side were full of superstars and winners. And they were ahead of the game in their thinking and approach. Woolmer and Reeve were architects of changing teams' approach to cricket, their brand of cricket - using modern day words, in an era before the advent of T20 cricket.

Remarkably, there wasn't room for any of these 'winners' in a then struggling England side.

"We had hardly any England call-ups. The team was overlooked for three or four years. I remember Ray Illingworth was asked the question why no Warwickshire player was selected and he just said we were average players, who weren't good enough. That is fine and his opinion, but I remember Mark Nicholas who was captain of Hampshire saying that if we're average players, what does that make the rest of county cricketers. I think a lot of people were surprised."

England's loss was most certainly Warwickshire's gain. "As we didn't experience call-ups, it meant our players really got to know each other. We had the same group of players over several seasons and that was very beneficial."

I asked Andy how he thought that great Warwickshire side would fare in today's game. "It's very difficult to say because the game has changed so much, with all of these ramp shots and scoops. Batsmen are able to score 360 degrees around the wicket against the quicks. We were the first team to bring in the reverse sweep and we were innovative under Bob Woolmer and I'd like to think we'd be successful now, but we're talking the unknown as the game is far different today."

In addition to his time at Warwickshire, Andy also played domestic cricket in South Africa. In three seasons for Griqualand West, Andy scored 1,989 runs at 64.16 and I asked him if he felt there was much of a difference, at the time, in the standard of domestic cricket in England and South Africa. "In England every county had magnificent overseas quick bowlers, Wasim Akram, Waqar Younis, Courtney Walsh, Sylvester Clarke to name just a few. When I went out to South Africa there wasn't the quality of overseas player. However, as you didn't play as many games the competition was harder. The ball bounced a lot more and the weather conditions were a lot hotter. I thoroughly enjoyed my time there. You played once every couple of weeks, you could properly prepare for games, relax when you needed to and it helped focus the mind. You knew you had nine or ten opportunities to get the very best out of your performance for the team."

Andy lists Wasim Akram as the finest bowler he faced during his career. "It wasn't just because of his pace, but as an opening batsman I didn't face that many left arm over bowlers at that time. The different angle made it very difficult. Also, we had Allan Donald playing for us and with Lancashire having a strong side Allan always wanted to do well against them and would try and bowl at the speed of light. But this of course would wind Wasim up so he would then try and outdo Allan and bowl even faster, which wasn't ideal for an opening batsman like me!"

But it wasn't just the overseas bowlers. "All of the counties had good English seamers to back up the overseas stars. There were no central contracts in those days so you used to play against the best players all of the time. You would be under pressure in every fixture so if you were fortunate to get runs, they were always good runs. Not many runs were handed out freely in those days."

Andy retired from first class cricket in 1997 and headed straight into coaching. Having played for many years under the late Bob Woolmer, he couldn't have had a better mentor and tutor.

"You always learn from your mentors. I tried to take the best from all of the people that moulded me as a player. Bob was a very good man manager. He challenged every single individual to get better, whether it was someone like me, as a senior batsman, who had played for many years, he challenged me not to stand still. He challenged us to improve our games and become better players. In my coaching career now, I always talk to my players about improving some part of their game."

Andy's coaching career began at Free State, in South Africa where he stayed for five years and I asked him how he found the path from player to coach, was it an easy transition? "The first area I had to get used to was the difference of being a player to being a coach. In my first couple of years in South Africa I found it difficult. I was drawn into having good friendships with the players and being part of social nights. I was too close to them, in that regard. At the end of a season you have to talk to these players about their games, some may be coming towards the end of a contract, you might have to have a difficult conversation. I found that hard in the early years because I'd been drawn into the dressing room culture. I learnt very quickly that wasn't the way to go forward. I quickly understood there had to be a line between the coach and the players, because you do have to have discipline and difficult conversations. At times you have to have words with players when you think they need to give more."

In 2001, Andy got his first appointment as the head coach of a national team, when he coached Hong Kong at the 2001 ICC World Cup. His spell in charge of Hong Kong was soon followed by spells in charge of Scotland and Kenya. His success in charge of these associate nations led to his appointment as head coach of Northern Districts in New Zealand where he guided the side to the State Championship. This success at Northern Districts led to Andy succeeding John Bracewell as New Zealand national coach in 2008.

"I look back on my time in New Zealand with very fond memories. I thoroughly enjoyed living there, I enjoyed the culture and the cricket was excellent. First class cricket in New Zealand is competitive and the Northern Districts had a great bunch of lads. It was probably one of my favourite appointments. During my time in charge of New Zealand there were issues, but those issues were there when I went on board. And who would turn down an opportunity to coach an international team? I was fortunate to be in charge for two Test series against the West Indies and India and we went to the T20 World Cup. I look back at that time as a magnificent learning curve for me as a coach. We had some very talented players who had some strong cricketing ideas, but as always you look back and review the work you did and it was a great learning curve."

In 2014, Andy was appointed batting coach for the Afghanistan national cricket team with the goal of preparing them for the 2015 ICC Cricket World Cup in Australia and New Zealand. Just weeks into role however, Andy was promoted to head coach to replace Kabir Khan, who had stood down from the position. Full respect to Andy for taking on the challenge of coaching a country who was in the middle of a well-publicised international conflict, particularly as the foreign office advice was to avoid all but essential travel to the country.

So how did this appointment come about and what was the experience like? Andy gives an incredible insight.

"I got the job because originally they were looking for a batting coach to go and help them for the World Cup. They got hold of me through an agency. I went over there to work with the players in Kabul which was just a different world. It was an absolute war zone. You would see armoured carriers going up and down the road and you would see literally hundreds of AK47s every day in the hands of very young teenagers, who had been employed as security guards outside houses, hotels and sports clubs. There was just so much uncertainty around with the Taliban. Security was massive as the threat of kidnap was so huge, especially for foreigners. A lot of foreigners had armed guards and cars to transport them around."

But for Andy, he didn't have the comfort of such security. "Sadly for me, the Afghanistan cricket board couldn't afford to put that in place. But they did look after me as best they could and did all they could to ensure that I was safe as often as possible. For the majority of the time I did feel safe, but there were times when the traffic was like central London and there just wasn't any movement. You could be stationary in the car for 10/15 minutes with 30 or 40 people milling around the cars begging and looking through the windows and obviously if they recognise you as a foreigner that could be an issue. I wore my hoody for a while and wouldn't shave just to try and blend in as best as I could. I would travel around in a battered old car. You basically had two options: 1) drive around with armed guards around you, but then that would draw attention, or 2) you go the other way and drive around in a real battered old car and just blend in and that is what I always did."

Under Andy's guidance, Afghanistan were one of the rising success stories of the associate nations and I asked him how big was the country's passion for cricket? "It's massive. Kids are playing cricket in the streets all of the time. They play a thing like tennis ball cricket. They wrap tennis balls in tape so it becomes harder and the ball swings all of over the place. Everywhere you go around Afghanistan kids are playing the game. You see open plains of massive land and there will 10 to 15 games of cricket being played. They have a first class structure there now, played by six different provinces and they have a good under 19s set up so they are in a position where they will have players come through over the next few years but they need to be given the opportunity to do more touring. They will get better the more exposure they have."

One can only imagine the experience Andy had in Kabul and as I write this, my respect for the guy just goes up and up. He has played a big part in helping people appreciate there is more to Afghanistan than conflict.

Andy's passion for associate nations' cricket extends to all nations though and he feels that if the likes of Afghanistan, Ireland and Scotland are to progress, they need to be given more opportunities to face the leading nations. "Statistically speaking all of the associate nations at the last three of four World Cups have all improved from where they were. They are far more competitive and getting better with every competition. But they need to keep testing themselves against better teams. The only way to get better is to play against better quality more often and be exposed to different conditions around the world. "We played Australia in the World Cup at Perth. It was the perfect storm. Here we were on the quickest wicket in the world, facing Mitchell Starc and co. They absolutely blew us away. We didn't have an answer. We tried to get players ready by throwing golf balls at them on concrete nets to get them used to the bounce which was going to come But it was all so alien to them as they don't come across anything like that back in Afghanistan. These countries need to play in different conditions around the world to get that database in their own mind about what they are going to come up against."

I think a number of us agree that the ICC should look to reverse the decision to reduce the opportunities for associate nations at future 50 over World Cups.

With talk of a two-tier Test system I asked Andy if this would give an opportunity for associate nations and would they be set up and ready for second division Test cricket?

"When I played county cricket in the 80s and 90s Sri Lanka came across to England as an associate nation and look where they are today. They have won the World Cup. Afghanistan and

Ireland are the leading associate nations at the moment. Afghanistan have played a lot against Zimbabwe recently and beaten them regularly so the argument can be made they do, along with Ireland, deserve the opportunity."

Yet Andy reiterates again, they need to be given the fixtures to ensure they are ready. "Ireland and Afghanistan have done enough over the last three or four years to be given the opportunity to play against countries like Bangladesh. But they need to be playing those teams more often and given the opportunity to go on tour and play the A sides, or Lions equivalent, of the leading countries. They need to go around the world. Not just to England, but to Australia, to India, to South Africa, to the West Indies and experience not only the higher skills levels but the conditions and just how the game is played in different parts of the world."

The associate nations have given cricket fans a lot of joy and if Test cricket is to go to two divisions I, for one, hope Andy's wish for the likes of Afghanistan and Ireland to be given the opportunities, comes to fruition.

And where is Andy right now? With his time in charge of Afghanistan at an end, he is just starting a new role back where his coaching career began, in South Africa. With all of the experience he has gained around the world, hopefully one day soon he'll be given an opportunity back in England so our young players can learn from him as he did from his mentor, the late Bob Woolmer.

16

GRAHAM THORPE
FORMER ENGLAND BATSMAN

Graham Thorpe was a left-handed batsman who played countless match-winning innings in both Test and limited-overs cricket. He helped transform England from the also rans of the 1990s to the battle-hardened, successful side of the mid-2000s. His ability to handle both pace and spin with ease, in all conditions, saw him go on to score nearly 7,000 Test runs for his country at an average of just under 45, in an era when a number of the greatest bowlers to have ever played the game were turning their arms over.

But, before we start talking through the highs and lows of Graham's career, I must start with a couple of did you knows...

Did you know that this great left-handed batsman, is actually right-handed?! "Totally true," admitted Graham. "I write right handed, I hit tennis balls with my right hand. In fact, everything is right handed, apart from cricket!" Apparently, at five years of age he kept getting out to his two older brothers, so of course there was only one thing to do. "I kept getting out and having to field all of the time! My Dad batted left handed in village cricket and told me to try batting left handed. I did and I started batting for longer periods of time!"

And now to the second. Did you know we could have lost this great 'left'-hander to football? "I probably loved my football more than cricket when I was younger."

And we're not just talking a fleeting love interest. Graham's childhood football career reached the levels of England under 18s. "I remember going through about 10 elimination days at Lilleshall, and I got all the way through to England under 18s. It was a brilliant experience and great fun. But in the end, I chose cricket."

We're glad he did.

And it was certainly the right decision. After some early successful seasons batting in the middle-order for his home county Surrey, Graham was selected for the 1993 one day series against Australia. Despite the side losing the three match series 3-0, Graham took confidence from the fact that he made 'starts' in all three of appearances, registering scores of 31, 36, and 22; performances, the selectors obviously took note of, as just a few months later, Graham was thrust into his first Ashes series.

With the side 2-0 down in the series and with four Tests to play, the selectors knew changes were required if they were to have any chance of turning around the deficit. "The selectors made a lot of changes. As well as myself, Martin McCague, Mark Lathwell, Mark Ilott and Nasser were brought into the team. I was full of nerves and the game didn't start well at all for me."

Batting first, an 86 from Robin Smith and 71 from the returning Nasser Hussain, saw England register a competitive 321 in their first innings. But for Graham his return was just six runs, caught by Steve Waugh off of the bowling of Merv Hughes. "I was edgy in those first three days. I didn't get runs in the first innings. I then dropped Michael Slater in the field when he was only on 10 and the Aussies were well ahead in the game."

But then came a rest day. This was the last series where the sides had a 'rest' day after the third day's play of a Test match. "I got on the train and went back to London on that rest day. I went to a BBQ and had a couple of beers and spoke to a few people, including my Dad, and just said that I didn't enjoy those first three days and that I felt quite tense. It really helped talking. I then went back up to Manchester telling myself just to give it a crack and don't worry if you balls it up. Don't worry about failing. Just give it a go. And if you go down, go down on your own terms."

114 runs (not out) later, it's fair to say the approach worked! "I had a great partnership with Goochie. It was a great experience for me batting with him and it was a brilliant feeling to get a hundred on debut. I was a lot more positive in my approach and that rest day really benefitted me. We ended up close to winning it. I remember we had them six down at tea time; it finished up a draw, but I remember walking away from those last two days thinking, this is brilliant."

2 balls into his next Test however, and Graham was quickly learning the harsh realities of Test cricket. "Talk about a big high followed by a big low. A second ball duck! But it was a good early lesson, not to get too high after a good innings and not to get too low after a low score."

Following a heavy defeat in that Test match at Headingley, and with the Ashes gone, captain Graham Gooch tendered his resignation and was replaced by Michael Atherton, in what signalled a new dawn for English cricket. "I remember Goochie telling us in the dressing room that he was resigning. It was a bit surreal. Here was me playing in my second Test match, sat in the dressing room with England and the captain was resigning. Looking back, when you started off playing for England in the 1990s there was so much insecurity. The team changed so much; it was one of the reasons it was hard to build team spirit."

The harsh realities of Test cricket also hit (quite literally) in the build up to the final Test of that series. "I then broke my thumb and didn't play in the final Test match at the Oval. It was quite ironic that it was by a bowler from my club side in Farnham who was bowling to us in the nets on the morning of the Test. What a first few Tests!"

That Winter, a new look England under the captaincy of Atherton headed to the West Indies, for a tour that in Graham's words, changed his approach to international cricket. "I learnt a lot on that tour. The West Indies were still the best team in the world. They had four quicks coming at you and I had never seen pace like that in my life, to be honest. As a 23-year-old, it was a massive challenge. At times, I felt under the pump and while I felt I could survive against their bowlers, I just couldn't break out and throw any punches back."

But things started to turn, at least personally for Graham, in the third Test in Trinidad. "I watched Brian Lara a lot in that series and I tried to take bits from him into my own technique. I would look at his movements and his pick-ups. I also looked at how the likes of Robin Smith, Alec Stewart, Mike Atherton and Desmond Haynes approached fast bowling. How they ducked and weaved, how they took the quick bowlers on and hit the bad balls and slightly good balls for four. We'd been blown away in those first two Tests and I'd been bowled four times. I went away in the nets and just practised. I changed my technique for the Trinidad Test and hit 86 in the first innings. Unfortunately, the second innings didn't go too well!"

This is of course, the Test match when chasing around 180 to win the game, a Curtly Ambrose onslaught, saw England bowled out for just 46! "Ambrose bowled brilliantly and he just got on a roll. They had a 180-run lead but it should have been so much less. I dropped Chanderpaul and Hicky dropped one. We should have restricted them to around a hundred. But Ambrose blew us away. It was a pretty humiliating being in that dressing room, but we realised and knew we had to keep going. We had two Test matches still to play."

And bounce back they did. After the humiliation of Trinidad, came one of England's finest wins of the 1990s in the next Test at Barbados – the West Indies' first defeat in Barbados for over 60 years, with Graham once again playing a key role, with an excellent second innings knock of 84.

"I felt I was coming out of my shell by this stage. Stewie got two hundreds in the game, I got a nice little 80 and it was a really good pitch to bat on. The crowd was amazing and it was a brilliant win. We'd gone from the lowest low to the highest high. We knew after Trinidad we just had to start again. Part of that era was that if you got beaten, get back up and get on with the next game; throw punches back in the next Test. That was our attitude. But I grew on that tour, especially my attacking game."

Graham's form continued during the following Summer - when he scored three 70s in two Tests - against South Africa and on the tour to Australia the following Winter, where he was the one batsmen who was able to consistently keep the Australian attack at bay, averaging 49.33 as England were heavily beaten in another Ashes series. But it wasn't just that series against the Aussies in which Graham was our rock. Throughout his career he was the one player we had who was able to 'play' Shane Warne.

In 16 Tests against the Aussies, his average was an impressive 45. So how was it that he was able to thrive against a bowler that so many others couldn't? "People around the world had the fear of playing Shane Warne. He didn't bowl much crap. He'd land the ball in the same place, time after time. He was good at verbals, but I quite enjoyed the challenge of it. We were similar ages and I was lucky that I could pick his flipper. I found him easier to pick than someone like Mushtaq Ahmed, whose arm was a lot lower and could get a lot more spin. But Warney was just so accurate and that's why he got me out a few times. I remember charging down to him at Perth, when I was on about 120, and tried to hit him out of the park – I totally missed his googly!! But I got runs against him and others in that Australian side and that was very rewarding and satisfying, because they were a fantastic side. I always felt I wanted to go out there and show that I was good enough to play against them."

During Graham's international career, Australia won six successive Ashes series and only once did England come close. 1997. "We always had our moments against Australia, but they were one off Test wins, once the series were dead. Our biggest chance, however, was in 1997. We beat them 3-0 in the one-day series before the Ashes started and then went 1-0 up at Edgbaston, which was a great Test match. It was the first and only time I played against them where we had the lead in an Ashes series. We played bloody well."

England bowled the Aussies out for just 118 runs and then thanks to a century from Graham and a double hundred from Nasser Hussain, England piled on 478 runs in reply. "Mark Taylor was struggling and you could tell little chinks were opening up a bit in their side." Despite the Aussies fighting back in their second innings, England went 1-0 up in the series with an outstanding 9 wicket victory. But as they always say, be wary of the wounded animal. "We got away with a draw in the next Test at Lord's – somehow we produced a green pitch which was tailor-made for Glenn McGrath who got eight wickets on it! But then all of a sudden Steve Waugh, Shane Warne and McGrath played out of their boots and they blew us away in the next three Test matches and our chance was gone. They just collectively were a very powerful side, that didn't change a great deal throughout that era. I always felt that was our best chance in getting close to them. But history will tell you they were one of the best sides to have ever played the game."

One of the advantages the Australians had over England in that era was that their players were centrally contracted and had been for a number of years, while England players didn't have that luxury. And that to Graham, was one of the big disadvantages the squad had during the 90s and when trying to compete with the likes of Australia. "Throughout that era we were pushing and pushing as players for central contracts. One of our big challenges was that we were never able to get the same bowlers out on to the park time after time. Australia had central contacts ten years before us. We'd finish a Test match and have to go straight back and play county cricket the next day. Whereas sometimes batsmen could deal with playing time and time again, for bowlers it would wear them down. We were playing cricket 25 days out of 28. Once those central contracts got in place it was no coincidence that we started getting the consistency and wins. If I look at my Test career, I won about 12 or 13 Tests of the 50 I played before central contracts. In the second 50, I won about 37 and a lot of that was due to central contracts, consistency in selection and less injuries to our fast bowlers. Those central contracts also bought about an England spirit. We felt we are England now. We belong to England. It was a big shift."

England finally moved to central contracts when the team was under the guidance of Duncan Fletcher and Nasser Hussain. And it was the period under this captain and coach that coincided with Graham's most successful time playing for England. One of the biggest highlights were the wins in the subcontinent against Pakistan and Sri Lanka. And who can forget that decisive win in Karachi, where Graham's 64 not out, in near darkness, was vital to securing a memorable series win.

"It was filthy dark and within ten minutes of us going off it was literally jet black. I'd been out there batting for two and a half hours, so my eyes had adjusted and could see the ball OK. But it was much tougher for the guys like Nasser who had to come in at the end and could barely see the thing. By the end we were literally just swinging and hoping. It was a great feeling at the end to get over the line. We had a great team spirit on that tour, one of the best I had played in. We had great support staff and there was just a real camaraderie in the camp. We definitely surprised them. A lot of people thought we were going to get hammered 3-0 and that we had no idea on how to play spin in that part of the world. But we thought we had a decent side and in Crofty and Gilo we had two strong spinners of our own, so if the pitches did turn, they would come to the party. We went into the tour trying not to lose to start with and just biding our time for an opening. And that opening came in Karachi, where they just felt the pressure."

With a 1-0 series win in the bag, the team travelled on to Sri Lanka, and another memorable series victory was secured. "The bigger performance that Winter for me was away in Sri Lanka. We were up against Murali on real turning tracks and really hot conditions. It was very challenging. To achieve the win there was as good as it got for us as a Test team. If we weren't going to win the Ashes, to win in the sub-continent was the next biggest thing to do and those two wins represented a fantastic achievement for us. It pushed us quite high up the rankings and the innings I got in Colombo was probably one of the best innings I ever played."

In searing heat, Graham hit a magnificent first innings 113 not out, with the ball turning square. With Sri Lanka bowled out for just 81 in their second innings, England reached their target of 74, for the loss of six wickets, with Graham, once again guiding the side home with an excellent 32 not out. "I felt I picked Murali well in that series. He hadn't quite formulated his doosra on that tour, but he was a real, real, challenge. However, I managed to get some good performances where I felt quite confident playing against him. When you're in that mind set, you have to make the most of it. But credit to our bowlers, they bowled brilliantly. We were 1-1 going into that Colombo Test and the pitch really did turn square. But that actually brought our spinners into play. Crofty and Gilo were brilliant."

I asked Graham how much of an influence did the coaching of Duncan Fletcher have on that tour. "Massive. He gave us ideas on what your way of playing spin should be. I found him a very positive coach, especially when it came to playing spin. For example, he said I should look to hit Murali over the top from a standing position, as I felt uncomfortable going down the pitch to him in case he managed to turn it past me. He said, 'Can you hit him from the crease?' Things like that gave you the license. His training sessions were always intense. I remember he would rough up surfaces to make it difficult to bat in the nets and that put us in a good place in the games as we felt we could go toe to toe with the Sri Lankans. Often the biggest battle at Test level, is not confusing the games too much. Keep a good clear plan. And that's what we had on that tour. We had good new ball bowlers in Gough and Caddick. Craig White was excellent at reverse swinging the ball. And we had two spinners in Gilo and Crofty. Duncan didn't always come across as everyone's favourite, but the lads who played under him in that period, held him in a very high regard. He had a good sense of humour in the dressing room, very dry. But the public never saw that side of him. He'd give us a few nights off and I remember we used to have some great fun tuk tuk racing around Colombo, which he laughed about. He wanted a team that was enjoying itself and which had a togetherness. He knew a bit of a laugh off the field would allow us to play better on it. He fostered that very well."

While things were going well on the field, off the field in 2002, Graham was going through a tough period in his personal life. "I was going through a very difficult divorce. Also, my Surrey team mate Ben Hollioake was killed in a car accident and I was going through a lot of mental trauma."

Despite this, on the tour of New Zealand in early 2002, Graham hit one of the fastest double centuries ever in Test cricket. "To be honest it was a very strange innings, in that I was in so much personal turmoil, I didn't really care at that stage. I remember I was dropped on four, third ball. I was out there batting with Freddie and we both said let's just give it a whack and see what happens. We did that for 50 overs and put on about 370 between us. It was bloody good pitch to bat on, lovely bounce, quick outfield and we piled it on."

What made this game interesting was the fact that despite setting a target in excess of 500 to win, New Zealand nearly chased it down. "Nathan Astle was unbelievable. He hit the fastest double hundred ever. We ended up winning by 70 runs, but Astle was batting so quickly that they only would have needed another six overs or so and they would have won. It was some of the most amazing hitting I'd ever seen. I've honestly never seen power like it. I remember he hit Caddick for a six straight out of the ground." But, win England did.

Following that tour, Graham took the hard decision to take an indefinite break from all cricket. In recent years there have been a number of instances of other players who have experienced health issues and mental illness while on international duty, and I asked Graham if he felt the team management today are better equipped to spot the various symptoms?

"A lot still relies in a way on how the lads develop. With players like Marcus Trescothick, Jonathan Trott and myself, things developed while we were away. You get married, you have kids, something might suddenly happen while you're away and it plays on your mind and those can be the triggers. We definitely have the systems in place now where players can put their hand up if they have a problem. But occasionally, players still keep it to themselves, so you can never be 100 percent sure. But there is an acceptance now that you should not be afraid to ask for help. Barriers have definitely been broken down. As a management team on tour we try to make sure everyone is alright, that no one is staying in on their own. Lads of course might still want some of their own time, but we make sure no one is staying in too much. There is definitely a lot more awareness and players know there is nothing to be ashamed of. In any walk of life, we all have our issues but there are people to help and that's a good place to be."

Graham made a return to the England side in 2003 for the crucial fifth Test against South Africa at the Oval, where he delighted everyone with a century that helped set up England's astonishing comeback to level the series 2-2.

"That was one of the best innings I ever played. I think because I was out of the side for such a long period of time, and at 34 I didn't know if I still had it in me. I'd not been in the team for a year. But I'd met my second wife and she said I should give it another crack with England. And that got me mentally wanting to play for England again that Summer. I was picked for the final Test after Nasser broke his toe and I got a call from David Graveney to say I was back in. It felt like a debut again. It was Alec Stewart's last Test match and I was pretty nervous as I didn't know if I was still good enough. But it was a dream innings. I managed to channel the nerves and we won the Test and drew the series. If I'd failed in that game I probably wouldn't have been picked for the Winter tour. Michael Vaughan had taken over as a skipper by then and even though I got on well with Vaughany you never know how a new captain is going to view some of the older players. So it was great to score runs. Later that evening he took me to one side and told me that I would be going on the tour that Winter, which was just great."

Following that innings, Graham went on to score 1,635 runs at 56.37 in England's successful run under Michael Vaughan, also reaching the milestone of 100 Tests, against Bangladesh at the start of the 2005 season. It was fair to say he definitely 'still had it'.

"It was brilliant playing under Vaughany. We won seven Tests out of seven at home in 2004 and something like seven series on the bounce, it was just amazing. The team had winners in it. Bowling wise we had Harmison, Flintoff, Hoggard and Jones that could all take wickets. Gilo was very under rated. He played such an important role in the side with the support he offered the quick bowlers. He never bowled $hit. He always kept it tight and picked up important wickets. It was a great side to play in."

The highlight of Michael Vaughan's captaincy was of course the 2005 Ashes series, a series that sadly Graham was overlooked for, despite averaging nearly 60 in the 20 odd Test matches he'd played since returning to the side.

"I was loving being back in the side and enjoying it, but do you know what? Vaughany and Duncan were no mugs. KP was always going to play in 2005, especially after what he'd done in the ODI series in South Africa and the ODI series leading into the Ashes. He was the type of player you needed against Australia, a young energetic, talented player who was going to throw some punches back at them. Don't get me wrong, it would have been great to have played in it, firing and performing, but that's life. And, if I'm honest, on that 2004 series in South Africa, I was starting to creak and Fletcher and Vaughany knew that. I played a couple of real dogged innings, one in Pretoria and one in Durban, but I knew I was starting to just tail off mentally. I was 36 and it was getting tougher and tougher. So it was probably the only time in my career, that I was left out of a side, when deep down, I wasn't surprised."

From a supporter's point of view and from the outside looking in, it was a crying shame, that someone who fought so hard against the Australians for so long, was not a part of what was such a glorious time in England's history.

"It was life, but when I look back at my whole career, I wouldn't change it. You could say I wish I won the Ashes, or a World Cup along the way, but you can't look at it like that. When you play cricket for England as long as I did, you feel blessed. It would have been great to have had central contracts sooner. I honestly believe they would have made a difference. Vaughany's team were in prime position to finally win an Ashes against what was still a very, very fine Australia team. Those central contracts led us to become a very fine England side. But we had some good times and I always look back at it fondly."

I asked Graham, when he looked back at his career, who were some of the best players he played with and against.

"Brian Lara was definitely the best batter I played against. He was a big influence on me as a player. I played in both of his world record innings, plus countless double hundreds and hundreds, so I got to see a lot of him! But I picked up so much stuff from his technique and took it into mine. Then of course there was Tendulkar, Ponting and Kallis. Batting wise for us, Stewie was probably the best we had who could play fast bowling. Michael Vaughan was an exceptional batsman. He got to number one in the world for a while and looked an awesome player for a period of time. Fred had the presence as an all-rounder – you could see he had something special and could win a game with bat or ball and he had bucket hands at slip. Bowlingwise, Shaun Pollock was an exceptional bowler who certainly gave me problems. As did Wasim Akram, Shane Warne, Murali and Courtney Walsh. In a strange way I didn't mind facing Ambrose or McGrath as they were line and length. Don't get me wrong they were bloody hard to play against, but you knew where the ball would be landing, whereas someone like

Courtney Walsh had a few more tricks up his sleeve. Sometimes he would pitch it up, he had a great slower ball that got me out a couple of times and he had a quick bouncer. He was awkward. Pollock would bowl very close to the stumps and move the ball both ways and could clip you on the head with his bouncer. He was a very intelligent bowler. While Wasim had all of the tricks with both the old and new ball. He'd run off of about eight yards and bowl 90 miles per hour plus!"

And who was the best captain he played under? "I played more Test matches under Athers' captaincy than anyone else. But I felt he was a slightly stubborn captain in many ways. He was a guy you wanted to impress. He was determined, dogged and led by example. You wanted to earn his respect, especially in the early days. You'd see how hard he fought and you wanted to match that. But I wouldn't put Athers at the top of my captain list, tactically, mainly because I didn't think he ever had the teams really to bring it out of him. So I'd say it has to be between Nasser and Vaughany. Nasser made the team harder to beat and really gelled a team, which some say, had some awkward players in it. He galvanised that team and put a lot of passion into it. You knew exactly where you stood with Nass. He had the right players at the right time. When he handed over to Vaughany though, it was the right time. Vaughany brought a little bit of what I would call, freedom. They were both very well respected and tactically good captains. Nasser would put a bloke on the boundary for Brian Lara and would bowl over the wicket to Tendulkar and not give a toss. He'd be in your face as a captain. Vaughany would give more responsibility to his players. It's hard to split them because it was different kinds of eras. I just think they were both the right captains at the right stages of our evolution. Domestically, however, Adam Hollioake was a very good captain at Surrey. He had quite a senior dressing room when he first took over, but he was such a strong personality, and the hardest bloke in the team, no one would ever pick a fight with him! But he dragged people along with him and I loved playing under him. He was a very positive captain."

I asked Graham about his time at Surrey, and he looks back at his county career with great fondness. "We won two county championships. We got to two Lord's finals and we won the Sunday league in 1996 under Dave Gilbert's coaching. We had a very strong team with a lot of home-grown players. Very fond memories."

After Graham's England career ended, he made the move down under to work for his former Surrey coach Dave Gilbert, who was then chief executive at New South Wales. "Dave asked me if I fancied coming over. I discussed it with the wife, and with the kids both under five at the time we just thought what an opportunity for a change of life. I wasn't totally sure what to do career wise; I'd played around with a bit of television work, but here was an opportunity to go over as a freelance batting coach. I actually went over as a player, I was on their registered list but that changed pretty quickly and I became batting coach for New South Wales, under Trevor Bayliss. I worked under Trevor for a year, before he took the Sri Lanka job, which was great. Matty Mott then took over and I became his assistant and also ran the New South Wales second team."

It was great experience for Graham, particularly leading a second eleven team, which consisted of the likes of Dave Warner, Steve Smith, Usman Khawaja and the late Phil Hughes. "It taught me a lot. When you move into coaching from a player, you're starting on the bottom rung of the ladder and it's like doing an apprenticeship. You know you've got a lot knowledge and experience as a player, but coaching is very different. If you speak the wrong way to players, you lose them. You have to be quite thoughtful and patient. New South Wales are a big state side, but I thoroughly enjoyed my time over there and it's been great to see how those players have now progressed."

After three years in Australia, Graham returned to the UK and to a coaching role at his beloved Surrey and he is now employed at the ECB as the country's National Lead Batting Coach. "It's a varied role. I'm involved with the England Lions, the Under 19s and I dip in and out with the England side, so I typically coach the one-day side and Ramps (Mark Ramprakash) does the Test side."

Graham is extremely passionate and you can tell he gets immense enjoyment out of his coaching. "I've always been quite clear on what I wanted to do with my coaching: to produce players to play for England. Sometimes you might hear some people say you can get away with being a good front foot player in county cricket but I don't want to produce county cricketers, I want to produce international cricketers. So my style of coaching is that you have to be a good player of the short ball and you've got to be a good player of spin. So players have got to develop a good technique and practice in that way. You do some really hard yards with the players, but you've also got to be compassionate with them and realise that players do develop at different times. I feel very lucky to do it and I have a lot of passion for the role."

Graham also gave a bit of an insight into the way Trevor Bayliss operates. "Trevor is a very open-minded coach. He's open to different coaches from the county set-ups coming in and out on training days. He's very keen to get them involved so they can see what's going on."

I asked Graham if he has to tinker his approach to coaching with the three different formats of the game, but similarly to Peter Such, he says the basics will always remain the same. "You're there to score runs. If you've got the intent to score runs, you'll pick the bat up better and you'll move your feet better. You'll also defend better. You try to keep the basics in that form. If you're a Test player you want them to have the intent. If you're playing 50 over or T20 you want them to have the intent. It's then the 'practice' that is different. The amount of power hitting we do now in T20 and 50 over cricket is enormous and it's actually quite dangerous for us coaches! But as coaches we try not to over-complicate stuff. We just need to make sure players develop 'game sense', tactical awareness and read the game well."

Since Graham has been in his role at the ECB, many of his charges have gone on to great things in the game. "The really pleasing thing for me is that a lot of the lads who were with the under 19s and the Lions four years ago have all now progressed into the senior side, the likes of Root, Stokes, Buttler, Roy, Hales and Sam Billings. They have become very successful international players. What I like about these lads is they also play with a smile on the face. They could very easily be playing on the local park, but there they are representing their country and having fun. It's great because young lads look at that and want to come through and be the next Joe Root or Ben Stokes. I'm very proud to have played a part in their development."

As fans we are indebted to Graham Thorpe. As a player, he gave us many memories. He was the player who made us proud to support England in those darker days and who we were proud to say was our number four. And now we are indebted to him for his coaching and the great work he's doing at the ECB.

A true England legend.

17

ROB TURNER
FORMER SOMERSET WICKET-KEEPER

Rob Turner was another Somerset stalwart that I was fortunate to interview. Rob took over 1, 000 catches/stumpings throughout his career and was one of the most accomplished and consistent wicket-keepers on the county circuit. He was a player that experienced the highs of Lord's finals and the disappointments of getting overlooked for international recognition, which many would say his performances (and career statistics) deserved.

Let's start at the beginning, as we always do. Cricket was part of Rob's life ever since he was born, but it was the famous Ashes series of 1981, like it was for so many, that really caught young Rob's imagination. "That was the most extraordinary series, wasn't it?" recalled Rob. "Although it wasn't my first recollection of cricket, it was the series that captured the imagination of the whole nation. Ian Botham was my hero as a kid growing up. It was great that in my career I got the opportunity to play against him, when he was still playing county cricket up in Durham – an incredible experience to play against your hero."

The admiration became mutual as Botham was kind enough, many years later, to write a piece for Rob's benefit brochure.

But with Botham as the 'hero' why did this youngster choose a career as a wicket-keeper? "I always wanted to be a wicket-keeper. My older brother was a wicket-keeper and for a long time I just copied him in everything he did; whichever football team he supported, I supported; he became a wicket-keeper, so I wanted to become a wicket-keeper! All that said, as a keeper you're always in the game and I just wanted to be involved all the time."

Rob's brother actually kept wicket for Somerset, for a while, playing with the likes of Botham, Garner and Richards, so it was inevitable that Rob would want to follow suit.

To achieve his first-class aspirations, Rob took up a scholarship at Cambridge University. "I used Cambridge University purely as a route into cricket. Oxford and Cambridge were playing against the counties all of the time, so it was my route into county cricket. Coverage of university games against the counties would be in the national newspapers every day, so if you did well, you'd stand out. If cricket didn't happen, at least I would have had an education. But, representing Cambridge meant I was able to play a really good standard of cricket and play against many of the first-class counties."

With the likes of Mike Atherton, Steve James and John Crawley, in his intake, the standard was certainly high. "It was a great experience and I had a great time. I did four years in total. I stayed on an extra year so I could captain the side. I did a one-year course in computer science just so I could play that extra year of university cricket. I really wanted to get some captaincy experience."

Sadly, the captaincy plan backfired a little as Rob broke a finger and missed the chunk of the season where games against the counties came up. "Greg Thomas bowled quite quickly and I broke my thumb. I missed the B&H cup, where I was going to captain the combined counties university side. Incidentally the guy who took over from me was Nick Knight, he went on and did alright for himself!"

Injury aside, the university route into first class cricket worked for Rob as a contract was on the table, upon completion of his life at university, with his home county Somerset.

"I was associated with Somerset anyway, as I'd played a bit for the under 19s and their 2nds, so I was sort of on their radar. But as soon as I finished at Cambridge they offered me a contract; that contract would certainly not have been on offer if I hadn't of gone to Cambridge. University cricket made me a much more mature cricketer."

Rob made his first-class debut for Somerset in a county championship game away at Glamorgan in 1991. "I got called up on the morning of the game because of an injury to Mark Lathwell. Neil Burns was wicket-keeper so I played the game just as a batter. Thankfully I didn't have time to think about it as I literally received the call and then I was on the motorway driving up to the game!"

A successful debut saw Rob retain his place, but it was a century at home to Nottinghamshire that cemented Rob's place in the side. "That hundred really kick-started everything for me. I remember Chris Lewis was playing and I'd never faced pace like that before. He was very sharp, especially on a quick deck at Taunton! It was an amazing experience. I remember he bowled a short one at me early on and the ball looped up in the air, but the guy under the lid at short leg didn't see and it just dropped down by his side and I went on to make a hundred. Luck was with me."

Rob took over behind the stumps and was soon making his name as one of the most promising young wicket-keepers in the country. This promise was acknowledged by the England selectors who picked Rob for an England A tour to Bangladesh and New Zealand.

"That tour was an amazing experience. It was incredible to experience a country like Bangladesh. The people there were all cricket nuts. They were incredibly harsh conditions to play in, what with the heat. But it was great just to witness a third world country for the first time. We started off in Dhaka, which you think is very third world, but then we got a flight over to Chittagong and it was a completely different world. Despite some of the things we saw in terms of how people lived, which were difficult to witness, the people were so happy and just fanatical about cricket. We'd turn up for matches and they'd be tens of thousands of people there watching. New Zealand was a bit more subdued! We were based in Christchurch and we played against a number of guys that went on to represent New Zealand."

It was a strong England A team squad that Rob played in. Under the management of Martin Moxon and captaincy of Mark Alleyne, others within the squad included Aftab Habib, Vikram Solanki, Chris Silverwood, Chris Schofield and David Sales.

"I started very well in a couple of the one-day games in Bangladesh, but then I didn't get a great deal of batting. My keeping went well throughout, but once we got to New Zealand I didn't get many runs. I started off well and got a 40 odd not out to see us home in the first game, but then didn't get many opportunities, and when I did get an opportunity, I didn't make any significant contributions. It was a shame, but it was great fun and it was a great bunch of lads to be on tour with."

Sadly for Rob, that was to be his only taste of international cricket. With the likes of Jack Russell and Alec Stewart in front of him, a call up to the senior side never came. "It was disappointing, of course, but it didn't really faze me. It would have been nice, but I don't think I'd ever have had a long England career but it would have been nice to have played a series of two."

Rob did come extremely close in 1999, when many had him named in the squad to tour South Africa under Nasser Hussain and Duncan Fletcher. "We played a Lord's final against Gloucestershire (we'll talk more about that final later) and I was up in London two nights before for a cricket writers' dinner. I was being interviewed by all the main cricket writers of the national newspapers. Throughout the season, I was aware that there were a few scouts watching me, including Alan Knott, so I knew there was a fair chance of me being selected. These journalists were interviewing me and telling me that I was going to be named in it. But then having breakfast on the morning of the final the squad appeared on Ceefax screens in the breakfast room and I wasn't listed. If there hadn't of been the hype, I wouldn't have thought about it, but after all the talk and being told by the journalists I was going to be in the squad, it was a little disappointing. But it's not something I look back on and am angry about. I enjoyed myself playing county cricket at Somerset."

Rob's life as a county cricketer was similar to many others in that period. He played for his county in the Summer months and looked for employment for the other six months of the year. "In those days you played cricket for six months and then you were left alone for six months. I had a couple of Winters where I played cricket in Perth, Australia, but other than that I was left to my own devices."

Fortunately for Rob, he got employed by a stockbrokers called Rowan Darlington, who employed Rob for a number of Winters during his time at Somerset. "A guy who was captain of my local cricket club was a partner at Rowan Darlington and he told me to come down and see what's it like; I did and I really got into it. I took some exams in stock broking and it was great fun. It worked out perfectly. They always let me disappear off to do my Winter training when I needed to and they just really supported me. Thankfully they were all cricket nuts, so they loved having me work there. The company actually went on and became our main sponsor at Somerset for a few years and they supported my benefit year later on down the line. I'm forever grateful to them."

On the pitch, Somerset were making great strides forward, under the captaincy of Australian Jamie Cox. In 1999, as we mentioned earlier, they reached the final of the NatWest Trophy, where although they lost to rivals Gloucestershire it was the start of a successful period for the west country outfit. "It was an amazing day at Lord's, despite the result. The fact it was Gloucestershire who were our big local rivals really made the day. I was good friends with a number of their players, Mark Alleyne, Martin Ball, Tim Hancock and Mike Smith. I remember batting at one point and you could hear the whole crowd singing "stand up if you're west country", it was incredible. Usually, you block out the crowd, but there were times like that, when the hairs on the back of your neck stand up. It was just frustrating to lose!"

Two years later and Somerset righted that wrong with a C&G Trophy win over Leicestershire. "Another incredible day. The crowd were again magnificent, but when you're winning, you take it in that bit more. I remember after the game we all drifted back to the team hotel and the bar was full of Somerset supporters. We were being treated like Gods. Those were the days you used to be among supporters, spend time with them, chat to them in the bars, you knew who they were. It was very personal, which I think is lost a bit now, which is a shame."

The team also finished runners up in division one of the county championship, 12 months after the restructuring of the county game, which saw all 18 counties split in to two divisions of 9.

"To be honest, we were nowhere near winning the championship. We won a few games at the end of the season that got us into second place, rather than we were challenging. But it showed how much we were progressing."

I asked Rob, how different it was to adjust from a division of 18 counties to two divisions of 9. "It made a big difference, especially at the end of the season, when you previously didn't have too much to play for. Suddenly you could be midtable, but you still had to win games to make sure you weren't going to go down, or to give you an outside chance of winning it. Also, as a player you wanted to be in the top division. The best players tended to migrate to division one because that's generally where the England players were being picked from."

Somerset reached the C&G Trophy final again in 2002, this time against Yorkshire, but sadly they were unable to retain their title. "We were a bit unlucky in that final. It could, perhaps should, have gone our way. I remember we got ourselves into a potential winning position, but a couple of decisions didn't go with us and we weren't able to see it home."

I asked Rob, what made Somerset such a successful side in that period, particularly in one day cricket.

"Our coach Dermot Reeve was brilliant. We used to rock up and everyone knew their jobs and what we had to do. We all supported each other and everyone believed in each other. We used to win games for fun. We had an incredible side. We had lots of bits and pieces cricketers who all had phenomenal seasons; players like Keith Dutch, Keith Parsons, Ian Blackwell and Richard Johnson. Trescothick and Caddick aside, we didn't have household names, but we came together as a team. We won so many games when we were out of it but believed we could get over the line. And we had Jamie Cox as captain, who was just sensational."

It was just after this run of one day cup finals that T20 cricket was launched in England and it's fair to say many didn't think it would grow to as big as it has. "I wouldn't say the competition was treated like a joke, but it was initially felt that 20 over cricket was something you did in club cricket. We of course wanted to win, but it was a bit of light relief in the middle of four-day and one day cricket. But it quickly became a major form of the game. The way it has developed cricket is incredible. It's revolutionised both one day and Test cricket."

I asked Rob what he thought was the catalyst for the change in people's perception of this short format of the game. "Financially, people soon started to realise that big money was being put into T20 cricket and with the big crowds it became a showcase and a platform for county players. It allowed specialist players to come through. I remember we started playing the same team that played four-day cricket! It is funny looking back. No one believed it would become so big!"

Rob retired from cricket in 2005, following a management change at the club. "I was intending to play on for another year to help with transition to a new younger keeper. But a new management team came in and the new coach Brian Rose wanted to basically clear out the old guard and start refresh. It just made me feel like it was the right time to retire and try and forge a new career elsewhere."

Rob took over 1,000 catches and dismissals in first class, List A and T20 cricket, not to mention just under 13,000 runs with the bat.

I asked Rob, among those 1,000 catches, and which he would

rank at number one. "It has to be a catch I took to get out Shahid Afridi in the final at Lord's against Leicestershire. He was a player that could take a game away from you in an instant. No matter what the score was, if he batted for 10 overs, he could destroy you. We'd played Leicestershire a couple of times leading up to that final and they were a very good one day side. But, they kind of relied on him. We felt if we could get him out, the rest of the team would fall apart and because he tried to blaze every ball, you felt there would always be a chance. Before he signed for them, I always felt they were always a tight unit but with him in the team you sensed there could be a bit of complacency from others as they thought Afridi would always win them the game. Richard Johnson got him to top edge massively and the ball went right up in the air, a real steepler. People said to me afterwards that the crowd just went completely quiet, as if the whole game hung on this catch. I was back paddling, but the ball was so high, it was extremely difficult to judge. Sometimes as a keeper you can get those horribly wrong if you don't judge it properly against clouds and stuff. As the ball came hurtling down I just thought this is going to drop behind me and I wasn't getting back quick enough. In that split second though I must have relaxed and next thing it was in my gloves and we were all off celebrating! It was only the 5th over of the game, but in that moment, we felt like we'd won the game. It was my most famous catch by far. Thank god I caught it!"

Rob scored 10 centuries throughout his first-class career and it was a hundred against Worcestershire during a Somerset festival game which Rob's ranked as his best. Each year, Somerset would host some of their county games at 'out grounds' as part of their annual festival. What happened in this game at Bath was an entertaining insight into county life during those old festival days.

"I was batting with Shane Lee, Brett's brother, who came over to play for Somerset for a couple of years and we put on a record partnership of 268 or something like that. In those festival days, we would camp out in that town for a week and a half, and if I'm in honest they used to turn into a bit of a party. In this particular year Shane and I, had, had a big night out. We'd had a bit of a laugh in several bars and got in at a ridiculous hour of the morning - completely unprofessional. Shane was batting in the morning and I joined him at the crease 10 minutes before lunch. I walked out to the middle and I'll be honest I could hardly see the ball! I remember saying to Shane that I was struggling big time but I somehow survived until lunch. After the break though, I lost any kind of inhibitions and just started to play like I'd never played before! Shane scored 160 and I got a hundred. I think it was just a case of being so relaxed that I attempted shots I'd never tried before! But I wouldn't recommend to anyone to play in that kind of condition! Truth be known all teams did it. Both sets of players would typically be out together. Nowadays it's very, very different!"

Rob's top score was a 144 in a county game against Kent; that came while Rob was going through a period of opening the batting.

"That was an interesting innings because Martin McCague was bowling at the time. I knew a bit about him from playing cricket in Perth but in this game, he'd lost it and was bowling flat ones; it just looked like he didn't know when to release the ball. He got warned by the umpire, but he then bowled another bad delivery and was removed from the attack. So, they were a bowler down. I batted pretty much all day, scoring around 50 runs a session. I was on 144 with six overs of the day left and I had this focus that I wanted to bat all day. I thought it would be such a major achievement to do it. I ended up trying to hook Mark Ealham down to fine leg and got out. I was gutted! Hooking was a common way for me to get out. I used to try and hook everything! Against someone like Mark Ealham you couldn't do it because he was such a clever bowler."

I asked Rob if it was easy or difficult to open the batting as a wicket-keeper. "If all areas of the game are going well it's actually quite good if you're opening the batting. You'd either get a big score and then still have time to rest up before going out to field. Or, you'd be out early and get time to rest up before going out to field. When you're batting at seven, it's hard to completely rest up mentally. It's difficult to relax if you lose a few early wickets; you're on edge all day waiting to go out. And then when you do bat, you could bat through and you're straight into keeping."

Rob was a one club man, having played all his first-class career at Somerset. So, what made Somerset such a great club to play at? "I was brought up in Weston Super Mare and Somerset used to do festivals down there all the time. When Somerset came to town, as a kid it was a big thing as it was the only time you got to see county cricket. The whole town would come out and see them. As a result, Somerset became my club. My earliest memories were at Weston Super Mare and I always wanted to be part of it. I played in the last festival there which meant a lot. I played against Malcolm Marshall there which was amazing."

For a county cricketer who didn't represent his county on the international stage, to face someone of Marshall's calibre was a big thing. "He was a brilliant bowler. He wasn't rapid in that game, but he swung the ball all over the place. I remember batting with Chris Tavare who was batting at the other end like an absolute god, while I couldn't land a bat on it. Marshall had such control of the ball and could swing it so late. I remember speaking to Tav in between overs asked him how he knew which way the ball was going swing. He just said that when he got into his bowling action, you could get a glimpse of the ball and could see which way the shine was. I remember thinking I can't even see that. It might have been a split second that he showed you a glimpse. The fact Tav could spot that, showed me that I was a world away from that top level to be able to see things like that."

Malcolm Marshall was just one of several great players that Rob played with and against during his career.

"Graeme Hick was incredible at county level and I was very fortunate to play against the likes of Waqar and Wasim, Walsh, Ambrose, Warne, McGrath. It was an utter privilege to play against them."

When talking through the great players he'd played against, Rob recalled a game in 1997 against the touring Australians – a game which saw a mutual respect emerge. "We played against Australia at Taunton in a three-day game. I was facing McGrath and I remember looking around and there was Ian Healey behind the stumps, and then a line of players in the slip and gully region, including both the Waugh's, Warne, Langer and Ponting – it was an incredible sight. Greg Blewett was fielding under the helmet at short leg and he used to bowl some filthy medium pacers at times. He got hit for a couple of fours the over before, one of which was a streaky one by me! So, as I was getting set to face this ball from McGrath, he's under the lid chuntering away me as McGrath was running in. Just as he was in his delivery stride, I walked away and went to confront Blewett to tell him to shut up. What I hadn't realised was McGrath carried on and bowled the ball; Healey caught it and as I walked out of my crease to confront Blewett, he tried to throw down the stumps, but missed them. As nobody was there, the batsman at the other end called me through for a single. The whole thing turned into a farce and for the next three or four overs I was just abused by pretty much everyone on the pitch! It was constant. I played alright though, defended well and got through it. Then in between overs someone tapped me on the arse and just said 'well done mate' and from then on there was total silence in the field. It was like I'd got their respect. Things like that were brilliant to be part of. It's a shame counties don't really get these touring games anymore. Both players and supporters miss out. These days the international tours are all geared toward minimal cricket; play the international games and go. It's a real shame."

I asked Rob who the best bowler was he kept to and one man came out number one: Pakistan spinner, Mushtaq Ahmed.

"Andy Caddick was brilliant and a delight to keep to as he just shaped it away and got good bounce. Goodness knows how many catches I took off Caddy but Mushtaq was an absolute legend! We became good friends and roomed together when he was over at Somerset. He was a little maestro who massively improved me as a player, especially standing up to the stumps. You had to put so much focus on watching the ball. Sometimes you don't do that properly but when you have someone who spun the ball that much you had to focus. He could bowl all day, which could exhaust me because of the focus and concentration. It could be so intense but totally worth it. Keeping to Mushy also helped my batting. I got a 50 against Shane Warne when we played Hampshire and I'm sure that was through all of the time keeping to Mushy and learning his tricks of the trade."

Rob's friendship with Mushtaq began in Australia when Rob was playing Winter cricket in Perth and it spoke volumes for the kind of man Mushtaq is. "I was in Australia when I heard Somerset had signed him and he was out in Perth touring with Pakistan. I went to see him at the WACA, during a Test match and just introduced myself as the Somerset wicket-keeper, even though I was playing in the 2s at the time. I asked him if he minded me video him in the nets as I'd be his wicket-keeper in England and it'd good to prepare myself for the following Summer. He was great. In the middle of an international game, he took me over to the nets and let me video him. I must have watched those videos over and over but he was still impossible to pick at times!!"

It wasn't just Mushy, Andrew Caddick and Marcus Trescothick that he held in a high regard at Taunton however, there were many others. "Mark Lathwell was an absolute genius at times. It was such a shame he didn't continue and enjoy county cricket. I don't think it was for him after a while. Keith Dutch, Keith Parsons, Michael Burns and Ian Blackwell also performed so well for us; Richard Johnson was an outstanding bowler who was high class when he got it right and Jamie Cox was a genius."

Rob doesn't use the word 'genius' lightly when he talks about Cox's captaincy. "He was very, very clever. He was always relaxed and measured and read a game very, very well. He'd make the right tactical fielding decisions and brought a completely new dimension to our side. When he came in it was difficult for him in that he wasn't a big-name overseas player; he wasn't an Australian legend. But, as soon as he came over, he demanded huge respect and was just a lovely guy. You could have beers and fun with him but you knew the line and everyone had the utmost respect for him. You always knew where you stood."

Rob is now enjoying life as a school teacher. "As soon as I retired I stepped into teaching. During one of my years in Perth I did some work in a school and helped with a bit of coaching and really enjoyed it. I knew stock broking wasn't the career I wanted long term, so when I finished playing, I wanted to try and get into teaching. I wrote to all the independent schools in the area as I didn't have any formal teaching qualifications, which were necessary to teach in the state system - there were quite a lot of independent schools at the time in Taunton. I ended up getting taken on by a school and was there for ten years and I've now just moved into the state system at a sixth form college in Taunton. It's really enjoyable."

Education's gain is most definitely cricket's loss. But batsmen beware in the west country as Rob still dons the whites at Weston Super Mare Cricket Club and the catches are still sticking!

18

PAUL NIXON
FORMER ENGLAND, LEICESTERSHIRE &
KENT WICKET-KEEPER

Throughout this book we have spoken to some of the country's leading wicket-keepers of the last 25 years and for this interview I spoke to another, former England, Leicestershire and Kent keeper Paul Nixon. What a golden generation we've had over the last 25 years.

Paul's energy and enthusiasm behind the stumps was always second to none and it was of course his contributions, with the gloves, the bat and in the changing rooms which made him a hero among England fans back in 2007, when following England's disastrous 5-0 Ashes defeat, Paul (or Nico as he's affectionately known), along with other one-day specialists, arrived down under and transformed our performances to give us long suffering England fans something to cherish on that horrible tour!

"The guys had lost their way a little bit after being heavily beaten by Australia and it needed us one-day guys who were arriving to be upbeat and positive and try to rally the troops; which we were able to do."

We'll come on to that series later. Let's talk Nico's journey through to international selection.

Before falling in love with wicket-keeping, Nico was a young 'all-rounder' who idolised the likes of Ian Botham, Viv Richards and David Gower. "I was around 10 or 11 when I tried wicket-keeping and I loved it. The feeling of being in the game every ball, was for me!"

In Paul's teens, his performances behind the stumps took off. He played representative cricket for the north of England and Cumbria Schools – a period that he looks back at with a great deal of fondness. "Those days were great fun. I always felt I was progressing on my journey."

His performances for the north of England and Cumbria Schools, saw him picked up by the Lord's Ground staff and it was this period at the Home of Cricket that saw the first-class counties begin to circle. "I went to Middlesex for a few weeks, but didn't get offered a contract, but then Leicestershire came in. I was fortunate that they needed a wicket-keeper so I took the opportunity to go up there and took it with both hands."

Nico made his debut for Leicestershire in 1989 against Warwickshire at one of the county's out grounds in Hinckley. "I remember we were playing on a very green wicket, but fortunately for me I had a good debut! I managed to get six dismissals, which I enjoyed and thankfully I was able to avoid having to face Allan Donald bowling what I'd call, legalised stoning at 92mph!"

What followed was arguably one of the most successful periods of Leicestershire's history.

In 1992, the Foxes reached a Lord's final. Wins against Norfolk, Derbyshire, Durham and Essex saw the Foxes head to Lord's to take on Allan Lamb and his Northamptonshire side. "At the time that was the biggest game of my life. Lord's was packed out but sadly we didn't get enough runs. If I'm honest, at times we batted quite safely and although eventually we got up to a competitive total, our bowlers didn't have a good day. Alan Fordham put us to the sword. I remember he had an aggressive partnership with Nigel Felton and we were always chasing the game after that and they romped home. It was disappointing not to come away with silverware and a winner's medal, but it was a great experience and I loved every minute of it. Being in the middle with a packed crowd just felt right. It was the kind of occasion you wanted to play in every day."

Thankfully, Nico and his team mates didn't have too long to wait to get a winner's medal - a medal which every county cricketer craves: A County Championship winners medal. 1996 saw the Foxes win only the second County Championship of their history, a feat they were able to repeat two years later. And if it wasn't for a crazy Summer of rain in 1997, it could very easily have been three successive county titles – an extraordinary feat for a club the size of Leicestershire.

"We lost over 1,000 overs to rain in 1997, if we hadn't of done so, I honestly believe we'd have won three out of three."

I asked Paul what made that team so successful. "Everyone in that team in 96 and 98 had something to prove. Several us had played together in the 2nds so we all knew each other's games. Alan Mullally and David Millns bowled beautifully. With Gordon Parsons, Vince Wells and Adrian Pearson we had great balance to our side. In 1996, we batted only once on ten occasions, that's phenomenal and I don't think will ever be repeated."

But it was not just in four-day cricket that Leicestershire were dominating; they were playing great cricket with the white ball and in 1998 they had another Lord's final - this time in the old Benson & Hedges Cup. Sadly, the game ended with a runners-up medal for Paul as Essex took the trophy home to Chelmsford. "That final was a damp squib really. Lord's was always renowned at the end of the season as a bit of a win the toss, win the game ground. It rained and rained. We waited around for ages and when we eventually did get out there, it was damp under the covers, it was wet and sticky. Essex bowled well to be fair and took some amazing catches, but we got bowled out for peanuts. It just didn't happen for us. We came back the next day on the reserve day, the weather had brightened up and they put us to the sword with the bat. We were well beaten and again it was very disappointing."

But what a period it had been for Nico, two county championships and two Lord's finals, more than I'm sure he could have dreamed of when he first put pen to paper at Grace Road.

With a benefit year looming, Paul was looking forward to building on this success, with a promising group of youngsters emerging. But, sadly for Nico the county had other ideas and he had to make a move away from Leicestershire. "I wanted an extension to my contract for just another year. I was next in line for my benefit year but for some reason Jack Birkenshaw didn't want to offer me that. I'd played so many games in succession, we were winning things so it was very disappointing."

Sussex came close to signing Paul, but it was a game against Kent which was the catalyst for Paul's career taking a new direction to the South East of the country. "We were playing a game against Kent, when Matthew Fleming said to me that Steve Marsh was looking to retire and they were wanted a vibrant keeper; a keeper they wanted to play for England and that; that keeper was me. They ended up offering me a contract I couldn't refuse. Kent was a big club, who had just finished second in three competitions and were on the cusp of something special. They looked after me well and it was just fantastic to know someone was desperate for me to go there. Chris Adams did want me to come down to Sussex with him and Peter Moores; they offered more money, but I'd already verbally given my commitment to Kent and I'm a man of my word and wanted to honour that. But I was close to going to Sussex. It just wasn't the right timing."

What followed was a debut season that ended with a call up for England's Winter tour to Pakistan and Sri Lanka. "We won the Sunday League which was fantastic and in those two seasons at Kent I was fortunate to play alongside the likes of Steve Waugh, Andrew Symonds and Rahul Dravid – we had some serious players. It was great!"

Paul also scored his career highest score while at Kent, a memorable 173 not out against, guess who, Leicestershire! "You always want do well against your home club!"

But his delight with an England call up was immeasurable. "I was delighted. I always knew it was going to be tough to get a game because Alec Stewart was an England legend and he was always going to play. But it was a case of making myself stay fit, be positive in the unit and make sure I gave as much as I could for the team. I just did everything I could to impress."

And in impress he did. In one of the warm up games he scored an excellent 47 not out. "I was playing nicely when Nasser decided to declare out of the blue! It would have been nice to get a 70 or 80, but it wasn't to be."

Sadly, his pre-tour prediction was right and he wasn't able to break into the Test side.

I asked Paul how frustrating it was as a wicket-keeper in that era when you knew international chances would be limited, when there is an England legend wearing the shirt and gloves. "Life is about timing at the end of the day. Alec was churning out the runs and his keeping got better and better the more he kept. Jack Russell could and should have played more, so as a keeper it is tough as there is only one place. So, yes there is frustration but ultimately you can only control what you can control and you just have to keep churning out the runs and try and force them to pick you. I tried to make sure that if anything ever happened to Stewie, I was there and ready."

After two years at Kent, Paul made a return to Grace Road, following the emergence of Geraint Jones at Kent. "I was on a good wage at Kent and Geraint was doing really well in the second team. He was scoring a lot of runs and keeping wicket well. I was a senior pro, who although I was playing well but was on a six-figure salary and it made good business sense for the club for me to move on, because Geraint Jones was developing well and we were doing the same job. He was the younger man so my contract wasn't renewed. Fortunately, an opportunity came up back at Leicestershire so it was a perfect fit."

I asked Paul, if things had changed much upon his return and how easy was it to fit back in to the dressing room. "I was lucky that I was able to fit straight back in, which was great. There were a lot of different names, but I was back home."

His return to Leicestershire coincided with the rise of domestic T20 cricket. For many counties, this new format of the game was a chance to swing the bat and have some fun, but for Paul and his team mates, it was a serious competition and one they felt they could win. "I remember in that first season we had the perfect start because we had a week off in the week leading up to the first game. So, we practised and practised to get some momentum, we played several practice games in the middle. It was fun and we struck upon a few things we felt would help us in games. It was fantastic because we could work on our strategies. I also remember we had a brilliant brain storming session during that week which really proved its worth."

This preparation certainly paid off as the Foxes went all the way through to the first four 'Finals Day' of the competition, winning it in 2004 and 2006. "We should have won that first year, but we had a few players that didn't stick to the game plan, which we worked on and we were on fire after that. We had a fantastic record. We should have won in 2005 which would have been three in a row but we got beaten by Somerset. We had an easy score to chase but lost a lot of wickets together and fell a few runs short. I loved T20 finals days as they were the nearest things you could get to playing for England. It maybe wasn't the pressure of an international game, but the atmosphere would be as incredible as an international fixture. It was the stage you wanted to play on. A great buzz."

I asked Paul, if he ever felt at that time, that T20 cricket would grow to the size it is today. "We honestly did. Because it was so accessible for people at weekends and in the evenings and it was just fun to play and watch."

I asked Paul where he stood in terms of franchise cricket and the proposed new league set to launch in 2020. "It's what is needed. It cannot just be about the counties. It's about getting youngsters into cricket and at games. And we need to make sure as many of these games as possible get shown on terrestrial television so the masses can see it. It's crucial."

Paul's form in T20 and domestic 50 over cricket saw his belated recall to the England scene in 2006 as wicket-keeper for England in the Commonwealth Bank one day series against Australia and New Zealand.

"If I am honest, I probably had given up thinking about playing for England. Of course, you always dream but realistically, I was 36 and I had given up, so it was a surprise. To be fair when I played against Yorkshire at the end of the Summer Michael Vaughan had told me to keep cricket fit, as you never know what might happen. I was in good form but it was a huge surprise when I received the call from David Graveney on Christmas Eve to say that I would be flying out to Australia to be the number one keeper for the ODI series."

An early Christmas present I'm sure Paul will never forget.

Paul flew out after the Test team had been hammered 5-0. "The boys were struggling and Freddie wasn't in a great place. They needed characters. They needed a lift. It's very easy when things aren't going your way to dwell on the negatives, so the one-day lads just came out and tried to be positive. It was crucial."

Paul made his ODI debut against Australia at the MCG. Despite being dismissed for a duck (we'll gloss over that!), he did catch the Australian's two danger players, Adam Gilchrist and Matthew Hayden. "It was magical. My Dad was present as he was already over there following England throughout the Winter, he as always does. Being in the twilight of my career, I just wanted to go out, wear the three lions and enjoy it. There was nobody prouder that day."

England won the series, beating Australia in a best of three match final. The abiding memory of that final was a photo of Paul celebrating with the fans in Sydney. It was an iconic photo.

"To win that series, having lost the Test series the way we did was fantastic. There was so much happiness in that dressing room after that game."

I asked Paul what he felt was the turning point in fortunes for the squad. "To be honest people just stood up at the right times. Paul Collingwood had a great series throughout, but Ed Joyce scored a brilliant century in Sydney and people started to deliver match winning performances. Our assistant coach Matthew Maynard played his part by insisting that we had a big celebration after every win. It all just worked well."

Following that fantastic series win, England headed over to the Caribbean for the ICC World Cup. Individually, Paul had an excellent tournament: 9 dismissals and nearly 200 runs with the bat at an average just shy of 40. But once again, collectively, England failed to live up to their potential in a World Cup tournament.

"I'd learnt in Australia that I didn't get the runs that I should have. When I went out to bat, we were generally always 20/30/40 runs behind, so I too often tried to run before I could walk. In the World Cup, I gave myself more time to get myself in, even if it was just a few balls. It worked well for me. We desperately wanted to keep that momentum from Australia going, but we just didn't score enough runs at the top of the order."

England exited the competition at the Super Eights stage. Prior to England's final dead rubber game against the West Indies, coach Duncan Fletcher announced that he was standing down as England coach. Fletcher had done a huge amount for English cricket and had also done a huge amount for Paul. His departure sadly signalled an end to Nico's blossoming England career.

"Duncan decided to hang his boots up and then Peter Moores came in. He decided to go with Matt Prior, who was a developing wicket-keeper, but a player who was a world class batsman. If Duncan had stayed on as coach, I honestly think I'd have made my Test debut that Summer. It was disappointing to have played well and been so fit – I was the fittest all-round cricketer in the side. I was loving every minute of playing for England and living the dream, but those memories and experiences can never be taken away."

England's loss was Leicestershire's gain and the following year the Foxes appointed Paul as first X1 captain.

"I'd always thought of myself as a leader anyway - you always want your senior players to be leaders – but it was a natural transition for me. It wasn't an easy period though. A lot of senior players had left the club and the management wanted to go down the line of youngsters, as there were financial rewards for doing so, for me it was frustrating because we weren't playing the best players we could have played. We were playing youngsters to balance the books. The positive was it gave these youngsters opportunities, but you don't want youngsters getting used to losing. It was frustrating."

You can understand Paul's frustration when you think of the players that moved on from Leicestershire: Darren Stevens, James Taylor, Harry Gurney, Stuart Broad, Luke Wright, Alan Mullally.

While the England dream had died, there was to be a swan song of overseas cricket for Paul when he got picked to play in the Indian Cricket League (ICL), a T20 competition that was a pre-cursor to the IPL. The league eventually folded because of a lack of support from the BCCI and the ICC. Paul played two seasons for Delhi Giants and joined fellow England cricketers Vikram Solanki and Darren Maddy in the tournament.

"The ICL was a great competition. Several young Indian cricketers started out playing in the ICL before going on to pick up big contracts in the IPL. That competition awoke officials in India to the fact that the world's best coaches and players from around the world would come to play domestic cricket in India and help mentor and develop their youngsters and make them much more rounded cricketers."

Paul eventually called time on his career in 2011. "My body was getting sore and tired so I knew it was the right time."

Paul's final game for the Foxes was against Warwickshire in the final of that year's T20 competition. A total of 166 was overcome by Leicestershire via Duckworth Lewis and Paul was held aloft by his team mates. "It was very emotional. You try not to immerse yourself in the emotions too much. You just try and get through your routines. I always wanted to go out on a high and I was fortunate to do that. It was funny because you were never sure when your last game would be. My last game at Grace Road was against Kent in the quarter finals, that would have been my last game if we'd lost, but we achieved an amazing run chase against my old team. But to win in the final with the first ever super over was special. There were a few sore heads for a few days after that final!"

Paul scored just under 24,000 runs throughout his career and took exactly 1,600 catches and stumpings – a truly remarkable record.

With all those dismissals, I had to ask which his favourite was. "It was a catch off Alan Mullally to get Robin Smith out. I had to go back and away and it was an enjoyable catch. Others up there were getting Kieron Pollard out just before my 42nd birthday at 10pm at night! I once stumped Alec Stewart at the Oval – it's not easy to get a stumping at the Oval and then of course my first international stumping off Monty Panesar. Great memories."

Paul kept to some great bowlers, so who were up there as the best? "Muhammad Asif was an incredible bowler. Alan Mullally was a high class away swing bowler to right handers. Martin Saggers at Kent another high class away swing bowler during my time at Kent. And then of course there was Mike Kasprowicz and Winston Benjamin."

Aside from these bowlers, Paul played alongside some of the world's best batsmen, Sehwag, Cronje, Dravid and Waugh - not a bad list!

When you add the players, he's played against - Lara, Ponting, Kallis, Tendulkar, Richards - it's clear that here's a man who can look back at a career full of wonderful memories.

But I had to ask Nico about sledging, especially given his reputation for enjoying a few chosen words with

opposition batsmen! "For me it was about making batsmen forget about their mental routines. I admit the last game I played I was probably a little bit over the top, but it was something that got me into the game, which I needed. It was a powerful thing for me but I always knew the line not to cross, that was absolutely crucial to me."

Paul is still involved in cricket, he often appears on Sky Sports, he has a regular column in the Cricket Paper, is involved with the PCA and coaches Jamaica in the Caribbean Premier League. Add to this several after dinner speaking engagements and working for a company called World of Payments, a PayPal type system of the gaming world and Paul is incredibly busy.

He may have only pulled on the three lions jersey a few times, but for England fans and especially those who were on that 06/07 Australia tour, he's a former player who is held in the highest, highest regard.

19

CRAIG WHITE
FORMER ENGLAND & YORKSHIRE
ALL-ROUNDER

Former England all-rounder Craig White was my very first interview back in 2016. Craig played 30 Test matches for England, scored a wonderful Test century in India, took three 5-wicket hauls and became the first bowler to dismiss the great Brian Lara for a golden duck.

Born in Morley, West Yorkshire, Craig was an attacking right handed batsmen who regularly bowled at speeds in excess of 90mph. I caught up with Craig, who is now bowling coach at Hampshire, to talk through: his career, his path to Test cricket for England, an incident that ended up changing his entire outlook towards the game, his fondest memories, together with his thoughts on the current England team and the domestic structure in England.

Although born in Yorkshire, Craig was brought up in Australia, in a small town called Bendigo, which is situated 100 miles from

Melbourne. "My Dad was a very, very, very, proud Yorkshireman and he used to take me down to the MCG whenever England were touring. I remember watching the likes of David Gower, Ian Botham and Bob Willis as well as other touring sides like the great West Indies team which included Viv Richards, Malcolm Marshall and Joel Garner." Like many children, Craig's passion was just picking up a bat and playing games of cricket. "I was a kid that simply loved cricket, but when I was starting to show signs of becoming a decent cricketer, my Dad promised me that one day he would take me back to England to have trials at Yorkshire. So even though I was brought up in Australia, the influence from my Dad was that I was English and one day I was going to play for Yorkshire."

Craig's dream move to Yorkshire became a reality in his teens when he moved back to England, and after successful trials, signed for the county.

However, such was Craig's early promise, he was selected for Australia at both under 17 and under 19 level, in squads that included the likes of Shane Warne and Damien Martyn.

"At the end of that first season for Yorkshire, I was selected for an Australian youth tour to the West Indies."

Craig knew that he soon had to make a decision on where his future lay, in Australia or in the country of his birth. "To be honest, even though I played representative cricket for Australia I thought there was no way I would reach the standard of being a full international cricketer. I just thought that was miles away and an unreachable goal, but I knew I was good enough for a decent career at Yorkshire and as a first-class cricketer. So, that was the decision I made very early, to make my future with Yorkshire."

What Craig didn't foresee, was that just a couple of years later, he would be making his England Test debut at Trent Bridge! In

2004, when Raymond Illingworth became the new Chairman of Selectors, he was keen to have an all-rounder who could bat at number six, and bowl first change. It was a shock for Craig to be thrust into the England set-up so soon. "It was just a bit of a shock, but a massive bonus. I had, had a decent year with Yorkshire the year before and I played for Yorkshire in a tour game against New Zealand where I bowled very fast and also smashed a quick 70. Ray Illingworth was there and I guess that is what got me selected."

In a Test team that included the likes of Atherton, Stewart, Gooch, Smith and Fraser, Craig made his debut against New Zealand at Trent Bridge in a Test where England won by an innings and 90 runs. During his debut, Craig picked up his maiden Test wicket, that of the prolific Kiwi batsman Martin Crowe, not a bad first Test scalp.

"It was a glove down the leg side. But 20 years later people would have classed it as an absolute jaffa!"

Injuries curtailed the first half of Craig's England career and he regularly found himself in and out of the side. Injuries, which Craig put down to his late development as a seam bowler. "Before I made my Test debut, I'd only been bowling fast for a year or so. When I first came to England, I used to bowl offies and then every now again I'd bowl some seamers in the nets and I was doing people for pace. During the odd county game when nothing was really happening, I was thrown the ball and asked to bowl quick to see if I could pick up a wicket and break a partnership. Every now and then, I took some wickets and I was given more opportunities to develop my seam bowling. But I think that played a part in the number of injuries I got in the first part of my career. My body wasn't used to bowling quick. I'm not the biggest lad, so suddenly going from bowling off spin to 90mph, my bowling muscles hadn't developed so something was always going to give as my body wasn't able to cope."

I also asked Craig if success as an all-rounder comes with experience and if that lack of experience also played a part in some inconsistent performances, early in his career. "Absolutely. If you weren't bowling well, in practice you'd naturally tend to work more on the aspects of your bowling that weren't working, but that was often at the detriment then of your batting. So your bowling would improve in the short term, but then your batting would suffer. You'd then work more on your batting but then your bowling would suffer again. As an all rounder you have to train on your batting, bowling, and fielding and it can be exhausting. With experience you learn how to get the balance and how to prepare properly, but that didn't happen for me until Duncan Fletcher and Nasser Hussain took charge. Once I did figure it out, I had quite a strong three-year period in Test cricket when I was at my best. When I look back, there was no way that I was ready to play Test cricket in 1994 and I still believe that if I was given another couple of years getting fitter and stronger with my bowling, before making my Test debut, I'd have played a lot more Test matches for England, but if you get selected at a young age, you're never going to turn the chance to play for England down."

In 2000, Craig suffered a mystery blackout, and collapsed in the street. The incident revitalised him as a cricketer, and his county performances earned him a recall to the England team for the series against the West Indies. "I was a different person after that incident. Before then I was always very harsh on myself. I wanted to make a hundred every time I batted and if I didn't, I'd beat myself up and get very down. That incident made me realise that every day was a bonus and it changed my outlook on cricket. In a funny kind of way, if that had happened earlier in my career, I also think that would have allowed me to have played many more Test matches."

When Craig was recalled for the West Indies series, the England set-up was a very different place. Duncan Fletcher was now

England coach and Nasser Hussain was England captain. This period was Craig's most enjoyable and successful spell as an England player. "Nasser was a fiery character, but that was what was needed at that time. He was a very, very good captain. He had a very strong relationship with Duncan and they worked very well together."

But what was the catalyst for getting the best out of Craig White, the all-rounder? "It was the communication. They would sit you down and tell you what was expected of you, how good they think you are and that you had a massive part to play for England. Just those words would put you in such a positive frame of mind. They created a new culture for the England team and you wanted to do well for them. Previously, it hadn't felt like you were in a team, it felt like individuals were playing to keep their places in the side, and that the result wasn't the important thing. There was no real team spirit."

I asked Craig if the introduction of central contracts also played a part. "Yes, definitely. They came in, in 2001 and I was one of the first batch and you definitely felt more of a 'team' after that and results picked up. People talk about 2005, but Duncan and Nasser played such a huge part in turning around England's fortunes that they deserve a lot of credit for the successes that happened down the line."

The new culture certainly coincided with Craig's most successful period as an international cricketer. In that series against the West Indies he cemented his place in the side, contributing useful runs, and became an important member of the pace-bowling attack, his bowling had improved to such an extent that he was capable of using reverse swing and consistently reaching speeds of 90 mph off his short run-up. He also has the honour of being the bowler to dismiss Brian Lara for the first golden duck of his Test career. "It happened at the Oval. I'd heard he'd been bowled around his legs a couple of times in the nets, so that had always been in the back of mind. In that series I was bowling around the wicket and taking it away from him, so he came out to bat and moved his guard over to off stump. I attempted to bowl him a Yorker, but it was probably more of a half volley, if I'm honest, but he over balanced and it knocked his leg stump out. I have to admit, when I released the ball, it didn't come out right, and I thought to myself 'oh no, that's four runs', but because he was so far over, trying to compensate for me usually moving the bowl away, he was so far out of position, his leg stump went flying out!"

After that series, Craig was one of the star players on subsequent tours to the subcontinent, with his most notable achievements being a 93 against Pakistan at Lahore and a 121 against India in Ahmedabad.

"When I started to play international cricket, all I wanted to do was make a Test hundred and get a Test fiver. The hundred in India was obviously one of the top highlights of my career, together with a Test five-for against the West Indies. But my best Test innings was actually against Sri Lanka in Kandy. I only got 20 odd but Murali was turning it square and we only had four wickets left in the tank and needed 50 more runs or so to win and Ashley Giles and I knocked them off."

I asked Craig, what it was like to face Murali and why he felt he managed to play a number of his best games for England in the sub-continent, where many players from England typically find it difficult. "To face Murali was amazing. He would pitch the ball and it would turn a foot and a half; it was a great challenge. I loved the challenge of facing the best spinners in the world in those conditions. I always tried to be positive and just thought you've nothing to lose. I think I enjoyed it more when we were up against it, in those conditions and situations. I performed better. With the bowling, I think my bowling was better on the flatter pitches. In England, I wasn't a big swinger of the ball, so if a pitch had a little more in it, the big lads would be picking up the wickets and I would tend to be more of the 3rd or 4th change bowler. But on Indian pitches for example, which were skiddier and flatter, I was able to get reverse swing and I came into my own more, ."

Craig's final Test series was the 2002/03 Ashes series where he played in the first four Tests of the series before an injury to his side prevented him from playing in the Fifth Test, in Sydney but he later recovered to play in the 2003 Cricket World Cup, his last appearance for the national team.

After the World Cup, bowling-related injuries began to take their toll on Craig again, and he re-invented himself as a specialist batsman for Yorkshire. In 2004, he was appointed captain of his home County and in 2005 led them to promotion from Division Two of the County Championship. However, he resigned as captain at the end of the 2006 season, having helped them to avoid relegation.

During his Test career, Craig faced arguably some of the best players who have ever played the game and I asked him who he found to be the most difficult of opponents.

"That's a tough question! Batting wise there was Tendulkar and Lara, but I actually enjoyed and had the most success bowling at left handers. That said, the hardest player I felt to bowl to was Matthew Hayden. I remember the opening day of a Test match in Australia; I was bowling before lunch, and felt in a good rhythm, I bowled a ball to Hayden, and he just took a couple of steps down the pitch and hit me over mid-wicket for 6! He was a bully to bowlers! Bowler wise, as a batsman I was facing the likes of Murali, Warne, McGrath, Ambrose, Walsh, Lee, Akhtar, every Test had a challenge. I am proud to be able to say I faced those guys, some of the best bowlers to have ever played the game. But certainly the fastest was Brett Lee."

I asked Craig, firstly as a batsman, was there much different between 85 to 90 or 90 to 95 mph when you're facing deliveries of such speed. "It's a different world. 90mph is obviously sharp, but when you're facing a Brett Lee or Shoaib Akhtar, it's a different world. You're batting on instinct and just trying to protect yourself, as you're no good to your team mates if you get carried off with broken ribs or a broken jaw. You know as a batsman, early on those bowlers will try and intimidate you and you have to get your head around that and plan for it and then hope after 18 balls or so it will become easier to score. I always felt it was a great challenge, it'd fire you up and looking back it was a great experience."

Craig recalled a Test match at the WACA, when Brett Lee was bowling perhaps his fastest ever spell. "In Perth you have what they call the freemantle doctor, which is usually a breeze that blows across the ground; on this day it wasn't just a breeze, but a full-on gale and it was right up Brett Lee's arse! He was steaming into bowl every delivery and smelt blood. A wicket fell and it was my turn to bat and I remember Alec Stewart meeting me halfway and said 'Chalks, you know you have to be up for this, he's bowling seriously quick'. I just said, 'No shit Sherlock I've been watching for the last few hours!' But I just remember being at the non strikers end and he bowled a bouncer to Stewie. Stewie was about two minutes too late playing a hook shot and it went through to Gilchrist, but to this day I can remember the sound of the ball hitting the pitch - it was like slapping your hand on concrete, just an amazing sound. But when you face someone like Lee, your first thought is just to protect yourself and then you'll start working out where your scoring shots will come from. But those first 18 balls are interesting stuff!"

Over the years, Craig played with a number of very good players for England. "Alec Stewart, Mike Atherton and Graham Thorpe were obviously very good players, but I was a big Graeme Hick fan. I just felt it was an honour to play with guys that I'd always looked up to and people I now class as good mates. Darren Gough is one of my best mates and I played a few Tests with Andrew Flintoff, towards the end of my career."

In total, Craig scored 1,052 Test runs and took 59 Test wickets in his 30 Test matches and I have no doubt that if his Test career had begun a few years later he would have played many more Tests for England and scored and taken, many more runs and wickets.

After Craig's first-class career ended, he moved on to the coaching staff at Yorkshire and also captained their second team, where among the youngsters who played under him were Joe Root, Gary Ballance and Johnny Bairstow. "It's been great to see how these guys are now doing and you like to think you had a little bit of an influence on their careers and where they have got to now."

Craig is now on the coaching staff at Hampshire, where three of his players have just been called up for this month's World T20 (James Vince, Richard Dawson and Reece Topley). "Giles White gave me a call after I left Yorkshire and said they had a coaching vacancy and would like me to fill it. It's been one of the best decisions I've ever made. Hampshire is a great club with some great people and I'm very happy here."

I asked Craig if he found it an easy transition from player to coach. "It's been OK. You have to get used to it's not about you anymore, it's about making others be the best they can be. I was never really a big fan of the limelight and I am quite an introverted person. I always found it a bit unnatural to perform in front of thousands of people, so to step into coaching has been quite natural for me, where I can sit in the background and help others. I think I am lot more comfortable in coaching."

The conversation with Craig then switched from talking about his career to that of another young all rounder and the potential of the current England team. "Ben Stokes is brilliant. I remember when he made his hundred at the WACA, I told people that for 20 years we'd been looking for the next Ian Botham, now in 20 years time people will be looking for the next Ben Stokes. And that was after that innings at the WACA! Look how he's developed since then; he could be one of the best ever. We've got an excellent team now and there's no real weaknesses. Encouragingly, there's also plenty of players in the background just waiting to pounce and they are all high quality as well, there's such depth which is healthy and enjoyable to watch."

I asked Craig if he puts this depth down to the strength of county cricket. "County cricket is very, very strong. The standard of some of the teams in division one is world class. I honestly believe, we have the strongest first-class competition in the world. I sit on the sidelines and what some of these lads can do, is amazing."

Craig though, is concerned about the future of Test cricket. "You'd like to think Test cricket remains the pinnacle, but there are so many tournaments now happening around the world, offering a lot of money, it's a worry. A player can play three or four tournaments a year, for four or five years and be very, very well off; you can understand why players can get drawn towards that, sadly."

With the T20 world cup this month, Craig is positive about England's chances. "We can go a long way. The team is now strong and we have matchwinners. We'll need a bit of luck, but we've a good chance."

And what could he tell us about the three Hampshire lads in the squad. "James Vince has been doing well in domestic T20 cricket for a few years now. It's great for him to get an opportunity on the world stage. Reece Topley is a new signing for us but is highly thought of with a lot of skills and Liam Dawson is a gutsy little cricketer. He has nice control with the ball and is a fighter with the bat who reads situations very well. If he gets a chance, he won't let anyone down."

Craig was an allrounder who went on to become an integral member of the England side in the early 2000s and should rightly be proud of everything he achieved. As supporters, we certainly remember a number of those batting and bowling performances with fond memories. He's been a credit to English cricket and someone his Dad can very proud of.

20

DEAN HEADLEY
FORMER ENGLAND, MIDDLESEX & KENT
FAST BOWLER

In this interview I spoke to a former England fast bowler who bowled England to victory in the famous MCG Test of 1998. Needing just 175 runs to win, Dean Headley's 6-60 steered England to a win that supporters still talk about to this day. It was one of those 'Do you remember when...' bowling spells.

"They actually outplayed us for a lot of the game but then we just got on a bit of a roll," recalled Dean. "Ramps took a great catch off Alan Mullally to get rid of Justin Langer and I then started to take wickets. It was just one of those days when you felt good and the ball was coming out all right!"

While that Test match was an obvious career highlight, there were a number of others in a career that yielded over 600 wickets.

Born in Stourbridge, Dean is a member of a famous cricketing family. He is the son of former West Indian cricketer Ron Headley and grandson of George Headley, widely regarded as one of the best batsmen to play for the West Indies and one of the greatest batsmen of all time.

"Growing up people knew who I was because of my family. If I played games of football, you could hear 'that's so and so's son', the reference to the family name was just part of everyday life for me. Quite often I was in the company of the likes of Michael Holding, Malcolm Marshall and Viv Richards, but they were just normal people to me as a youngster. The family name was never a burden, it was just the way it was. People often ask if it helped or hindered me, if I'm honest probably both. I would come across people who didn't necessarily like my Dad that much, for whatever reason and then I'd come across people who wanted to help me in my career because of my name."

One of those people was West Indian legend Clive Lloyd. Dean started his career at Worcestershire, but at the end of his initial contract, he wasn't retained. On the advice of Clive Lloyd, Dean headed north to play professionally for Leycett Cricket Club, who were based just outside Newcastle-under-Lyme. "Clive Lloyd advised me to go and play league cricket for a year and set me up with a club up north. I was earning more money playing club cricket for two days a week than if I'd carried on at Worcester. It was crazy. I felt a lot of responsibility but it was good grounding for me. The club played in the Staffordshire and Cheshire League and they have a Talbot Cup competition – we were the first second division club to win it. It was an enjoyable year. I ended up with 800 runs and 80 odd wickets. To give you an idea of how small the village was, eight of that team were related!"

At the end of that season, Clive Lloyd, intent on guiding Dean in the right direction, career-wise, arranged net sessions at three counties, Somerset, Derbyshire and Middlesex. It was the latter that secured Dean's signature. "I had a two-hour net session with all of them and each of them offered me a contract. I chose Middlesex. Clive, felt they would be the best option for me to get myself in the spotlight."

With the likes of Mike Gatting, Mark Ramprakash, Paul Downton, John Embury, Phil Tufnell, Angus Fraser and Desmond Haynes, Middlesex were one of the strongest sides in county cricket.

"It was a good side, with nine internationals. Playing in that dressing room was interesting, as it was so volatile. When you talk about honesty, nobody in that dressing room held back."

Dean made his first-class debut in a season curtain-raiser against the MCC. "As county champions, we played the MCC, in the traditional curtain-raiser for the season. I didn't think I would be playing in the first team so soon, but because of injuries to the likes of Neil Williams and Norman Cowans I was suddenly bowling to the likes of Graeme Hick and Neil Fairbrother."

But it was his full county debut where he began to make a name for himself by taking a wicket with his very first ball. "The ball went down the slope a bit and Ashley Metcalfe nicked off. It was a nice start. People often ask if that was one of my most memorable moments, but if I'm honest we all have loads don't we and they are all as memorable as the others. When I got in to my county side at under 13s it was a memorable moment, then going from under 13s straight to under 15s was a memorable moment; when I made my debut for the second team it was a memorable moment and so on. Every new stage is memorable as you begin a new challenge. I cherish them all."

Middlesex won the Sunday League in Dean's time at Lord's, a campaign that saw the county win the first 12 games of the season. "We just teed off in every game. I loved playing in that competition. The games were sandwiched in the middle of the county championship games. You played three days, then the Sunday league game, and then the fourth and final day. Because you knew what you were going to face on a Sunday - 100 overs - so you knew you could enjoy a Saturday night and know what was coming the following day!"

After two years at Middlesex, Dean made the move to Kent. "I was offered a contract extension, but I'll be honest I refused it. That was probably unusual for Middlesex as no one ever really turned down a contract, but they just didn't offer me a very good contract. I wasn't being greedy at all; it just wasn't a good contract offer."

It was a great move for Dean. What followed were a string of career highs and doors being opened on the international front.

"I played my best cricket at Kent. We had good pitches and we developed a strong squad. At the beginning, it was a hard team to break into, but Daryl Foster and Mark Benson were great at giving me the confidence to kick on."

I asked Dean what the main differences were between Middlesex and Kent. "Middlesex had international players ready to play, while at Kent we had hard working players. It was a great place to play cricket and we did well. I enjoyed playing with the likes of Carl Hooper, Aravinda de Silva, Andrew Symonds, Mark Ealham, Matthew Fleming, Alan Igglesdon, Martin McCague and Min Patel – we had a good team."

And it was a team in which Dean thrived. Hard work in the Winter of 1993 saw Dean add a few yards of pace which in his words took him from "someone reasonably above medium to someone who could be quite potent". Kent got the rewards as the team won the Sunday League and finished runners up in the county championship on a few occasions.

But individually, Dean was developing himself nicely into an international-ready bowler.

The 1993/94/95 seasons yielded over 120 first class wickets and despite being ready in many people's eyes, the national selectors thought otherwise and Dean didn't earn a place on an England tour in the Winter of 1995. "It was very disappointing but all I could do was just get on with it. Selection is subjective at the end of the day. I saw Wayne Morton, England's physio, in a game at Scarborough, just after the announcement and he said I'd been a bit unlucky not to be selected and to keep myself fit."

But a week later, an injury to Middlesex seamer Richard Johnson on England's main tour to South Africa saw a place for Dean open up on the England A tour to Pakistan. "Peter Martin got called up to the seniors so Tim Lamb phoned me up and said would I like to tour Pakistan. We played against the likes of Shoaib Akhtar, Shahid Afridi and Azhar Mahmood. It was a tough tour, but I struck up a good friendship with Nasser who was captain. I played a few warm up games and got selected for the First Test and didn't look back from there. The pitches were good for seamers and in some cases, were a lot quicker than we'd expected. It was interesting tour off the field as well. There wasn't a lot to do in Pakistan and there was only one public bar that you could drink in. To get served you had to sign a form saying that you were alcohol dependent – the entire squad signed!"

Back on the county circuit and Dean returned from that tour to Pakistan and equalled a world record the following September by taking his third hat-trick of the season in a game against Hampshire, at Canterbury.

Dean's career was progressing nicely towards senior England recognition.

The Winter of 1996 saw him selected for his second A team tour, this time down under in Australia. "That was a great tour. I enjoyed it immensely and we all had a lot of fun! And we were successful."

The team won two of the three first class games they played and won two of the other three list A games played.

Both A-team tours saw Dean return as top wicket-taker and a senior call-up was surely not far away.

"I hoped it would be on the tour to New Zealand but it wasn't to be." But the debut did come in the Ashes Summer of 1997. With the series level at 1-1, Dean was called up for the third Test match at Old Trafford.

Four wickets from Dean saw the Aussies reduced to 235 all out in their first innings. It was only a Steve Waugh hundred that rescued the Aussies. "The wicket was a little bit green and I thought I bowled as well as I could have done on debut."

As was often the case in the 90s England's batting failed and England went on to lose the Test by 268 runs. "I got eight wickets overall and got all of their left-handers out. It was funny, I was suddenly the best bowler in the world to left handers!"

Dean went on to take 16 wickets in the series but the Ashes were lost. I asked Dean what it was like facing that great Australian team and how wide he felt the gulf was between the sides. "It was good to play against them as they were the best team in the world. If you want to pit your skills against somebody, it might as well be against the best in the world to see if you can or can't bowl at that level. For me it was just fine lines. Their fielding was outstanding and that was a big difference. I remember on my debut we dropped Paul Reiffel, he went on and got 30 odd which allowed Steve Waugh to get a hundred and suddenly we had a deficit, when we shouldn't have. That kept happening and happening and happening. At Headingley Matthew Elliott got dropped and we didn't take another wicket for 300 runs. If that catch was taken, they were 50 odd for 4. It really was fine lines and you need good fortune against the best sides. And good fortune continues to this day. Would we have won the last Ashes if Joe Root wasn't dropped on nought at Cardiff, before he and made a hundred? Would we have won in 2005, if they'd have got those two more runs at Edgbaston? They were the breaks and good fortune the Aussies got in that period. You need breaks in sport."

Dean was also making a name for himself in one day cricket. In the Winter of 1997, England's one day team won the then much-famed Sharjah tournament, under the captaincy of Adam Hollioake. "Adam Hollioake was a really good captain. He led from the front and we played well in that tournament. We had a very good squad and a great team ethic. But we then went to the West Indies, lost a few games and the team got dismantled. It was no coincidence that the best teams were consistent on selection while, if we lost a couple of games, we'd have a clear-out and change our whole strategy. As a player, it was hugely frustrating. In my time, I always said England were a team I'd be going to represent, now it's very much a club you join. If you ask Jimmy Anderson now who he plays for, he'll say England and Lancashire, it won't just be Lancashire. Success is based on continuity of selection. Take the football world cup, Iceland did well because they picked the same group of players; in England we'd use 45. We may have had better quality players, but Iceland played as a unit, they knew their jobs. Playing for England in the 90s was like going into work and every Friday you'd get told if you were still in the job for the following week. You'd go in, work hard, but the uncertainty meant you could only perform at certain levels for so long. You can only manage people with a stick for so long. All that said I wouldn't have changed any of it, it was great times."

As well as that Sharjah tournament, the Winter of 97/98 saw Dean tour the West Indies for the first time as an England Test player. It was a special moment for Dean and his family. "It meant three successive generations of our family had played Test match cricket. Only a family in Pakistan have done the same. It was a good tour. The wickets were slow. I received a good reception in Jamaica but because of the big inter island rivalries, Barbados was a completely different story!"

This was the series when the first Test match had to be suspended after just 10 overs after the England batsmen had been struck several times by balls which lifted dangerously off a length. After lengthy discussions, the match was abandoned. In its place the teams played two Test matches in Trinidad. The West Indies won the first and England bounced back to win the second. A victory which included Dean taking an important 4-77 in the West Indies' second innings. The West Indies fought back in the next Test and England headed into the final Test of the series in Antigua trailing 2-1.

"That Antigua Test was over for us on the first evening. They left the covers off the pitch and it rained heavily. We missed two sessions of play and then the umpires felt it was fit enough to play; it wasn't. The ball was taking diverts out of the pitch. We batted that evening and found ourselves five down for next to nothing. The following day the pitch was all rolled out, became flat, the sun came out and that was the end of our Test series."

Straight after that defeat, captain Michael Atherton announced his resignation as Test captain. "Athers was very well respected and liked by everyone when he captained England for five years. It was quite an emotional moment for a lot of the players."

The following Summer the South Africans were in town and if any of you watched Mark Butcher's excellent documentary on England in the 90s will have heard the story of Dean's hilarious encounter with Allan Donald at Lord's. "We had a plan that series to try and take him out of the series by bumping him. I followed the plan, others didn't! We bowled them out with 35 minutes to go of the day. Everyone was telling me well done as I'd followed the plan and bowled several bouncers at Donald, but it had clearly ruffled them and the whole South Africa team reacted. We were reduced to 48-4 and I'm told to go out as night-watchman. I just thought are you kidding me! I had to walk out to face Donald and co who were hell bent on revenge. I was literally just thinking survival! I heard that one commentator said that Donald wasn't trying to bowl me out, but just to hit me! But, if you give it out, you've got to take it. I guess it was one of the more amusing stories. The thing is in his book Donald said that he'd hit me at Canterbury once with a ball towards the throat and that my bowling was some kind of vendetta, but it was honestly the plan that Bumble had given us."

I asked Dean if, that spell aside, he enjoyed the role as night-watchman. "Let's just say as a bowler you work your socks off bowling all day, so the last thing you want to hear when you get in the dressing room is that you need to be a night-watchman! It's no different in my mind to a bowler turning up one morning seeing the wicket is flat and asking the batters to have a bowl instead! Bowlers should bowl, batters should bat!"

In the Winter of 1998, the Ashes had come around again. "That Ashes tour was brilliant. But again, we didn't have the breaks. At Brisbane Gus Fraser dropped Ian Healy and Healy went on to make a big hundred – he didn't score a run all series after that. We gave a good account of ourselves at Perth and Alex Tudor bowled well. We then went to Adelaide and on day one it was 46 degrees, so both teams knew whoever won that toss would win the game. We lost it and had to bowl and field in those conditions. It was ridiculous. By the time, we got them out, they were so far ahead and the pitch was turning square. Just a horrible Test match."

Then came Melbourne and Dean's heroics. "It was such a memorable win and we then went on to Sydney knowing if we won, we'd level the series. Goughy took a hat-trick and I bowled well again. But then in their second innings the umpire didn't give Michael Slater out when he was clearly run-out. He went on to score 66 percent of their runs in that innings, which was the highest percentage anybody had ever scored in a team's innings. We should have been chasing 180 to win, in the end it meant Mark Taylor could put men around the bat and you couldn't do that against Australia in that period."

The team lost the series 3-1 but they came out of it with credit.

Having cemented his place in the side, Dean sadly played just two more Test matches for England as injury brought a premature end to his career. "It all happened very quickly. I had been complaining throughout that following year that I couldn't bowl, but I was being told I had no obvious injury symptoms. I shouldn't have played those Tests against New Zealand. I went on the tour to South Africa and the warm-up game against Oppenheimer was my last game of professional cricket. My back went and finally I was told that what I had been saying for so long was right. I had a crack in my spine which was opening up. I was cooked. It was hard to accept. I had come back from Australia and a lot of people thought I had cemented my place in the team, but that Test match against New Zealand at Lord's was awful. I was bowling and not knowing where the ball was going it was not nice to play like that. It was disappointing not to have played more Test matches for England, but who knows I might have had a stinker and they might have dropped me anyway, I'm happy with the memories I have."

Looking back at his career, I asked Dean who were the best players he played with and against. "Domestically, Ramps, Graeme Hick and Darren Gough. Overseas, Brian Lara and Steve Waugh, but for different reasons. I admired Steve Waugh's toughness and Brian Lara was just immense. He was a nice guy and it was a total privilege to play against him. It wasn't just the amount of runs he scored, but the way he scored them. A beautiful player to watch."

And the best captain? "Difficult one. Nasser got the most out of me. I loved playing under Adam Hollioake, but Stewie, Athers, Mark Benson they were all very good captains and I was fortunate I didn't not like any of my captains."

Looking at the England team now, Dean sees a bright future. "England have turned a corner in recent years. They hunt as a pack and a unit. I love the way our one-day team approach the game. The likes of Buttler and Billings have lifted the lid off our game. One of the criticisms in all our sports is that we are conservative; trust me these boys aren't conservative. They've been great to watch.

And what's Dean up to now. "I'm at Stamford School where I coach. I really enjoy it. It's a nice life and good to be involved with the kids. I get to coach rugby and hockey, as well as cricket which is nice. It's good fun and I get some nice long holidays which allow me to do stuff for the PCA."

So still pulling on the whites? "A few games but I'm definitely getting to the end. When you don't practice, you don't warm up and you're playing against 25-year-old cricketers it's not easy!

Dean may have only played 15 Test matches for England, but his haul of 60 wickets is full of memories that supporters will long cherish and talk about.

21

NICK KNIGHT
FORMER ENGLAND, ESSEX &
WARWICKSHIRE BATSMAN

Nick Knight was a former England opener who scored over 3,500 one-day international runs - at an average of over 40, a batsman who played in 17 Test matches and someone who is now excelling as a presenter on Sky Sports.

Over the last two years I'd interviewed many former players but from speaking to Nick one thing is abundantly clear, no one matches his passion for cricket!

"I am just absolutely absorbed by all things cricket!" he told me. "I fell in love with the game at such an early age. I remember at school, cricket was such a big part of my sporting education. I was fascinated by all aspects of the game and it's a fascination that continues to this day."

We spoke to Nick on his return from New Zealand where he had been commentating for the under 19 World Cup. And so, it seemed the right place to start: his career at Sky Sports. Was it where he saw his career heading once his playing days came to an end?

"It was. I did quite a bit of commentating while I was still playing and I got very interested in it. When you're as passionate about cricket as I am, having a job where I can talk about it and listen to others talk about it, is a dream. To be honest, I don't really see it as a job. I just see it as an extension of my playing career and I love it."

Such has been Nick's rapid rise in the media, he now fronts many of Sky's cricket productions. "I'm really enjoying the presenting. It's different to being a guest or a pundit and I really, really like that."

As fans we get used to switching on our TV sets and seeing the polished productions, but I was interested in finding out just how much work and preparation goes on in the lead up to big matches and series. "A lot. It's funny when you speak with players who don't do a lot of media work and come on to do a day with Sky; it's amazing how many of them afterwards tell me that they didn't realise how much was involved. But why should they? Take things like the man of the match interviews, pitch reports or interviews at the toss, it's amazing how much preparation goes in for those few minutes. It's important that you're asking the right questions, that you understand and know the person you're going to be talking to, all to get the moment right. Of course, you don't always get it right and you can't always control what goes on, but as long as you've prepared properly that's all you can do."

And what about those dreaded rain breaks that can hit at any time in an English Summer? "I love the rain breaks! They give you an opportunity to do an in-depth analysis into a topic that you would normally only get a couple of minutes for. So, when it rains and you have some really good guests, which we always have, I love, as a presenter, to have the opportunity to really get to the bottom of a problem. Don't get me wrong you don't want to do it all the time, it would get dull, but there are times when those breaks are great for us."

Cricket commentating has evolved hugely in recent years, particularly with the advent of T20 cricket. Commentary teams can be speaking to different audiences for the various formats of the game and also in different environments from the studio in Test match cricket, to the now famous T20 'pod'. "I love the pod! And I love T20. It's great being so close to the boundary edge and not being behind a glass screen. You can really feel the atmosphere and it's great fun! I played the first year of T20 cricket in England and loved it. I wish I could be involved now; it definitely suited the way I played!"

Nick's playing career is one he can be incredibly proud of. He was one of the most consistent opening batsmen England has ever had in limited overs cricket, and while he only played 17 Test matches, he can count himself unlucky that he played in an era when England had established Test openers such as Michael Atherton, Alec Stewart and Mark Butcher, with whom he was competing for a place.

"It's actually quite funny that Butch and I played a lot of cricket for England at the same but never in the same team! He played Tests and I played the ODI's and while I played 17 Tests, he incredibly never played a one day international. But he was a better Test match opener than I was, there was no doubt about that and the selectors were right to go with him over me at that time. That said, I do feel when I look back at my Test career, that I could have done a good job batting at number 6. I was better in my first-class career - at that time - batting at five or 6."

We'll come on to Nick's international career later, but I was keen to learn how Nick's love for the game began.

"When I was young, I was inspired by the likes of David Gower, Ian Botham, Graham Gooch, Allan Lamb and Robin Smith. Cricket was always a massive part of my life. I think it's fair to say that by the time I was six or seven I was completely obsessed by the game."

And it wasn't long before people realised this cricket obsessed youngster had some serious talent. "I was at a public school in Essex where Gordon Barker - who is well known in Essex cricketing circles - was the school professional; so, I was incredibly lucky that I was able to work every day I chose with Gordon, who knew everything about the game. To have that expertise enhanced my game in those formative years. To get that kind of guidance at 13 or 14 I was extremely lucky."

Nick was quickly part of the Essex youth set up, and he excelled in their under 15s, 16s and 19s. "I know I keep saying the word 'lucky' but it was true. I knew that I was lucky to get the opportunities I did and I'm very thankful to Gordon for a lot of those. Gordon clearly had an influence at Essex, so I can well imagine he would have said to Essex that I was a lad they should take a look at. I always had sympathy with lots of talented youngsters who didn't make it because they didn't have that lucky moment to be seen at the right time, at the right place, by the right coach. Of course, I had to be good enough but there's no question that I was lucky to be given the opportunities that I was."

Nick was offered a professional contract by Essex at 18 years of age, a contract he was excited to sign. But he did so with a degree of maturity. "I wanted to get a university degree so I signed a Summer contract, which allowed me to go to university and when I finished my studies in June I could then play for Essex. At that time cricket wasn't what it is now financially and I felt it was important to always have a plan b."

Nick's early success as cricketer saw him named as the Daily

Telegraph's young cricketer of the year in 1989. It was an award that gave the young Essex opener a huge amount of confidence. "Awards like that gave me confidence and a boost that I was doing OK. But when I look back, I was proud that I never tried to get ahead of myself. I also played for England under 19s at the time, but I viewed all of those accolades as a good starting point for my career rather than think I'd made it and then become complacent and take things for granted."

Nick spent four years at Essex and using that word 'lucky' he recounts the influence of two Essex stalwarts, Keith Fletcher and Graham Gooch in his early development, another example of the opportunities that were presented to the young batsman. "Keith Fletcher was a great player and when I started playing in Essex's 2nd XI Keith was still playing and I had the opportunity to travel a lot with him to games, as he lived not far from me. That was great for me as we'd talk cricket all the time and I was just soaking everything up - I loved all that. Then having the opportunity to open the batting with Graham Gooch was fantastic. Not many players can say they did that. He was one of my heroes growing up and it was a fantastic feeling to walk out at Chelmsford to open the batting with him. He was such an amazing player and when you're standing 22 yards away from someone like him, you learn very quickly. It was a great way to develop my game. Also, at the time, Essex had a terrific side. Probably the best side in the country. It was a squad of players where the majority of them were reaching their peak together. And we were led by Graham Gooch, who at the time was playing the best cricket of his career, so to be around that environment as a youngster I again was very fortunate."

The strength of that squad had its drawbacks, however. Because of it, nailing down a regular start spot was difficult and in 1994 Nick made the switch to Warwickshire in search of regular 1st XI cricket. "Essex had such a good side that I didn't always play. As well as Gooch, we had the likes of Nasser Hussain, Paul

Prichard, John Stephenson and Mark Waugh was our overseas player. There was a stable top six. I knew that I wasn't always going to be a regular at that time. There was two or three of us competing for that openers birth. Warwickshire came in for me. I'd made a big hundred against them earlier that Summer and they were keen to snap me up. It was a big decision to go from a big club to another big club who played at a Test match ground. Warwickshire at the time were winning a lot of titles under the captaincy of Dermot Reeve, who was a quite brilliant captain. But it was a decision that I had no regrets over. I'll always have a huge gratitude for what Essex did for me."

Nick spent 10 plus years at Edgbaston and it was a period of successes and transitions which culminated in a two-year spell as captain which saw him lead the county to another county championship – more on that success later.

"We had a tremendous squad of players when I first joined. I remember walking into a dressing room which had won three trophies the previous year. We then won two trophies in my first year - it was just an incredible feeling. We would take to the field knowing that any one player could do something special on any given day. We had Allan Donald and Brian Lara in those early years and Dermot Reeve was tactically the best captain I played under. They were great times."

Nick's form for Warwickshire brought international recognition in 1995 when he was called up to make his Test debut against the West Indies. If you want to test your abilities at the highest level, I guess opening the batting against Ambrose and Walsh is one quick way to see if you're good enough!

"I was petrified! But it was a dream come true. I'd been on a couple of A tours so I thought I could be getting close. However, I was always realistic that other players were around. There were a number of injuries at the time so it was slowly getting around to the point where I was thinking I might be next in line and I was playing well. I got the call and the West Indies had a brilliant attack with the likes of Courtney Walsh, Curtly Ambrose, Ian Bishop and Kenny Benjamin. I opened the batting with Michael Atherton and just being in that environment was a real thrill, but incredibly nerve-racking. I didn't eat much the night before, or at breakfast, but we fielded first which I think was good as I could settle into the game."

'Luck' again became evident as Nick was out first ball, caught at short leg, off of the bowling of Ambrose, but thankfully it was a no ball. "I managed to bat for an hour and a half until I got out to a slower ball from Courtney Walsh. A little ironic given I'd worked so hard against all that pace to get out to a slower ball! But it was a terrific experience and a dream come true. I scored 50 in the next Test, which was a real moment for me. I think whenever you get your first milestone you start to believe. I think that was the point that I thought that I could do this international cricket."

12 months later and Nick enjoyed arguably his best Summer in international cricket. He scored two one day international hundreds against Pakistan, which was followed by his first Test century. "I was in the form of my life. My game just felt in good order. I was so confident in my batting that year I just had a fearless attitude. I was very technical early on in my career, but the more I played the freer I became, in my mind and attitude."

That Winter England travelled to Zimbabwe. Think David Lloyd and his 'we murdered them' comments. This was the Test match that England were chasing a win and fell just short. Nick was man of the match thanks to his outstanding 96. "It was a run chase we got close to, but we should have won the game. My view is slightly different to others in that I should have won that game for my country."

England visited New Zealand after that Zimbabwe tour and it was there that Nick, using his words 'lost his way a bit'. "I was thinking too much about my game in New Zealand. Technically I was all over the shop and I then got a badly broken finger, which put me out of cricket for five or six months."

It was during this period that Mark Butcher emerged in Test match cricket and Nick found opportunities to win his place back difficult to come by. "I don't know whether the selectors would have stuck by me for the Ashes series that Summer but injury made the decision easy for them. Before that injury I played eight or 9 Tests in a row and it was a great feeling to be part of the side. But I lost my way in Test cricket for a couple of years after that injury. I'd get picked then dropped, picked then dropped. It was fair enough if I'm honest. I wasn't where I needed to be technically to open the batting in Test match cricket."

Nick's journey in one day international cricket however was a different story. His approach to the game suited the shorter format and he became a mainstay at the top of the order through until his retirement in 2003, notching up exactly 100 one day international appearances. But as I spoke to Nick about his one-day achievements he was honest about areas he could have done better, despite an average in excess of 40.

"When I came into the one-day set-up it was a great time to be involved. New powerplay regulations had been introduced encouraging players to give the ball a trash; they wanted teams to make flying starts and that suited my game. I'd done it for Warwickshire and felt I revelled in it. Alec Stewart and I were both keen to have as much fun as possible. In my first 20 games I got a lot of runs and it seemed to be a format that suited me. But the game changed in terms of our approach. I played 100 games and scored five hundreds, yet I got past 50 on thirty occasions. I began viewing myself as a main player and the approach changed to if I got us off to a good start, it was important that I then saw us through to the end. I think I took that the wrong way and I wasn't quite as imposing once I reached 50 as I was at the start of the innings because I was conscious about preserving my wicket. The fact I only converted five of my starts into hundreds highlighted to me that I was getting obsessed about being there at the end. In hindsight I should have just carried on in my attacking vein. It was what brought me my initial success. But overall, I look back on my ODI career with great fondness. It was great going down the wicket to the likes of Ambrose in Barbados and scoring a century; to take on Allan Donald and Brett Lee; to reverse sweep Shane Warne in Sydney and get a hundred. Those audacious things brought some great memories I'll never forget."

Nick's final appearances for England came in the 2003 World Cup in South Africa and one of those appearances went down in history as he became the first batsman to officially have a ball bowled to him at over 100mph.

"I just remember opening the batting with Marcus (Trescothick) who looked comfortable sitting on his bat at the other end. I think he was happy to take on Wasim bowling at 85 mph!"

I asked Nick to talk through that experience as Shoiab Akhtar was getting faster and faster with each delivery. "It was definitely a quick spell. I remember thinking I had to go backwards in my crease – there was no way I was going forwards – and to make sure I had my off stump covered. But it was almost like a game within a game. I'm not sure he was too bothered about getting me out and his focus was more on reaching 100mph. In that period, they had a speedo which showed the mph bowled. He was looking at it after every ball, and the faster the ball the more the crowd were cheering. His run up was getting longer and longer with each delivery. The ball before I remember I was late on to it and it hit the top of my bat and went over the keeper for six. I think that was the moment I realised just how quickly he was bowling. I managed to ride the actual 100 mph ball down to square leg, but I couldn't get Michael Vaughan to take the single! Shoiab is a good friend and he actually joked with me before the game that he was going to bowl quickly at me and he was a damn difficult bowler to face - a bit like Wasim. It was always difficult to pick up the ball out of their hands."

Rather him than me. I asked Nick could he tell the difference between the pace of that spell to others he'd faced who bowled in the early to mid 90s. People say there's a big difference between 85mph and 90mph but was there a noticeable difference in pace between 90mph-100mph?

"To be honest, you're just attuned to playing fast bowling. You're not thinking about hitting the bowler over his head for 6. You just have to figure out how to get through that spell. If there was no speedo in South Africa would I say that ball was the fastest I'd faced? I'm not sure. Brett Lee has bowled some incredibly quick spells. And sometimes if you're a batsman out of nick you think a ball is quicker than what it is and if you're in nick you think it's slower than what it is. I'd just say that 90mph+ is pretty quick bowling!"

Nick retired from international cricket straight after that World Cup in 2003 (and the Winter tour to Australia where he had a fabulous series). "I knew the time was right. Many people said I retired too early and I could have carried on playing international cricket. I'd had a really good tour of Australia but I was just mentally shot, I knew I was done. I'd actually said to my family before I went to Australia that Winter, that, that was going to be my last tour. I wasn't one of the most gifted players so it took a lot out of me preparing for games and series, mentally. I had come to the end. So, I put everything into that last tour and as I walked off at Port Elizabeth when we lost that game against Australia that we should have won, I lifted my bat up and no one knew apart from me and my family that that would be the last time I would play. I just knew myself. I was also of the opinion that I wanted to go out when I was at a high with my batting."

As Nick reflected on his international career I posed two further questions, did he think central contracts would have made a difference to his international career and how frustrating was it in that period that the ODI side wasn't more successful, given the players they had at their disposal?

"I think we'd have loved to have been on central contracts because really we were just a disparate bunch of county cricketers coming together to play for England. On any given Sunday we'd listen to the radio to find out if we'd been selected to play for England on the Thursday. There was the core group of players that would play regularly, Atherton, Stewart, Thorpe, Hussain, Gough, but there were three or four of us that were always in a revolving door and that was a hard place to be at times. Central contracts would most definitely have helped that, but I'd never blame the system then. That was the system we were in and it was up to us to make the most of it. In terms of the one-day side it was incredibly disappointing. When I look back at that dressing room, we had players like Hick, Stewart and Gough. We had everything we needed. We'd head to tournaments and people would look at that England side. But we didn't know how to win games, and that's what cost us. We changed the team too often and there wasn't enough continuity with the group of players we had. And because of that we were fearful as a group and not fearless. We'd think 250 was a good working score rather than aim for 275. We became conservative and that's what crept into my game after my first 20 or so games. As a group we didn't have the right approach. However, if we're honest its only really been the last couple of years that any of our ODI teams have got the approach right and you can see the dramatic difference in the results. There is no question in my mind that we had the players, we just weren't able to beat the big sides often enough when it came to tournaments."

With Nick's international career at its end his county
Warwickshire, who had by then gone through a period of
transition after their mid 90s successes, appointed Nick as first
team captain. "It was a great honour, but I'll be honest, I wasn't
keen on accepting it. I just didn't feel it was something that I
would be good at. As a player, I was always a bit selfish and quite
obsessed with my own game. It's very different being a captain.
But as I'd finished my international career I thought if I was ever
going to give captaincy a go, now was the time. So, I took it on. I
told the club I'd do it for two years. I didn't want to do it any
longer than that, and I'd give it my all but they'd have to let me
do it my way. I wanted my own team and I had some very strong
views on how I wanted to do things and the club were terrific
and said yes to everything and it worked out. I had a good core
of senior players around me such as Dougie Brown and Ashley
Giles and I had some quality youngsters emerging including Ian
Bell and Jonathan Trott. Players who could push the squad on."

It certainly did work out as The Bears once again won the
County Championship. Nick's retirement from cricket followed
not long after and in 2006 he put his bat back in the case for
final time. "Similar to international cricket I could have carried
on, but I had achieved everything I wanted to achieve and the
thought of going back to the nets, fielding practice, preparing for
games, just didn't appeal to me anymore."

And so Nick headed off into the world of media and cricket's
loss was Sky Sports' gain.

I had to ask Nick who was the toughest bowler he faced, as
during the course of our interview he'd named so many great
bowlers. "Only one name for me. Wasim Akram. He was so
skilful with both the new and old ball. He had such a difficult
action to face, he had a quick arm, and he always made me feel
quite uncomfortable. It was quite ironic that I actually had quite
a lot of success against him, but I always found it a really great

challenge facing him. So, to have success against someone who I found difficult to face gives me a great deal of satisfaction."

And what about the best player he played with? "There were so many good players that its difficult to name one but what I would say is I always had a huge regard for those players that played regularly in that Test side. Atherton, Stewart, Hussain, Thorpe, Gough. I always had huge admiration for those guys because they were doing something that I wasn't able to do. To keep a place in that side and score runs and take wickets in Test Match cricket against those oppositions. I hold them in high esteem for that, and they just achieved more than I did because they were better than me."

Nick already listed Dermot as his best captain but what were his reflections on the other captains he played under? "They were all so different. Dermot really was outstanding in terms of game awareness and tactics. Nasser was a very, very good captain for England. I thought he was always very honest with the players and he made the dressing room a more honest place to be. If someone hadn't done well it wasn't someone else's fault. The environment set by him and Duncan Fletcher was a good one. I always had a huge amount of respect for Michael Atherton. His great

strength as a leader was that you wanted to follow him. He wasn't someone who would stand up in front of the team and shout at them but you just watched him quietly go about his business and think I want to do that."

I closed our conversation by asking Nick about his thoughts on the current England sides in Test and limited overs cricket. "The ODI side is a special team of players. I think they could become one of the finest sides to have ever played one day cricket. I said publicly two years ago that this was the best ODI side that I'd seen and they have come on considerably since then under the leadership of Eoin Morgan. They have a little bit of work to do on some of their smartness in certain situations but I'd be massively surprised if they are not one of the favourites for the World Cup next year. I think Joe Root is the right man to captain the Test side. I think he will become a terrific captain. They had a tough Ashes tour but they have some special players. The interesting challenge for this side will be the transition of the bowling attack over the coming few years after Anderson and Broad. They need to find an attack that can stay fit and strong. That will be key. If they can maintain a 5/6-man attack which is strong and ready to play they will have a real chance."

Nick's playing career brought many great memories for supporters and it's terrific that, because of his excellent presenting, his experience has not been lost to the game.

22

KEITH PARSONS
FORMER SOMERSET ALL-ROUNDER

The word legend is often overused in sport but in the case of this interviewee, there is not a better word to describe this former Somerset stalwart who, alongside Ian Botham, is the county's only player to have scored over 5,000 runs and taken in excess of 100 wickets in both List A & First Class cricket.

Born and raised in Taunton, Keith Parsons was part of the Somerset family from a young age. I suppose it would have been difficult for him not to have fallen in love with Taunton as a child, especially when the likes of Viv Richards, Ian Botham and Joel Garner were strutting their stuff on his doorstep. "We were lucky down here in the 70s and 80s having Richards, Botham and Garner. Somerset was thriving and with the cricket ground situated right in the heart of the town it was hard not to fall in love with the place and I used to enjoy heading down to the ground after school had finished, to watch these guys play."

It was a love affair that led to 17 happy years playing for

Somerset County Cricket Club. But where did it all begin for the popular all-rounder. In youth cricket, Keith was one of the county's bright young talents. Alongside his twin brother Kevin, he had the honour of representing his country at both under 15 and under 19 level, in squads that contained the likes of Jeremy Snape, Mal Loye, Tim Walton and Philip Weston. "We were in decent under 15 and under 19 sides," remarked Keith. "Quite a few of us went on to achieve reasonable first-class careers."

Unfortunately for Keith and the Parsons family, one of those that didn't go on to achieve that first-class career was twin brother Kevin. "It was tough for Kevin to get released having only played a handful of games. He was only at Somerset for three years but he has his own career now as an accountant and he's still playing a very good standard of club cricket at the weekends. I actually think he became a better cricketer once he left Somerset; he just developed a little bit later than others."

Keith however, was offered a professional contract and having progressed through the various youth ranks at the county ground, went on to make his first class debut against the strong Pakistan side of the early 1990s; a side, which just a few months before, had won the 1992 World Cup, thanks in part, to the intimidating bowling of Wasim Akram and Waqar Younis. "I remember it was 1992, and I'd got off to a reasonable start to the season playing for the 2nd XI. I'd scored a couple of hundreds and I received a phone call and was told that I would be playing in the touring game against Pakistan. I had only just turned 18; so it was pretty daunting if I'm honest, coming up against Wasim, Waqar, Mushtaq, Javed Miandad and all of these characters, that you'd only ever seen as a kid."

Sadly for Keith, he only scored one run in the game. "I didn't do particularly well and I only scored one run, but it was a good experience at that age, to play in front of a big crowd. And experiences like that, were invaluable for your career."

Keith's next game for the 1st XI, came 12 months later, against another touring side – the all-conquering Australians. "It was another real baptism of fire! But that Australia game and my first dozen or so games, I wasn't able to make any telling contributions. It was hugely disappointing, as I was scoring a lot of runs in the seconds, but every time an opportunity in the firsts came up, it didn't happen for me. It was a mental thing. I think I was just a little bit star struck and maybe got overawed."

But it didn't take long for that first telling contribution to occur and from that point a Somerset star was born. "We played a game at Luton against Northants, who had Curtly Ambrose in the team. I made a couple of scores of 30 and 40, and that made me feel part of it. My confidence began to grow and I felt I had found my feet. I think it's like anything in life you need confidence and once I had that, I felt part of the squad. People don't always realise that it's a big step up from 2nd XI to 1st XI cricket, as it is in club cricket when you progress up from seconds to the firsts. Each step up takes a bit of getting used to. Some people can do it quickly, but for most people, it takes time."

Once established in the side, Keith's career didn't look back and what followed was a period of success and enjoyment at both an individual and team level, as Somerset went on to become one of the most competitive counties on the circuit. Cup finals and man of the match performances became commonplace.

It was in the Summer of 2000, that Keith went on to get his highest career score, against the touring West Indies. Scores against touring sides became a bit of a norm for the all-rounder. "My first hundred came against Australia and in total I got two or three hundreds in those touring games."

But it was the 193 not out against the Windies that was the obvious big highlight. "It was my career best score. At the end of the first day I was 130 odd not out and Brian Lara came up to me as we walked off the pitch and shook my hand. That was a big moment for me. It would have been nice to have got a double hundred, as you don't many chances to do that, but it's not bad to have a career best against a West Indies side!"

With tours now cut so short, the opportunities for county players to repeat Keith's feats and pit their skills against the world's best have been reduced. I asked Keith if this was disappointing for county players that touring games had been reduced. "Definitely. We always got full houses for those games at Taunton. It was a big occasion. And for me, it inspired me, and my stats kind of suggested that. You did always look forward to playing those touring games and playing against people you watch on television; it was nice to challenge yourself. It's a shame for the counties that they don't get the opportunity to host these games much these days. Touring teams might now only play one or two games before a series starts, when it used to be four or five and they got taken around the country. These games were big opportunities to get the crowd in and a chance for supporters to see your side take the best sides in the world on."

The early 2000's saw some of Keith's most memorable games for the county. In 2001, his 60 off 52 balls helped Somerset win their first silverware for over 18 overs, as the county won the C&G final, against Leicestershire, at Lord's. "What a brilliant day. In 1999 we lost to Gloucestershire, which was frustrating as they were our local rivals. But against Leicestershire we got the win. I know it's a bit of a cliché, but you play to win trophies and it was well known down here, that we had not won anything since Richards, Botham and Garner in the early 80s, so it was a big occasion for us to come away with the trophy. And of course it was a big day for me, to be made man of the match and have such a good impact on the game, was special."

In 2003 a new format of the game was introduced in England -

T20 cricket- and Somerset were one of the first counties to take the competition seriously and went on to win it in 2005. But interestingly, as Keith looked back, not many of the players at the time believed T20 was going to grow into the competition that it has now. "The new format came as a huge shock to the players. I remember going up to Edgbaston for a PCA day, where we were told about the new format and I think we all thought that this would never catch on! And now you look at it and the finances it's created and it's fantastic. Every game at Taunton has been full here since it started in 2003."

So what about Somerset's early success in the competition. "It was a great occasion at the Oval. The Finals Day is so special to play in. We came up against a Lancashire side in the final, who were full of internationals. On paper they were far better than us, but we managed to turn them over and it was just another good occasion for Somerset cricket. Confidence was a big thing for us in that final. We were lucky we had three bowlers who could bowl at the death, and we had batsmen who could score quickly. Graeme Smith was an inspirational captain for us at that stage and everyone played well. We all knew our roles. We had certain people who batted at the top and others who could play around them. But most importantly, we could all clear the ropes and we knew if we could get the rate up, we had the bowlers to get us home, if it was tight at the end."

Lifting trophies, reaching finals and solid performances in the county championship became the norm for Somerset. They didn't just 'compete' with the so-called bigger counties, but they thrived and silverware was regularly being inserted into the Somerset's trophy cabinet; but what did Keith put this transformation down to? "Jamie Cox joined us in 1999 as captain and he was a big influence on everyone. He got us tougher on the field and managed to drive us on. Dermot Reeve also came in just before that and his coaching brought us different ways of thinking that we all bought into. In one day cricket we developed a method that proved really successful. But of course all of that will only take you so far, we had a good side. Obviously, we had the likes of Trescothick and Caddick, who were also playing for England at that time, but we had a number of very good county cricketers such as Mike Burns, Pete Bowler, Ian Blackwell, Richard Johnson and Keith Dutch. It was an exciting time to play one day cricket, in particular, down here."

Jamie Cox and Dermot Reeve are certainly two individuals Keith holds in a high regard, so much so, that he lists both as the biggest cricketing influences on his career. "My family were huge influences, but inside the game Jamie Cox always backed me as a player. He helped me develop as a one-day player, in particular; Dermot Reeve as coach also gave me ideas and the confidence to back my own ability."

Somerset's ongoing success on the field made the county an attractive option for overseas players, and in Keith's time, some of the world's best were able to call Taunton 'home'. "Graeme Smith made a big impact here, as did Jamie Cox and Justin Langer. And Ricky Ponting was down here as well as an overseas pro for a few weeks. Just to be able to play with and pick the brains of players of this calibre was unbelievable. They all offered us different things. Ricky was pure class with his batting; Jamie Cox was a big team man who pulled everyone together; Graeme Smith was so inspirational, especially in that T20 final. I remember we weren't chasing a huge score but he was like 'don't worry lads, I'll sort this out' and he saw us home, not out. They all gave us so much belief that we could achieve things. They were just great players for us."

The attraction of quality overseas players at Taunton, continues to this day. "Chris Gayle and Chris Rodgers are here now. We are very lucky at Taunton and going all the way back to the 70s and 80s we have had good overseas players, who have come in, enjoyed it and made an impact."

In Keith's time at Somerset he achieved a lot of personal success in all three formats of the game, I asked him how easy or difficult it was as a player to adapt your game between the three different formats. "It does throw up a few challenges, but I never found it particularly difficult switching from one format to the other. Certain roles are difficult, for example if you're an opening batsman who would play it around for a day and a half, you wouldn't be able to bat in that style in T20. But personally, I didn't find it hard and I enjoyed the diversity of the three formats."

In 2008, after a career of huge success at Somerset, Keith moved on. "It was disappointing. You always think you can play a couple of years longer, but I knew it was coming. I hadn't played an awful lot of four-day cricket for a couple of years and the one day game was becoming a little bit faster and I wasn't involved as much as I had been earlier, so mentally you prepare yourself that it would be coming to an end and 2008 was the natural time for me to move away."

But it wasn't the end for Keith. He was asked to lead the Unicorns side. The Unicorns was a new initiative by the ECB, who created a side which would be made up of young players who had previously been released from different counties. The idea being that it would give them a window to try and get back into the professional game. Keith was delighted to come in and captain the side.

"I had four years playing for them and it was a nice little tag on to my career. It proved hugely popular and it gave players around the country a real window to go and play against the best and a number of players who played for us went on and got signed by counties. It was a huge shame it ended, but we set out to achieve what we wanted to. I enjoyed being involved and it gave me a lot of pleasure trying to help find the next county cricketer."

The team played their home games at Wormsley, a favourite spot for the Addis Army. "Using Wormsley was fantastic. Tremers and his team always produced decent pitches, but they were probably too good for the Unicorns! The wickets always had good pace and bounce, so county players loved it and they were probably a bit too good for our young lads. I should have persuaded him to make them lower, slower wickets to even up the contest!!"

Keith stopped playing altogether in 2012, but it was a career that he can quite rightly look back on with great pride. He is regarded as a Somerset legend and played with and against some of the best players to have graced the game. So who were the best bowlers and batsmen he played with and against? "I always said Wasim Akram was the one bowler you didn't want to wake up in the morning knowing you'd be facing. Someone who could swing the ball at such a nasty pace! But I don't think it was just me that didn't fancy facing him! Andrew Caddick was the best bowler in county cricket for a while and it was always good to field in the slips to him. Ian Blackwell didn't play as much for England as his talent suggested he would, but he always did a great job for us with the ball and was able to hit the ball out of the park when he wanted to. Batting wise, Marcus (Trescothick) has done as well as anyone, across all three formats of the game, and continues to do so. In my early career, I thought Mark Lathwell was one of the great players who could turn a game. He was a phenomenal batter who stopped playing far too early."

Despite the many match winning performances for Somerset and scores against touring elevens, Keith never got the international recognition some in the game felt he deserved, especially in limited overs cricket. "To be honest, I was probably never really good enough to play international cricket. Maybe I could have had a go in the one-dayers, but in the four-day game, I never got enough runs to push my case, which you have to do. I have no regrets at all. I was very lucky to have had a career with Somerset for 17 years and I was more than happy with what I achieved."

Our discussions then moved towards the state of the game now and Keith thinks cricket in England is in a very good state. "I think the game is very strong. The central contracts have taken the England players out of the county scene and they don't get to play as many games as they used to, but I think the game overall is so much more professional now. Players are a lot quicker, fitter and stronger than when I first started. TV coverage in England is now great, it's just a shame it's not free to watch on terrestrial TV, but Sky Sports' money is what funds the game now."

However, one thing Keith doesn't agree with in the modern game is the idea that players play too much cricket and are a bit over-protected. "I was always someone who was happy to play lots of cricket. I felt if we were lucky enough to be paid to play cricket, then we should play cricket. You can do as much training as you want indoors against bowling machines, but you only really feel in nick, if you are scoring runs, or taking wickets, in the middle. So if you're a player in a rough spot, get out and play; if there are no county games, go and play club cricket and score yourself a hundred. I think there is a little over protection going on now where 2nd XI and fringe players don't play that much club cricket, or minor counties, which can be beneficial. Going back to play club cricket can get you used to winning games of cricket and gives you the opportunity to put in match winning performances and get back into the county 1st XI. If players are struggling at first class level, get out and do it at another level."

The debate continues to rage in English cricket about the structure of T20 cricket and having played in the competition for many years Keith is of the strong belief that the counties should maintain their own identity, rather than head down the franchise route. "Personally, as a player, I wouldn't like to join forces with your nearest rivals. Counties have their own identity and you can't expect supporters to suddenly jump ship. There is too much tradition. If all of the counties can survive and the competition can remain competitive, I think it should continue. If it does go down the franchise route it would lessen the number of professional cricketers getting an opportunity."

Having retired from the game in 2012, Keith is not only still involved in the game, but is still a regular fixture at his beloved county ground. "I now work at the cricket shop, Somerset County Sports, down at Taunton. We sell all of the cricket stuff, team wear etc. So, I'm still at the ground every day, it's just a different part of the ground to the changing rooms."

As I say, the word 'legend' is often overused in sport, but definitely not in the case of Keith Parsons. Across all formats of the game, Keith scored over 12,000 runs and over 250 wickets during the course of his career; you'll be hard pushed to find a Somerset CCC member who would disagree with the legend status.

23

JEREMY SNAPE
FORMER ENGLAND, NORTHANTS, GLOUCESTERSHIRE, LEICESTERSHIRE ALL-ROUNDER

What has Shane Warne, Gareth Southgate, Jose Mourinho, Sir Alex Ferguson, Sir David Brailsford, Sir Mo Farah, Sir AP McCoy (note all the Sir's!) and Mathew Pinsett all got in common? Answer: They have winning 'mindsets' and have all been interviewed by one of the World's leading sports psychologists, former England, Northants, Gloucestershire and Leicestershire all-rounder Jeremy Snape.

"I think having a winning 'mindset' is one of the last hidden frontiers," said Jeremy. "We had a decade of fitness, where everyone had heartrate monitors and were educated on healthier eating. This was followed by a period which saw the growth of analysis and tracking, where we had cameras installed in parts of grounds: in cricket Hawkeye and Hotspot were introduced. Now the only thing left is something that is hard to measure, the intangible psychological element inside people's heads."

And this is why Jeremy set up Sporting Edge – a high performance consultancy that blends powerful insights with proven psychology to give sporting stars and businesses a competitive advantage. (www.sportingedge.com)

"I've been fortunate to get access to some top performers and interview them about how they built their own success and/or created environments that allowed others to thrive. I love sharing these stories and experiences with the aim of helping other people to perform at their best under pressure. I've stood to face Brett Lee; I've bowled to Sachin Tendulkar in front of 120,000 people at Eden Gardens; I know what it feels like to be under pressure. A little bit of theory is never going to help you, so I've developed some practical techniques that have since worked for some of the best players in the world. Some of whom still phone me up now, five years after we first spoke, for advice."

"Honestly, the difference between your best and worst days will always be your mindset; not your technique."

"For all of the hours I spent in the nets I'd spend 1000th of that time focusing on my mindset. Your mindset is the biggest influence on winning and losing yet nobody likes to talk about it."

One person who has spoken about it, however, is former Australian spinner Shane Warne. In Warne's recent book he lavished praise on Jeremy having originally been very sceptical about his initial proposed presence with the Rajasthan Royals in the IPL.

"It's fair to say Shane wasn't a massive fan of 'psychobabble' as he called it! He actually told me later that he'd bought me a flight back to England, so convinced was he that my presence would be a waste of time! But I managed to forge a really strong relationship with him. And I think Shane changing his views helped knock a lot of barriers down for others. The fact he was publicly praising me in interviews and in his book fascinated people."

And it certainly fascinated me. There are countless examples of players who had the 'ability' and 'technique' but for whatever reason were unable to succeed at the highest level in their chosen sport.

But, more of Sporting Edge later. Let's look back at Jeremy's playing career. A career that saw the all-rounder achieve considerable success with three, I think it's fair to say 'unfancied' counties, and eleven appearances for his country.

Jeremy was born in Stoke, a self-acknowledged 'hyperactive' child. "I was always a sporty kid and as my Dad was best friends with the Northants stalwart David Steele. The Summer holidays would often see me and my brother (and David's sons) venture off to watch him around the county circuit. I loved cricket. We'd often play in the garden and on the beach and it wasn't until a few years later that I joined the local club Kidsgrove Cricket Club."

So what kick started his early cricket pathway? "Well, one day my Dad was decorating and understandably wanted me out of the way. He read the local paper and saw an advert for a day's cricket training. This was obviously too good for him to turn down – a chance to get rid of me for the day. So, he packed me off. At the end of the day I was asked to wait behind. My Dad was given a call and asked to come down for a talk. His initial assessment was I'd obviously broken something, so he came armed with his wallet to pay for any damages!"

But, what neither Jeremy nor his Father had realised was this was not just a 'training day' but a Staffordshire under 11s trial day!

"I was asked if I could go forward to the final trials on grass, which was all a bit of a shock. I got into that Staffordshire under 11s team, then progressed into the under 13s and then on to the under 15s where I also got picked for England."

It was a rapid rise, and the family friendship with David Steele saw Jeremy receive an invitation to Northants for Winter nets. And at the age of 16, he was offered his first contract. "My parents were keen for me to continue at school and then go to university; so for five years I had what was called a Summer contract, whereby I could continue my education and then play cricket during the months of June, July and August.

Around this time, I was spotted playing for Staffordshire by the teacher from a local private school. After scoring a century and taking five wickets, he asked me how much I played at school. I laughed as the local comprehensive I went to didn't do any representative sport at all because the Head Mistress didn't believe in competition. This meeting changed my life and very shortly I moved to Denstone College where I played cricket every day and both my ambition and skill advanced. I ended up as Head Boy at Denstone and I still look back fondly on my time there as it set me up to handle the later success."

The young all-rounder continued to advance and international recognition came again when Jeremy was selected for overseas tours to Canada and Pakistan with the England Under 18s and 19s respectively.

After five years, the Summer contract became a full time one and the challenge now was how to break into what had become a stellar Northants line-up. "The Northants team was full of talent. Lamb, Larkins, Cook, Bailey, Capel, Curran and Ambrose. We had a really strong side, so it was difficult to break through. I captained the seconds, which was a nice experience and played quite a bit for the one-days teams in those early years, but I was never really able to breakthrough. When I look back at my time at Northants, I view it as my 'apprenticeship'. I could have stayed there and possibly coasted but I wanted to take my cricket seriously and push and test myself."

So, in 1999 Jeremy made the move to Gloucestershire - a move that culminated in four trophy-laden years. "It was sad to leave Northants, but John Bracewell and Mark Alleyne at Gloucestershire were looking for an all-rounder to strengthen their team. If I'm honest, they were much more structured and hard working than Northants, in that they couldn't rely on their pure talent and past successes as top international players. We had to work incredibly hard for everything."

And what success that was. In 2000, Gloucestershire won the 'treble', and 12 months later followed that up with a 'double'. "It was a fascinating period. We had the right game plans, the right strategies and everyone knew their roles. We loved being the underdogs, without any pressure on us. But we were desperate to prove we were individually and collectively good enough. My own batting improved during that period In one season I scored four centuries which was great for my confidence."

And what was the key to success? "John Bracewell was instrumental. He came with new very 'left-field' theories, but theories which were thought-provoking. He was incredibly disciplined. I remember one day we did a 9-mile run, which was about seven miles further than I'd ever run before! He very much wanted us to be athletes that played cricket, rather than a cricketer who had to just be fit enough to reach the other end. This mindset shift definitely gave us a competitive advantage over other sides. For example we had one of our best fielders running from third man to third man between overs where previously that was a position for a tired bowler to relax. We knew every run counted and found novel ways to get an edge."

Then of course there was the individual talent. "Jack Russell was an incredible player behind the stumps who galvanised that team. He was one of the world's best wicket-keepers. We then had Ian Harvey who was a firecracker of an overseas player, the brilliant nous of Kim Barnett, the discipline of Mike Smith's bowling and a very good captain in Mark Alleyne. It was a special time."

Jeremy's performances for Gloucestershire brought full international recognition in 2001 when he was selected for England's tour to Zimbabwe.

"Lots of people were talking about it, but Gloucestershire weren't a particularly fashionable club. To receive a call from David Graveney and be told I was going to Zimbabwe was amazing. Sharing a dressing room with your heroes like Goughy, Thorpe and Nasser - players I'd long watched and admired and then suddenly being sat next to them on the team bus was incredibly exhilarating."

Jeremy's ODI debut saw him take the wickets of both Flower brothers, no mean feat, and his figures of 2/39 off 10 overs helped restrict the home side to just 206 runs. England won the game by five wickets and the Gloucestershire debutant was named man of the match.

"It was a special time. Robert Croft's time with England was coming to an end and I think they saw me as a dynamic all-rounder who could bowl spin, bat and dive around in the field."

Jeremy ended up with seven wickets from the four ODI's he played in that series and a tour to India followed soon after. "I felt comfortable in those games in Zimbabwe and didn't think it was too much of a big step up. Well, not as big a step up as playing in front of 120,000 people in Eden Gardens! That game was incredible. I don't think anything could have prepared us for it. We certainly didn't talk about the mental challenges. I remember having to bowl to Tendulkar and the noise was incredible, but all my focus was on making the first ball land somewhere near the spot! When I batted, I was out there with

Freddie trying to chase the runs down. I remember I called for a second run and he didn't hear me amidst all the chaos and noise and was run out. When he walked back, I was just left out there alone in the middle of this cauldron knowing it was now down to me, a nudger and nurdler who knew he'd have to hit Harbajhan Singh for about 15 in the next over. I panicked and played a terrible shot and got out. As I walked back to the pavilion, being pelted with onion bhaji's, I realised there was more to this game than we were talking about and that's where my interest in the mental side of the game begun."

Jeremy went on to play 10 one day internationals for England. It should have been a lot more. "I know I was very privileged to play for England. There were many better players than me that never got an opportunity. I have my England cap framed at home. It's the only piece of cricket memorabilia I have in my house."

I asked Jeremy if he felt it should have played more?

"I went on the 2002 tour to Australia. I was unfortunate that in the first warm-up game in Sydney I went out to face Brett Lee and four balls later my thumb had been fractured in six places! I went out to bowl with my thumb hanging off, but it was pretty obvious I needed an operation and get metal plates inserted. I had to fly home and was an obvious doubt for the World Cup that quickly followed that tour. Ashley Giles went instead of me and the rest is history. Was I frustrated I didn't dominate World cricket? No. I was always realistic and just very privileged to have played the games I did for my country."

Domestically, Jeremy made the switch to Leicestershire, 12 months after that final England appearance. "Leicestershire was another county that wasn't fashionable, and the 4-day side had been struggling for a while."

So, why Leicestershire? "I felt it was an opportunity to re-prove myself. The strategic and mental side of cricket had also really started to fascinate me; so, choosing Leicestershire as my final county, meant I could do my master's degree at nearby Loughborough University."

And the Gloucestershire success followed him over. "We built a great one-day side and excelled in those early years of T20 cricket. I tried to replicate some of the principles that had delivered success at Gloucester and we won the competition twice and reached finals day in each of the first four seasons. Those periods of T20 cricket were great for me. I scored the winning runs at finals day, which was an amazing feeling and I also took a T20 hat-trick."

I asked Jeremy what made Leicestershire so successful in the shortest format of the game? "We were a poor four-day side and the shorter format suited our bowlers. In four-day cricket we struggled to bowl a side out twice, while in T20 cricket our bowlers were effective at mixing up deliveries and not getting hit too far. With the bat, we knew how to manipulate the ball around the field. I think we just quickly realised there was an opportunity for us in T20 cricket. We built a strategy to outthink and out manoeuvre the opposition who invariably had bigger names. I remember in that first year we set up a practice game between ourselves at the start of the season. The team who batted first were all out for 46 off of about 3.5 overs! We learnt quickly through failing and realised that even though it was a ludicrously short innings there was still time to 'build' an innings. Partnerships and momentum are key in T20 cricket with both bat and ball. An accepted norm now is you can't be three wickets down after six overs. And we quickly realised that, back then. If we lost a wicket we had to re-group."

"We were also quite innovative in that we ensured every single player was sat there ready and padded up from the first ball. While it looked completely stupid it meant we could be flexible in the order. If a certain bowler was bowling, which a particular batsman really fancied, we could switch our order around with ease. We always had a strategy and that suited our squad. One of my career highlights was captaining that winning T20 side in 2004 and hitting the winning runs!"

I asked Jeremy if at the time he thought T20 would become the giant that it has become today. "I think what we did know was that it would take a big effort to fill a stadium in any other format of the game, yet in T20 cricket Grace Road could become full with relative ease. So, very quickly we knew it would be big commercially for the club. In my time as captain I tried to create a season within a season. When T20 cricket came around we'd go away for a day like we would in pre-season and discuss tactics and roles etc. It was a refreshing change in what could be an attritional season of cricket."

Jeremy's performances in T20 cricket saw another chance with England - 12 months after dipping his toes in the water on the coaching side with England. "It was funny. I went from playing for England, to working for England, to playing for England!"

Jeremy was selected for the first T20 World Cup in 2007. "What a fascinating experience. If I'm honest I feel we got our strategy wrong. We had some fantastic hitters like Freddie and KP, but at Leicestershire we found success by having the balance of hitters and rotators. Two hitters batting together could often become an 'ego off', which would fail more often than not. In that World Cup we had Freddie and KP at each end. Vikram Solanki was told to go out and whack it and so was Darren Maddy. It was just all fireworks and suddenly we'd be four wickets down very quickly and couldn't rebuild from that. But it was a great experience to play with and against the best players in the World. In one over I remember having two dropped catches and then being hit for six off of the last ball. That over could have been very different, yet it ended up being my last game. Cricket can be a ruthless sport!"

In 2008, Jeremy was invited by the owner of Rajasthan Royals to go and be part of the coaching team in the first season of the IPL, as we alluded to earlier – a wonderful experience. "We ended up winning the IPL and those seven weeks in India were my first real coaching experience with a really top team. We created a winning culture that over-delivered."

Jeremy's psychological skills meant he could bring so much more to a team dynamic than just throwing balls at batsmen. Such was his impact at the IPL, Graeme Smith invited Jeremy to become part of the coaching team with South Africa. It was a move that brought a premature end to his own playing career.

"2008 was actually my benefit year but I ended up retiring three or four months into it, so I cancelled my benefit and took up the offer with South Africa. My first series was against England, which was interesting, having played for them a year earlier! It was fantastic to work with the likes of Kallis, Steyn, de Villiers, Amla, Morkel and Graeme Smith. We went from number four to number one in the world, despite all of the political tensions. That period with South Africa was a great opportunity for me and an amazing experience to be touring the world with that group of players as a respected coach."

After that spell with South Africa, Jeremy became part of the Sri Lanka coaching team for the 2015 World Cup in Australia and New Zealand. "That was another great experience, especially to work with Kumar and the guys and to get to know the Sri Lankan culture. The one downside was being the only foreigner in the camp meant that I had to tackle some of the hottest curries I've ever tasted day-after-day. I'd walk into the dressing room after a hot training session and the chef would just smile and say 'enjoy'!"

It was another fascinating experience. "I was in an environment giving presentations around mindset to players that didn't speak English too often. It was a fantastic, cultural and technical experience to adapt my style to what the players needed."

Since that spell with Sri Lanka, Jeremy is putting all his energies into developing Sporting Edge. He has worked on the board with the football LMA (League Managers' Association) for the last six years, which has given him great first-hand access to the likes of Sir Alex Ferguson and Jose Mourinho, and he has also worked with Eddie Jones and the England rugby side.

I think over the coming years you'll hear a lot more about Jeremy and his work across all sports.

Not a bad journey for a boy who was packed off to a cricket day so his Dad could concentrate on decorating!

I wanted to close with Jeremy though, by returning to cricket and asking him who were the best and toughest players he played with and against?

"Curtly Ambrose and Allan Lamb at Northants. Curtly was an incredible professional. One of his greatest strengths was his ability to manage his energy throughout a county season. He'd still be able to bowl in September like he would in May. He could also work out how to get a batsman out in four balls. He also never chirped anyone; he'd just give a batsman that stare. Lamby was a mercurial talent. He was charismatic, funny and a great influence for me. Jack Russell was an inspiration and Ian Harvey was transformational for us. He was probably the biggest piece in the jigsaw for us at Gloucestershire. Finally, at Leicestershire, Sehwag was just an enigma – beautiful to watch and so destructive!"

"In terms of playing against... Andy Flower was an incredible player of spin. Brian Lara was a great player. Sachin would bleed you dry and Sehwag and Gilchrist would just embarrass you!

Then there were the fast bowlers. Walsh, Brett Lee, Ahktar, but the one who makes me still wake up in the middle of the night with a cold shiver is Wasim Akram! It was a privilege, as an average player to face these lads and fight the mental battles."

With 9 career trophies, 8,633 runs and 387 wickets across all formats, combined with 11 appearances for his country, one would say Jeremy did a bit better than average!

24

ADAM HOLLIOAKE
FORMER ENGLAND & SURREY CAPTAIN

When people are asked to name their most admired captains from the late 1990s one person's name comes up more than most: former Surrey and England one-day captain, Adam Hollioake. And when you look at his record it's a difficult one to argue: three county championships, two Benson & Hedges Cups, a NatWest Pro 40 League title (and division two title), a Twenty 20 Cup and then throw in the Sharjah Cup with England, and you have a truly phenomenal haul.

Yet one man who doesn't want to take the credit for any of the above is Adam himself! "I can't take any credit for the skills that Surrey team had," remarked Adam. "Some people have me down as this genius captain who put fielders in positions that others didn't. I don't see it that way. The best bit of my captaincy was my ability to manage a group of difficult individuals and being able to take that squad out on to the field in the right frame of mind and happy. Anyone could have captained on the field and got the success we did. Decisions like whether to have three slips or four didn't win us those championships; it was keeping that squad motivated, focused and wanting to win, oh and not killing each other!"

More on Adam's captaincy and achievements later. Let's begin with his journey to England and a county cricket career at Surrey.

Born in Melbourne, Adam travelled around the world a lot as a youngster. His father's job as an engineer saw the Hollioake family move from country to country. In fact, by the time the Hollioakes arrived in England when Adam was 12, he'd already attended 10 different schools!

But the move to England brought stability and more importantly a real love for cricket. "Growing up I liked watching the exciting players, players who could bowl quick and whack it hard!" Dennis Lillee, Viv Richards, Imran Khan and Ian Botham were the four players who immediately sprung to Adam's mind. With the likes of Khan and Botham as talented all-rounders it was probably little surprise that he would end up becoming an outstanding all-round cricketer himself for both county and country.

"I actually started as an out and out fast bowler, but I got injured and those injuries cut my pace back so whilst I was injured, I practised my batting. I had a year out because of a stress fracture so I spent the whole year focused on my batting. Then when I was fit again to bowl, I was suddenly an all-rounder."

Adam's performances at St. George's School Weybridge, saw him fast-tracked through Surrey's youth teams. "I played in all of the Surrey age group sides, then at 15 I was asked to go and play for Surrey's under 19 side. I went along and did really well and Ian Greig offered me a contract. I'll be honest; I didn't even know what a contract was! I rang mum and dad up and all I could think about was I was going to be the richest man in

England on £5,000 a year! At the time I was on £5 a week
pocket money! My parents wanted me to study and go to
university, but I was keen to get my hands on the money! I
signed the contract. I was still at school at the time, so I was
being paid while I was at school and then, when I finished, I
went and played the second half of the season for Surrey."

It's quite an achievement for any 15-year-old to play and
perform at under 19 level, but Adam put it down to his early
development. "At the age of 12 I was just a big kid, as big as I
am now, so I was a very early developer, which definitely helped
my cricket."

Adam made his 1st XI debut in August 1993 against Derbyshire
and despite being picked as an out and out bowler, scored a
magnificent hundred. "I was fortunate that we had a long tail, so
even though I was selected as a bowler, I was put at number
seven in the order. I got a hundred and never looked back. The
next game I got picked as a batsman and was moved up to
number six and scored 80, and my career just went from there.
But that period out injured where I concentrated on batting
really helped me. Two years earlier I was batting at number 11.
Now, when I coach players, I encourage them if they are injured
to practice other areas of the game, to try and become all-
rounders. If you're an injured bowler, go and hit a thousand balls
a day and get good at it. The more strings to your bow,
particularly in today's game, the better it is."

Returning to Adam's Surrey debut… the Derbyshire side that day
had the likes of Devon Malcolm and Dominic Cork in their
bowling attack and what makes Adam's debut century even
more remarkable is he scored it, against that attack, without a
helmet! "It wasn't me being brave, I'd just never ever worn a
helmet batting. I didn't want to make my debut with a helmet on
when I'd never worn one before. I didn't think I'd be able to
perform so I went out with my cap on! Eventually Alec Stewart

said to me that I had to start wearing one or I'd get cleaned up at some stage. So I practised and practised and learnt how to bat with one on. It's pretty crazy when I look back and now I see the equipment that players have, I just had this mindset that I'd rather get hit than get out."

I asked Adam if he thought not playing in a helmet in those early years actually helped his reflexes? "Funnily enough from speaking with older players from the pre-helmet era, they tell me they never got hit, and I never got hit when I didn't wear one. It was only when I did wear a helmet that I got hit. It may well have helped the reflexes but also, I think wearing a helmet you take more risks; you take on a shot you wouldn't have taken on without one. At the end of the day, in today's game, it's just not worth taking the risk of not wearing one."

Adam's early success at Surrey saw him named captain for the first time when he was just 22 years of age. "With Alec Stewart away with England they needed someone to captain in his absence, I was shocked they when they asked me. I'd never captained any side. I was quite a rebellious and fiery teenager so I'm not sure why they chose me. I guess it was because I was quite competitive and I think people respected the fact I played hard cricket."

The appointment soon became permanent and I asked Adam how easy/difficult it was to be a young captain with a side full of internationals.

"It was an intimidating thought to captain that Surrey side. But you're not going to say no. If I'm honest, I was nervous captaining teams with the likes of Alec and Graham (Thorpe) and other England guys in. These players had played international cricket and had a lot more experience than me. That was the thing I had to get over. But like anything in life, you get some success and your confidence grows. As your confidence grows the better you become."

At the time of Adam taking over Surrey, they were a county who had flattered to deceive, but within a few years they were winning championships and one day competitions. In fact, it's fair to say they were probably the old Manchester United of cricket.

9 trophies were won during Adam's time in charge, including country championship wins in 1999, 2000 and 2002. What were his highlights?

"The county championship is the one competition all players want to win. It's the competition that takes up the most time. We played 16, 4-day games, to win that title. That's a lot of cricket. Ask anyone who has played a 4-day game and they'll tell you how hard it is to win. You have to take 20 wickets, sometimes on flat pitches against very good sides. So to win how many we did over a season to win a title, says something. The hardest things in life are the best things in life when you overcome them. Of course the shorter games and cup competitions are nice and it's nice playing in finals at Lord's, but the championship is always the one. I can honestly say that I can remember everything about those title wins, I can't say the same about Sunday league wins etc."

So, what was the key to Surrey's success? "We had very good cricketers, but we also had very edgy characters. We didn't have guys who would just turn up in their tracksuits, take their pay-checks and not challenge their team-mates; our squad had so many different characters who were quite rebellious and outspoken. My role on the field was easy. Managing them off the field was the hardest! Half of the time we hated each other! But every one of us had professional respect for each other. We had players who would go to bed at 10pm, we had others that would go to nightclubs, to strip clubs, to play chess, we had everything! But every single player had professional respect for one another. You sometimes hear about how important it is to have team spirit, to do everything together like meals etc, but for me the most important thing is to have professional respect and play hard."

And I was intrigued to know how difficult it was to manage international players coming back into that Surrey team that had being winning, and having to leave players out despite them maybe making important contributions?

"Really tough and probably the toughest part of the job. We really appreciated the players that came in when the Test players were away and we always made sure as a squad we showed our appreciation. At times one of them would score a hundred or take five wickets, then Alec Stewart, Graham Thorpe, Mark Butcher and Alec Tudor would come back in for the next game and they weren't going to play. It was a unique situation that needed managing, but as a team we always made sure we showed our appreciation for those guys that came in. We made everyone aware that if we were to win Championships we needed those players. I think that's why those back up players stayed with us and didn't move to other counties. They would have walked into any other county side, but because they stayed we were able to win trophy after trophy.

Adam played many crucial innings for Surrey and put in many great bowling spells, but what were his favourites from his time at the Oval? "My hundred on debut definitely and the season I got the most wickets in the Sunday League, but for me it was never really about those centuries or five wickets hauls; it was more the periods of having to get us over the line in tight situations with bat or ball. Those contributions in pressure situations meant much more to me than big scores."

Adam's performances for Surrey saw him selected for England in the one-day series against Pakistan in 1996. Adam was selected for the 2nd game of that series at Edgbaston where he took an impressive 4/23 with the ball. He followed that up with another 4-wicket haul (4/45) in the third game as England won the series 2-1. "It was great to make my debut, and to get four wicket hauls in my first two games was a great start to international cricket."

The Winter of 1996 saw Adam appointed captain of England's A team tour to Australia. A tour that Adam calls "the greatest touring squad, ever!"

"We were unbeaten throughout the whole tour. We had the likes of Mark Butcher, Glen Chapple, Dean Headley, Ashley Giles, Michael Vaughan, Owais Shah and Craig White. We won all the games against the State sides, who were unbelievably strong. It was also the best drinking tour ever! It was a stag party who played some of the best cricket ever! One day in Adelaide, David Graveney, the tour manager, had waited up because he heard some players might have been out drinking. Two players got back in at 1am to be met by an angry David Graveney in the hotel lobby. The following morning at breakfast David wanted to speak to me to say that we had a bit of a problem; he'd caught two players coming in at 1am. I asked David if he'd then gone to bed, he said he had, to which I replied, 'well you missed the other 9 of us getting in a 6am then!'. He'd gone to bed thinking he'd caught the culprits when in fact he'd just caught the two who had come back early! We went on and won the game, playing some fantastic cricket. It sounds incredibly unprofessional, but that team just functioned on going out, having a good time and playing hard cricket. It sounds ridiculous now, but that's just how it was then. The class of 96; what a great collection of blokes!"

The following year Adam's England career went from strength to strength as he was named man of the series for England's impressive 3-0 Texaco Trophy win over Australia. In each of the three games Adam saw England home by hitting the winning runs. But it wasn't just the performance of Adam during that series, another Hollioake came on to the scene, Adam's younger brother Ben.

"I received a call from the selectors saying you're in the squad and we're thinking of picking your brother. Ben was just 18 and if I'm honest, I didn't think he was ready. But they did pick him and he went on to do what he did."

Chasing an imposing 270 to win, Ben came in at number three and took an Australian attack of McGrath, Warne, Kasprowicz and Gillespie to pieces, scoring a breath-taking 63 from just 48 balls. "He came out and hit Warne and McGrath to all parts, it was one of the biggest highlights of my career seeing my little brother go out and do that, to that attack. They had a crazy bowling attack, but he destroyed it. As he went out, I just thought, 'get to 20 and anything more than that is a bonus; you can be happy with your contribution,' but he just kept going and going and going. He hit Warne into the top of the Mound stand! All of that said I still didn't think he was ready. There was no doubt he was talented and had the ability to do that, but I do think the selectors should have waited a year or two. It'd have been better for his longer-term development."

There was a real buzz around the country after that ODI series. Could this be the series that England finally win back the Ashes? England rode the wave and comprehensively won the 1st Test match of the series, before the Aussies bounced back emphatically.

Despite the success of the Hollioake brothers in the one-day series, the selectors didn't pick either of them for the 1st Test and neither got the call until the 5th Test match of the series, when England were then trailing by two Tests to one.

"I was disappointed not to be picked for that 1st Test. I did see where the selectors were coming from in that they wanted to stick to a format which had worked well for them and not to break it just because someone had, had a good one-day series. But I felt I had an edge over that Australian team. I felt as though I had them psychologically beaten. On the field I was not scared to have words with them. I was doing well, scoring runs, and they hadn't got me out. I was on top of Warne and I wasn't intimidated by them. Of course, none of that guarantees success, but I felt I should have been picked for that 1st Test. And that's hard for me to say because who they did pick, Mark Ealham, was one of my best friends in cricket, so while I was frustrated, I was delighted for him."

By the time Adam and his brother Ben did get the call, the Australian side was on a roll. "It felt like we were getting beaten by Australia so let's pick these guys and they will sort the problem out. But by that stage Australia were performing, winning and were full of confidence. At the end of day though we were proud to be making our debuts."

The gravity of Adam and Ben being picked together didn't dawn on Adam until recently when Sam and Tom Curran played together in a one day international in Sri Lanka. "I only really realised the gravity of it when the Curran boys got picked and it was mentioned that they were the first brothers since the Hollioakes. I love those two boys. I played against their Dad and I've seen them up close when coaching England Lions. I take no responsibility for their performances but I'm very close to them. It was when I heard that, that it dawned on me how a big a thing it was for me and Ben to play in the same side. At the time we were young. We were earning good money, cruising around London in our cars, playing for England. Life was good. You never appreciate what you have at the time."

The following Winter, Adam had the honour of being named England one's day captain for a tour to Sharjah where the squad were to play in a tournament against India and Pakistan. A competition the side went on to win. "We had a squad of players that had been completely thrown together. Athers had been rested, Gough had been rested, as had a few others. We weren't expected to compete with India and Pakistan in those conditions. The selectors threw together a number of one-day specialists and the tournament wasn't covered on television back home. There was no real interest, so the pressure was off us. The backroom staff on that tour consisted of three people: David Graveney, the tour manager, David Lloyd, the coach and Wayne Morton, the physio. David Lloyd got ill so our tour manager and physio had to take training and warm-ups! But the whole tour had a relaxed feel to it and we could just go out and play our cricket. We had an incredible group of guys who felt we were out there on our own. The team spirit was unreal we kept winning games and gaining more and more confidence. In the end we felt invincible."

England won the tournament and I asked Adam how frustrating it was for him personally not to be able to build on that success - Adam remained captain for just 14 games. "We were never able to get a full team out. I never had the luxury of a stable team. Thorpe was out, we had all kinds of problems with the batting line up and we never were able to play the same bowling attack. At the time it felt like the Test side was more important and the one-day side more an afterthought. Don't get wrong; we were treated professionally and given support, but if someone had had a hard Test series, they'd be rested for the one-day series and never the other way around. Everything was geared around being successful in Test cricket. Now, I don't think the side that won Sharjah would have won the World Cup in England in 1999, but it could have formed a nucleus of a side. We just needed to bring in Gough and a couple of others. To discard all of that Sharjah side on the eve of the World Cup I believe was a massive error. It should have been the backbone of that World Cup squad."

One cannot argue with that, particularly as England went on to be knocked out before their World Cup song had even been released!

Was it disappointing to lose the captaincy? "I guess so. I didn't really feel I was given the best opportunity to do the best I could with the injuries that we had, but on the other hand, in my whole time of captaincy either for Surrey or England I never valued the job of captain as the be all and end all. I think that was my strongest skill as captain was that I never had the desire to be captain, so in a way I had nothing to lose. All I wanted was to play cricket for England and Surrey. When I lost the captaincy, I was more disappointed that I felt I didn't have the opportunity to do my best rather than losing the captaincy itself. I must have tried to resign from the Surrey captaincy five times over the years! I was a reluctant captain at times. Sometimes I just wanted to play games of cricket and win and captaincy got in the way of that. I was always talked back into it by my good friend and Surrey coach Keith Medlycott. Every year we'd talk and I'd say why are we having the same conversation? Every year I wanted to resign, and every year he'd talk me back into it! I'd say to him that you can't be a very good coach if every year I want to resign; he'd just reply I must be a bloody great coach because I always talk you back into it!"

Reflecting on his England one-day career I asked Adam what his personal highlights were. "My first few games obviously and the Australia series at home. But I also loved the tours to Australia where the crowds hated me. They'd call me everything from traitor to Judas, to turncoat - I loved it! I just loved the battle. The more banter I got from the crowd the more energised I became. Ultimately, I just loved being the centre of attention, so when I got sledged or received banter from a crowd, I loved it! I remember going out there in 1999 and we had to come up with individual tour goals. Goughie's was to get Steve Waugh out x number of times, Alec Stewart wanted to be leading run scorer, I said I wanted to leave Australia as the most unpopular person in the country - I wanted everyone in that country to hate me! We played the first game at Sydney in front of a full house of 50,000 and the whole crowd, probably including my Mum and Dad, were singing 'Hollioake is a w$nker!'. Ben was there and just said to me, 'it looks like you achieved your goal then'!"

Adam's one-day career saw him play 35 times for England, scoring 606 runs and taking 32 wickets. I asked Adam if he was disappointed not to play more than four Test matches?

"I would like to have played more Test cricket but I also understand how these things happen, and the timing of my career. There have been a lot of better players than me who never played Test cricket, and a lot worse players than me who have played a lot, so you just take the cards you are dealt . In another era I might never have got one game. I'd love the opportunity to have played more. I had two Test matches against Australia and two against a good West Indies side. Three of these Tests were on bad wickets (one of the Tests against the West Indies was abandoned). It would have been nice to have played a series against another side, but I have to be happy with what I achieved."

In March 2002, Adam's brother Ben was killed in a car crash in Australia at the age of 24. Ben had gone to play 20 one day internationals for England as well as man of the match appearances for Surrey in Lord's finals. He was beginning to come into his prime.

I asked Adam how big a star Ben would have become.

"I really don't know if I'm honest. For his ability to play cricket, his athleticism and his talent he was equal to anything I ever saw in my time in cricket. To give you an idea, Ben played in the same under 19 side as Freddie Flintoff and Alex Tudor and both said he was by far the most talented. But I also know my brother! Was he as talented at Alastair Cook? Yes. Would he have had Alastair Cook's ability to turn up every day and be professional? I doubt it very much. But we'll never know. I don't think he would have ended up with long and amazing statistics in cricket because he would have been one of those players who would have done amazing things on a cricket field when his team needed it, but then would have left other games to others. I think he would have been a unique cricketer. There was a player who played for Australia called Keith Miller who, if the team were winning games, didn't care and wouldn't try, but when they needed him to, he'd always deliver and I think that's probably what Ben would have done. He'd be fired up for the big occasions. He played in two Lord's finals and got man of the match in both. He smashed Australia everywhere at Lord's. He would have been a big game player. Would he have scored in his 13th season of county cricket 130 to save the game at Derbyshire? I doubt it! He was a big match player. I definitely think he would have had a long international career but was like me he got bored very easily! He'd always want the next challenge."

A year after Ben's death, Adam retired from cricket. "I was 31 when I retired. My body was strong and good; I was heading into my peak years but I was just mentally shot after my brother died. I felt I needed to go back to Australia with my parents and my wife at the time hated England. So I decided to retire."

After retiring, Adam set up a foundation in Ben's name and raised a considerable amount of money. One impressive fundraiser saw Adam complete 'Adam's Journey', which involved walking a marathon a day from Edinburgh to Brighton, then sail from Brighton to Dieppe. This was followed by a bike ride from Dieppe to Gibraltar, and Adam then rode from Gibraltar to Africa. "It took us two months and it was an incredible experience. The following year we ran a marathon. We managed to do lots of great things and raised lots of money."

It's hard to imagine what Adam and his family went through, but I think it speaks volumes and hopefully brings a small degree of comfort that so many people to this day speak about Ben and that innings at Lord's. In his short career for England and Surrey he gave so many wonderful memories to supporters. That alone speaks volumes.

Reflecting on Adam's cricket career I asked him who were the best players he played with and against. "The most professional was Alec Stewart. Saqlain Mushtaq had the ability to turn games. Mark Ramprakash was the best county batsman. In all forms of cricket, Graham Thorpe was the stand out. He was just brilliant in all forms, Test matches, ODI's and in both attack and defence. To have Mark and Graham, two amazing guys in charge of England's batting now, are great appointments by the ECB. For sheer excitement, Waqar Younis. But my favourite was Azhar Mahmood. We used to bat and bowl at the death together and we saw out so many games."

And playing against? "The toughest was Shane Warne. He wasn't the best bowler, I thought Murali was better, but as a character Warne was tough. He was such a competitive bloke."

Adam also named Shane as the captain that he admired most from his playing days. "From a purely tactical basis he was very, very, good. But so was Andrew Strauss. He had the respect of his team and I would say he was the only captain who truly challenged me as a captain, when he was captain of Middlesex. I felt when I could always get on top of other county captains, but Strauss was the one who I felt really challenged me. He was a very good captain."

Most people take things easy when they retire, but that's not in Adam's nature. He loves a new challenge and after cricket, he turned professional at MMA. "I found MMA easier than cricket. In cricket I always struggled to hold concentration for a full day, but with MMA it's very short and explosive. People who don't understand it just think it's a fight, and of course there is an element of that, but there are so many skills involved. In total there are probably over 1,000 moves. If you think of all of the skills involved in cricket, there are so, so many more in MMA. I understand it's not for everyone, but for me it was the ultimate competition and something I loved competing in."

Adam's progress in the sport was quick and in 2016 he was meant to fight for a world title, when one morning he just woke up and realised he didn't want to fight anymore. "I've never ever struggled with training. I was always the hardest trainer, but one morning, seven weeks out from a World title fight, I just woke up and I didn't want to do it. I was sick and tired of being punched in the face and thought I don't want to do it anymore. I had no interest in fighting. It was time for the next challenge."

And that next challenge was a return to cricket. Adam got involved with the ECB, supporting Andy Flower with the England Lions. "It was an amazing experience which I loved. We had a great bunch of kids. Andy Flower is an amazing coach, I learnt so much from him. I always thought coaching was easy, but then I realised I needed to do an apprenticeship. I was very thankful to Andrew Strauss for giving me that opportunity."

After impressing with England, Adam was approached by Queensland to become their assistant coach, a role he took up. "I loved the coaching with England, but with the other coaching gigs I was doing I was away from home eight months of the year; when Queensland approached me, it was the perfect role. I can be at home close to my family and coach a brilliant State side. It's the perfect job. I really want to develop as a coach and I'm loving the role at Queensland."

Adam's role in Australian cricket makes him an ideal person to give his thoughts on this year's Ashes series between the two countries. "It's going to be a really good series. In England you have to make England favourites, but Australia won't be easy.

With Warner and Smith, they will have two top 10 batsmen returning with a point to prove and they have a very good fast bowling attack. It's set up to be a great series, it could genuinely be like 2005."

And the World Cup? "This has to be the first time an England side go into a World Cup as favourites, but rightly so, they are the best England one-day side I've seen. Just amazing."

And 'amazing' is a great word to summarise Adam and what he's achieved in the game. His captaincy record is up there with the best, and he and his brother brought so many memorable moments, moments that will always live on. I wouldn't be surprised in a few years' time if the name Hollioake is being bandied around as a future England coach. You read it here first!

25

CHARLOTTE EDWARDS
FORMER ENGLAND WOMEN'S CAPTAIN

With over 10,000 international runs to her name, Charlotte Edwards was England's cricketing rock. I spoke with Charlotte, 24 hours before she boarded a plane to India for the women's World T20 tournament in 2016. The team headed into the tournament under the guidance of a new coach, Mark Robinson, and on the back of successful T20 and ODI series in South Africa. Sadly, the team were knocked out of the tournament at the semi-final stage, falling just short of chasing Australia's 132/6. However, on a personal level it was another successful tournament for England's captain who ended the competition with 202 runs, the second highest total.

So where did the journey from schoolgirl cricketer to England captain begin? Born in Cambridgeshire, Charlotte grew up in a cricket loving family. Her Dad and brother's love for the game meant a bat and ball were never far away. "If I wasn't at a local cricket ground, I was playing in the back garden. Living on a farm, there wasn't a huge amount else to do!"

Her talent with both bat and ball, was obvious for all to see, and from a young age she was encouraged to play the game by everyone that was close to her. "My Dad encouraged me to play and I was very lucky that I had two parents that gave their all to me and allowed me to go on and ultimately play for England. I was also lucky that my school and local cricket club didn't see it as an obstacle that I was a girl. They knew I was as good as the boys."

During this time, women's cricket was nowhere near the level that it is at now and, as a child, Charlotte thought that if she was to fulfil her ambition to play for England, it had to be for the men's side! "I didn't know women's cricket existed. All I had played was boys' cricket."

So how did Charlotte suddenly become the youngest player to ever play for England? "I was just in the right place at the right time. I was playing for my boys' team, when a guy that knew an England women's selector was watching the game and he passed my details on – and that's how I stumbled across women's cricket."

In 1993, the England women's team won the World Cup and from that moment on, it became Charlotte's ambition to both play for, and captain, her country. "From a very early age I was always pretty determined in what I wanted to do."

Charlotte was quickly selected to play representative cricket for East Anglia. However, all county cricket for women consisted of at the time of a five-day tournament held each year in Cambridge. "It was pretty amateur, but I was lucky that I got spotted early."

Such was the early impression that Charlotte made, she was playing for England under 19s at just 12 years of age and went on to make her full England debut at the age of just 16.

"I'll be honest, if I hadn't of played cricket with the boys, I know I wouldn't have played so soon. I felt ready at 16 to put on an England shirt. Nothing fazed me."

Despite feeling ready, news of her selection was a shock. "I remember I was at home one evening, knocking a ball against the wall and my Mum ran out saying there was a lady on the phone and I'd been picked for the 3rd Test against New Zealand at Guildford and that I needed to report there on Monday night. It was just amazing to think that my dream had come true. Can you believe I made my debut in a skirt! Thankfully that was the only game in a skirt and we quickly changed to trousers! I was just over the moon to finally get the opportunity."

Charlotte went on to make 34 and 31 in that debut Test match. "I was really nervous, but at 16 you could kind of take it in your stride. If I had been older, I suspect it might have been worse. Nothing really fazed me at that age and I felt ready to play. I had some great senior players around the group who helped me and I felt I fitted in well from the beginning. Playing a Test match in my first game was hard though; I'd never played in a four-day game before so it was a long four days, but four days I'll never forget."

Charlotte quickly became a run machine for both club and country. In 1997, she enjoyed a golden year where she reeled off 12 centuries for her respective sides. "It was one of those years. I just wish I could have another one! I was always pretty ruthless in how I approached my cricket and every time I went to the middle; I knew I had to make the most of it."

Within that golden run was her first century for England, off of just 118 balls against the touring South Africans.

The day before her 18th birthday, Charlotte went on to score a then-record ODI score of 173 not out in a World Cup match against the Ireland and her maiden Test hundred came in 1998/99 against India.

It was a rapid rise for Charlotte, and in 2005, when Ashes fever was hitting the men's game in England, Charlotte's second childhood ambition was fulfilled, when she was named England captain. "Initially, I was asked to stand in for Clare Connor who, due to injury, was unavailable for the tour of India. After 9 years of playing for England, I felt ready and I loved it."

The role became permanent the following March. "When I got the call I was over the moon. Of course it was disappointing when one of your close friends decides to step down, but it was a dream come true for me."

I asked Charlotte what it was like making that transition from player in the ranks to captain. "It was tough actually. And if I'm honest, it took me 12 months to get my head around captaincy. I was given one of the biggest jobs in cricket and suddenly I felt I had to do things differently. I put too much pressure on myself to lead from the front, make all of the decisions and be the one to score runs. It probably affected my batting more than anything else, but once I adjusted to captaincy, I felt more relaxed. I learnt that when I'm batting, I must be Charlotte Edwards the batter and when I'm in the field I'm Charlotte Edwards, England captain. Once I was able to separate the two roles, I felt captaincy became a lot simpler to me and I started to enjoy it."

Under Charlotte's guidance the team has enjoyed tremendous success. Ashes series were won and retained, the World Cup was won in 2009 and the final of the World T20 was reached. "Winning the World Cup in 2009, in Sydney, will always be the biggest highlight of my career. It was my first major world trophy and to win it in Australia, made it even more special."

On an individual level, Charlotte was winning many accolades. She was named ICC Woman's Player of the Year in 2008 and was a Wisden Cricketer of the Year in 2014, only the second time a woman has won this award. "Sometimes I do have to pinch myself about some of the stuff I have achieved because when you start playing the game, you have no idea what will happen and how your career will span out."

But with all of the plaudits for Charlotte's captaincy and batting, we shouldn't forget about her abilities with the ball. "I've got the best golden arm going! No-one wants to get out to me!"

Charlotte laughs, but through the years, her bowling displays have been invaluable. Her four wickets against New Zealand in the 2009 World Cup got England into the final. "I do love bowling, but the biggest issue for me was having the time to put into it. I was always a part time bowler. The reason I'm not doing it now, is I haven't the time and energy to put into it. And you have to have that at international level. I used to love it though, as I always felt I was in the game. If I hadn't scored runs it was nice that you could have a bowl and try to pick up some wickets. I do really miss it, if I'm honest."

But of all the games Charlotte has played thus far for England, it was an Ashes winning knock in Hobart that she lists as her most memorable. "I would have to say the 92 I made in a T20 in Hobart, which won us the Ashes. I have scored a number of 50s 60s and 70s against the Aussies, and sometimes they can feel more valuable, but that game in Hobart stands out for me just because it was one of those series that kept swinging from one team to the other. They scored 160 or so batting first, which is a really high score in women's T20 cricket and we just went out and chased them down in 18 overs, which was unbelievable."

On the subject of T20 cricket, Charlotte played in the inaugural Women's Big Bash T20 league in Australia this Winter, a tournament that ran parallel to the men's competition. "It was brilliant, I really enjoyed it. I played over in Perth, where they really looked after me. Some of the games were double headers with the men's games and they were great events to be part of. Especially Adelaide on New Year's Eve when there was over 20,000 in the ground at the end – I've never experienced that before in domestic cricket. Everyone in Australia bought into it and it's a fantastic thing for the women's game."

This Summer, the ECB launches its own franchise T20 competition, with the introduction of the women's Super League. "Having experienced the Big Bash in the Winter you realise what a difference a domestic competition like this can make to the women's game. One of my biggest concerns over recent years is the strength of the domestic game, so introducing the women's Super League is going to be huge for us and will help prepare our players for international cricket. It will give county players a better level of cricket and it will hopefully generate a lot of interest for girls wanting to play the game. Hopefully the six teams will deliver a great product."

Both T20 and ODI cricket have always been the pinnacle of the women's game, so where does Test cricket stand? "Test cricket is hard for us, because we don't play much of it, so we don't get the opportunity to practice our Test skills. We don't play four-day cricket domestically, so it's always difficult for players making their debuts, as they won't have played four-day cricket before and it can be hard to adjust. ODI's and T20's are the two formats we are most comfortable with, but we do love playing Test cricket. We just wish we could play more of it so we can understand the game better and get more out of it."

One recent change in women's cricket was the introduction of a points system in Ashes series. Previously, the women's Ashes series were won or lost based upon one, one-off Test match. Now points are collected for winning Test matches, ODI and T20's, so every contest counts. "We found that Test matches were becoming a bit negative. With a one-off Test, whoever held the Ashes wouldn't necessarily play a positive brand of cricket as they only needed to draw to retain the Ashes, so it became a bit of a non-event. Adding the other two formats has been a fantastic introduction, it has allowed the two best teams in the world to really fight it out and the series has become a true test of our abilities."

And what of the old rivalry, is it as intense as the series played by the men? "It's no different whatsoever. Any contest in cricket between England and Australia will always be competitive. They are our biggest rivals, and I'm sure we are theirs. Every contest we have with them is tightly fought but played with a huge amount of respect. Every run you score, or wicket you take, always seems to be worth more when you play Australia."

The old enemies have definitely been at the forefront of the huge development of women's cricket, globally and Charlotte hopes other countries' boards will support their players as much as the ECB have done here in England. "Us and Australia definitely lead the way with the financial backing from our boards. Players from most of the top countries now have some form of contract, but many are still part time. We have had enormous support from the ECB. They have been absolutely amazing. I never thought I'd be a professional cricketer but that's happened."

Charlotte also gives a lot of kudos to Sky Sports and the BBC. "The media support has been absolutely fantastic. Both Sky Sports and the BBC cover most of our games. There's a real momentum behind women's sport now in this country. We're playing our games in front of lots more people and there's a whole new audience watching women's cricket. We're selling out grounds at Chelmsford and Hove - with fans of the women's team, not just supporters piggy-backing on the men's game."

It's obvious the pride that Charlotte quite rightly feels. "I'm proud of seeing all of this happen and where the women's game now stands. 20 years ago I was playing for England in a skirt, I'm now a professional cricketer. Sometimes you have to pinch yourself. I've been on a wonderful journey – I just don't want it to end!"

Charlotte's achievements haven't just been recognised by the cricketing hierarchies. She has been a proud recipient from the Queen of both an MBE and a CBE. "I'm immensely proud. I'm the luckiest person in the world to do what I do."

As Charlotte heads into her 20th year of playing international cricket, what are her aims for 2016? "We have an important series against Pakistan in the Summer and of course the Super League. Then at the back end of the year we head to Sri Lanka and the West Indies for two important tours as we prepare for the ICC World Cup next year."

Charlotte has become an icon of women's cricket and she encourages all young girls to give the game a try. "The great thing now is that there are all girl cricket teams which wasn't the case when I was younger, so there are lots of opportunities for girls to play the game now, so give it a go!" and she urges parents to give their daughters the chance that her parents gave her. "Give them the opportunity. If they get half the pleasure out of it that I have, they'll be very happy."

As cricket fans we owe Charlotte so much. Her journey is inspirational and she has been an ambassador for not only women's cricket, but women's sport in the UK. She tells me that she "owes the game more than it owes me." I beg to differ. England cricket owes Charlotte Edwards a huge amount because women's cricket would not be in the position it is now, if it wasn't for her.

26

OWAIS SHAH
FORMER MIDDLESEX & ENGLAND BATSMAN

A player who can most definitely count himself unlucky not to have played many more times for England, particularly in that problem number three position is former Middlesex star Owais Shah.

"I was fortunate to have played with some fantastic players throughout my career. Ricky Ponting, Jacque Kallis, Mark Ramprakash, Marcus Trescothick, Michael Vaughan and Kevin Pietersen to name a few. Of course, I wish I could have played more for England but it is what it is," said a philosophical Owais. We'll talk more about Owais's international career later. But where did it all start for this batsman, who during his teenage years carried many great hopes on his shoulders?

Owais was born in Pakistan and enjoyed nothing more than playing games of cricket out on the streets of Karachi. "I grew up in Pakistan and Pakistan was very similar to India and other sub-continental countries where cricket was hugely popular. We used to live in a flat and I loved going outside and playing games of cricket with the other kids on the streets. We all wanted to be the next Javed Miandad. When I was eight, we moved to England."

Upon arrival in England Owais joined his local club side Wycombe House Cricket Club; a club where through the years, he has broken a number of club records. It wasn't long before this talented youngster was attracting the attention of the first-class counties. "I joined Middlesex at under 11s and went on to play under 12s and under 14s – I missed the under 13s as I was pushed straight through to the 14s and then I started playing second eleven cricket when I was 15. Cricket had certainly taken over my life!"

Such was Owais's rapid rise that he made his first-class debut against Nottinghamshire at the age of just 17. I asked Owais how daunting was it to be walking into a dressing room with some very established players in it at such a young age? "To be honest, it was a lot of fun. Mike Gatting was in the team, so were Mark Ramprakash, Angus Fraser and Phil Tufnell. I was probably a bit too young to be intimidated. If it was a few years later and I was 20 or 21, I might well have been, but at 17 I just felt I was turning up to play another game of cricket. I obviously knew these guys had achieved a huge amount in their careers, but I was just relishing the opportunity and enjoying being in their company."

Did going into the side at such a young age accelerate his development?

"Yes and no, if I'm honest. I was pushed in at such a young age that I was having to learn first class cricket as I went along. A tiny bit of me, when I look back, thinks I wish I could have played a bit more 2nd XI cricket to learn my game more and then maybe move up into the 1st XI when I was 20 or 21. I could then have gone into first class cricket with a better understanding of my own game."

Owais's career at Middlesex spanned 16 years – a period where he scored 13,377 first class runs for the county. However, despite being one of the most consistent batsmen on the circuit he and his team mates only had the one trophy to show for their efforts: the 2008 T20 title – the final of which saw Owais score a match-winning 75 off of just 35 balls.

"At that time, I was playing for England, so I remember I only played in the quarter-finals in the lead up to finals day. Ed Joyce was our captain who led the side really well. We had a very good side. Tyrone Henderson had a really good semi-final where he smacked Durham around the park. We then batted first in the final against Kent and put a big score on the board. We defended the total and lifted the trophy. It was a wonderful evening."

I asked Owais if it was frustrating that, despite all of his personal achievements with the bat, that trophy was the only major honour he was able to win during his 16 years at the county. "We were in a rebuilding phase and we accepted that; the club had, had a lot of success but that group then moved on and us young guys had to come through and rebuild Middlesex. It was of course frustrating on occasions. At times we didn't perhaps sign the right players, which disappointed the playing group. For example, we'd sign a fast bowler, when we really needed to sign a spinner, or we'd sign a spinner when we really needed a batsman. It was bizarre at times. But that was life and all you could do as a player was to get on with it, try your best, score runs and hope success would follow. Thankfully it finally did with that win in 2008."

One of the big benefits of playing for Middlesex was that his home ground was also the home of cricket. "Everyone who played for Middlesex was fortunate that your home is the home of cricket. For me Lord's is the best ground in the world, and I just felt like part of the furniture there. I was very fortunate."

Owais's success at Middlesex brought inevitable international recognition. Firstly, in 1998, where impressive performances in his first couple of years of first-class cricket, saw him named as captain for England's under 19 World Cup campaign in South Africa – a campaign they went on to win.

"That was a great experience. We had the likes of Rob Key and Paul Franks in the team. It was a really good time in my life, when cricket was just fun, there were no pressures. Yes, we wanted to win the World Cup, but we were a bunch of lads that just wanted to play cricket."

Owais's success in that under 19 World Cup campaign soon saw him elevated to full England honours, when he was selected to make his debut against Australia in a one-day international in 2001. Many hoped it would be the start of a long and successful international career, but for many reasons, a number of which seemed to be out of his control, he just wasn't able to nail down a consistent run of games in the side.

"I'd been scoring a lot of runs for Middlesex and I had been asked to come and join the one-day squad. On the morning of the game Michael Vaughan got injured and I was suddenly told "Owais you're in!". We batted first, lost a few wickets and then me and Ben Hollioake put on a decent partnership to get us up to a respectable total but Australia were far too good. Ricky Ponting scored a very good hundred and that was that."

Owais went on to play 71 times in one-day international cricket but the selectors didn't give him the backing that players of today most definitely appear to get. "The year before I got dropped for the final time, I was the highest run-scorer for England in white ball cricket and playing some of the best cricket of my career. We'd been to India where I scored runs, I then had a very good series against New Zealand; it was just bizarre. I think it does help now when you have a dedicated one-day captain, whereas when I played, we had many different captains and coaches, and they were always captains and coaches for both the Test and ODI sides and at times I think it's fair to say their heads and thinking was perhaps more towards the Test side. You just had to hope you fitted in people's plans which I obviously didn't."

Owais finished his one-day international career with a batting average of 30.56. You feel it could have been much more if he wasn't under the constant pressure of having to prove himself. But what were some of his big highlights?

"I scored 98 against South Africa in the Champions Trophy, against the likes of Dale Steyn – that was probably my best innings for England. Then there was my hundred against India at the Oval, where I scored 107 not out off of 95 balls. Those two knocks were my favourites, for sure."

It was a familiar story in Test cricket, where despite a debut knock of 88 in Mumbai, Owais only went on to play five further Test matches for his country.

"It was an amazing feeling to be picked for your Test debut. Similar to my ODI debut, I wasn't meant to be playing but Alistair Cook was feeling ill, so I was given the opportunity to bat at number three as they pushed Ian Bell up to open. I scored 88 in the first innings and 30 odd in the second, so over 100 runs in total on my debut, which I thought was a good return. For me, I'd had a wonderful Test match. Then at the start of the Summer I was told I wasn't in the team. I didn't get another opportunity for two years. It just didn't really add up. But what could I do? All I could do was go back and continue scoring runs for Middlesex which is what I did. But a Test recall didn't come for another two years."

The call eventually came in a Test series against the West Indies, but after scores of six and four in the match, he was immediately dropped again. Owais was given another chance in the 2009 series away in the West Indies, when he was brought in to replace an out of form Ian Bell and despite an excellent half century Owais never played Test cricket again.

For someone of Owais's undoubted talent, six Test matches seems an unfair return when you think back to many players who were given perhaps many more opportunities.

12 months after his last Test match for England, Owais parted company with Middlesex, in what was a bittersweet moment for the Middlesex stalwart.

"It wasn't my decision to leave Middlesex. Angus Fraser decided to release me. I wanted to stay but at the same time I was a little frustrated with the way things were being run at the club. I was a little bit surprised they didn't offer me a new contract as I felt I had performed very well over many seasons. I admit I had a poor 4-day season in my last year, but I was the leading run scorer in one-day and T20 cricket. I hold my hands up about my red ball form in that final season, but one bad season in all those seasons batting well at number 3, I thought they might cut me some slack. I moved to Essex and looking back I think it was the best thing that happened to me."

With T20 cricket growing exponentially, Owais concentrated his efforts on the shortest form of the game. And it was a start of a wonderful journey that saw him play in all of the big T20 competitions around the world. "I took the opportunity to really look at my T20 game and I decided I was just going to focus all my efforts on T20 cricket. It was obvious I was never going to get picked for Test cricket again. I played four-day cricket, as any player does because they dream of playing Test match cricket so with that dream gone it made sense to concentrate on T20 cricket. I ended up playing in the IPL, the Big Bash and all of the major leagues. So, that decision by Middlesex was a blessing in disguise really."

I had many questions for Owais on T20 cricket, but I did have to begin by asking him that when T20 cricket was born in England back in 2002, did he ever believe the format would grow to the levels it is today?

"No one did! I think we all felt, what is this competition that's getting in the way of the County Championship and one-day cricket. That was the attitude of everyone. It was just a bit of crash, bang, wallop. But as time went on the popularity grew and now everyone is desperate to play in the IPL and T20 is very much here to stay."

Owais was one of the first English players to play in the IPL and having represented a number of the big franchises I was keen to hear what was it like playing in what is the biggest tournament in world cricket?

"The atmosphere at the games is just amazing. If you could perform in front of those big crowds, you got such a buzz. There'd be 60 or 70,000 people chanting your name. You were a hero of the night. And it was just a great opportunity for me to play alongside the likes of Sehwag, Dilshan and Gilchrist. You'd talk to each other about the game, you'd watch how those players prepared for games, see how players batted differently, or bowled differently. It just gave you a broader sense of the game."

Having played in all of the major leagues around the world I asked Owais how our domestic tournament ranked?

"The IPL is a tough tournament and the most financially rewarding. It's tough because you play a lot of cricket. While in the Big Bash, which is a very good competition, you typically play less games and those games tended to be more at the weekends. The quality of both were amazing, which is what you want as a cricketer. They are by far the best two tournaments. With the Blast we don't have the noise in the grounds, or the build up around the competition. At times that can make our competition I guess a little boring or just another game of T20 cricket. But there is no reason why we cannot have a wonderful competition in England, because our competition definitely has the talent."

Could the proposed 100 ball competition make the difference? "It's a tough one to say as no one has actually played this kind of game before. People are rubbishing it, but it could be a genius of an idea. Until a game is played none of really know and remember back in 2002 people thought this T20 idea was daft!"

It's a good call. T20 brought a great climax to Owais's career and he is pleased that players in England today are now encouraged to play in various leagues around the world. "You'll get left behind if you don't. These competitions grow you as a person or cricketer. People of course have different motives; some are career-oriented, some are driven by money. But playing in these leagues was a wonderful experience for me and I'm very grateful that T20 cricket gave me the opportunity to tour the world, play cricket and meet different people."

Owais still hasn't officially retired from cricket and if the right white ball opportunity arose, he'd be keen to take it, but he is accepting that his playing career is reaching its end so much so he has already starting to make strides into coaching. In 2016 he coached the UAE in an interim capacity and is keen to do more. "I was head coach of the UAE for a small stint, which was a good experience. I've done other bits and bobs since and I'm enjoying it. I'd definitely like to do more. Cricket is who I am."

Reflecting on his long career, I asked Owais to name some of the best players he'd played against together with the hardest bowler he faced. "Tendulkar, Ponting and Lara for sure. It wasn't great being on the receiving ends of some of their hundreds, they were three greats of the game. In terms of the bowler it has to be Glenn McGrath. He was just so accurate and didn't give you anything. He was so tough to get away."

And the best captain? "I played a series under Adam Hollioake. He was great to play under and has very good man management skills. As Andrew Flintoff had; the results didn't necessarily do his captaincy stint justice, but he was a good captain and very good man manager."

Owais finished his career with over 16,300 first class runs, at an average just shy of 42, and with a further 10,500 List A runs and 5,500 T20 runs its fair to say despite some poor decisions by various England selectors it was a career fulfilled. And as a Middlesex fan writing this I can definitely attest to many happy memories watching this lad in the middle! Owais – thank you!

.

27

GARETH BATTY
ENGLAND & SURREY SPINNER

It's often said that hard work will always pay off in the end and that couldn't be truer for this interviewee, Gareth Batty; a player who after an 11-year absence from Test cricket got his much-deserved recall for the 2016 Winter tours to Bangladesh and India.

He may not have played in all seven Tests but his Test appearances (and wickets) in Chittagong and Mohali were reward for years of consistent service in the county game.

I met up with Gareth at the England team hotel, midway through the India series, to talk through his selection for the tour and to look back through his career at Yorkshire, Surrey and at New Road, Worcester.

"I was surprised, but very pleased, to get the call for these tours," remarked Gareth. "It capped off an interesting few weeks. Alec Stewart had put it on my radar that I might be getting a testimonial and then we had our first daughter on the 31st August, followed by the news of my selection. It was really pleasing and I felt if I could manage to get a game out here I could do well."

Gareth capped his return to Test cricket with four wickets in England's Test win in Chittagong and admits that despite those wickets he felt nerves that he'd never experienced in the game. "That first game was absolutely nerve-wracking; I never thought I would be like that. The first day was tough, but once that first day was out of the way it was fine and it felt like playing any other game." To be honest, many would argue that Gareth should not have waited 11 years between his seventh and eighth Test match appearances, so it's only natural there would be a degree of nerves.

Prior to the tour of Bangladesh there were a lot of column inches used up on whether it was safe to travel so I asked Gareth, as a player, what that unique situation with such security was like. "I don't know much about security but it felt like there was more security than would guard Buckingham Palace! As players we never felt in any danger. Some horrific things had happened in Bangladesh in the past but it's very easy to say things when out of the country but I think it was a real positive for Bangladesh and Bangladesh cricket that everything went off without a hitch."

A real competitor, whether as a spinner or useful lower order batsman, Gareth started his career at his home county Yorkshire, but it's perhaps surprising that a number of his boyhood sporting heroes were from the sport of rugby. "As a kid, it was always cricket and rugby for me. Ellery Hanley and Gareth Schofield were massive heroes as was Will Carling and Jeremy Guscott, but cricket wise you couldn't go past the great West Indian sides!"

His cricket loving family meant despite his love of rugby, cricket was always going to be first choice. "My Dad was involved for many years at Bradford & Bingley cricket club. I remember sitting on the rollers and collecting balls as they were hit out of the nets; as a kid if there was ever a day without doing anything, I'd be disappointed!"

And how much of an honour was it to don the white rose? "Representing any club is an honour and particularly one with the history of Yorkshire. But, bizarrely deep down I always knew it wasn't going to be a forever thing - I don't know why. I think I just always wanted to truly explore the game and not just the game in Yorkshire. Bowling spin was a big thing for me and at Yorkshire, spin was always a little more secondary in terms of how they won games. They had an excellent four-pronged seam attack which included the likes of Phil Kerrick, who was a wonderful bowler, but it just wasn't spin based so I knew that if I wanted to develop my game I'd have to look for opportunities outside Yorkshire."

In 1998, Gareth made the move south to Surrey for his first spell at the south London county. "When Micky Stewart got in touch, I jumped at the chance. I remember the strange feeling I got when I first walked through the gates at the Oval to go and sign my contract – it felt like walking into your house. It just felt really comfortable. Even now, when I walk into the Oval I always get the same feeling, which is brilliant. I had four and a half years at Surrey during my first spell. I remember walking into changing rooms with the likes of Stewie, Thorpey, Butch, Adam Hollioake and Saqlain - it was different gravy. I think we had 14 internationals on the staff, which was amazing. I doubt that will ever happen again because of the salary caps that are in place now, I was very lucky."

With so many star players on their books it was no surprise that Surrey were the team to beat. Silverware was never far away, but the flip side for a young player like Gareth was again opportunities became limited and despite playing crucial roles in cup quarter finals and semi-finals, he would often lose his place for a final when the group of England players would return. "It was just great to be involved in that changing room and seeing how the senior players went about winning; how they conducted themselves; how they prepared to perform in games. I learnt so much and that was invaluable for me at that stage of my career."

And the biggest learning? "Enjoy winning. People don't really talk about it, but if you don't enjoy winning what's the point. We play a team sport with 10 other blokes - or these days with 20 or 25 blokes - in a squad and with backroom staff. It's a massive thing how you celebrate winning and how you conduct yourself around the group when you win. It has to be special and seeing how those boys went about it was a pretty big thing for me."

After four and a half years at the Oval, Gareth knew, with a dressing room full of star performers, to further develop his game he'd need to make another move. And that move would be to New Road, Worcester, where he was finally able to come to the fore as one of the country's most promising young spinners.

"I had a few counties interested in signing me but Tom Moody was the sole reason I went to Worcester. He was big friends with Alec Stewart and Stewie had told him he could trust me and it took about a one-minute phone call and I was ready to sign whatever contract they gave me. Tom had a fantastic vision and, to be fair, for three or four years that vision played out brilliantly. We signed some quality players and we challenged in every competition. I suppose as a bunch of players we have to take responsibility that we didn't win more trophies than we did, at that time. We got to two Lord's final and blew up, that was the players' fault. A bit further down the line we did win the Pro 40 but for the quality of the group we had, we probably should have won a bit more. But the club was great. I'm very fortunate that I got to meet some terrific people there. Vikram Solanki is a very, very close friend and will continue to be way after cricket has gone from a playing point of view. Stephen Peters is a great friend of mine, as are Kabir Ali and Graeme Hick. It was a wonderful time at Worcester and I wouldn't change anything."

Gareth went on to take 318 wickets during his time at New Road and it was his early form with the ball that brought him to prominence with the England selectors.

In the Winter of 2002, Gareth was among the second intake of players to attend England's academy programme, which launched 12 months earlier.

"I got on really well with Rod Marsh and I really enjoyed my time at the academy. It was hard work and I think a lot of people came back to the season tired, but I really enjoyed it. It would be long days which would often start at 6am, get broken up with an hour rest here and there, but we wouldn't finish until 4.30pm/5pm. The days were a combination of fitness, which really tested you, and cricket. The fitness element was like a military style training programme, but that was my bag, I enjoyed it. However, what it did teach me was that in the sport we play, yes it's great to be really, really fit and I see that as a positive; but cricket is played by lots and lots of different people and people find success in different ways; just because something is right for one person it doesn't mean the approach is right for another. You have to be open to what makes different people tick. I've taken that into my captaincy all these years later."

Gareth's work ethic at the academy certainly paid dividends as he, along with Jimmy Anderson, was pulled out of the programme to join the main England touring squad who were suffering with a number of injuries during the 2002/03 Ashes series.

"Jimmy and I got called in. It was a bit surreal if I'm honest. Everything seemed to be happening very quickly. I'd moved to

Worcester that previous season and Jimmy had just played his first year of first class cricket up at Lancashire; I was lucky that I knew a few of the guys, such as Stewie and Thorpey. I suppose, looking back, I wonder if I was ready? No. I was a bit like a rabbit in the headlights. I think that's down to the way you think as a person in a lot of ways. As a young player you look around the dressing room and you're in awe of those around you. When you're older you respect them, of course, but they are just other players."

Gareth made two appearances during the tour, in one day internationals at Melbourne and Sydney. But it was in 2003 where he won his precious first England Test cap on tour in Bangladesh.

"Bangladesh was an interesting place to tour back then! I remember in the hotel in Chittagong the room was full of cockroaches and other creepy crawlies, but I think those experiences always make for better tours as all the boys stick together and you have a great time. The kitchen in the hotel was condemned so we had to eat in a restaurant up the road every day. We won the tour relatively convincingly yet bizarrely enough it was the fast bowlers that cleaned up with the wickets."

Gareth took 1-43 in the first innings of his Test debut before taking 1-65 in the second, as England won by seven wickets. Gareth also played in the third ODI between the two sides, taking figures of 1-35 as England won by seven wickets as he started to establish himself in the squad.

The second part of that 2003/04 Winter tour saw England travel to the hot and humid conditions of Sri Lanka, where Gareth made three further Test appearances. "They had a wonderful team and it was a tough tour. We managed to snuff them out up until the last Test match in Colombo when we were badly beaten."

For Gareth it was a mixed tour. "In the first game in Galle, things went pretty well for me. I got a few wickets and batted OK. The pitch spun a bit and I felt good. We then went to Dambulla and the pitch couldn't have been flatter and I got whacked everywhere. At Colombo I had a few lbw shouts, there were dropped catches and overall, I felt the tour was a case of what could have been. Maybe it just wasn't to be. It was an interesting and big learning curve. They were an emerging and talented team, especially on flat pitches. Murali was the only spinner to get anything out of those pitches."

I asked Gareth what he was able to learn from Murali on that trip that could he take into his own game. "Murali was the best finger spinner ever. You were able to take tiny bits but there was no way I was ever going to be able to replicate how he spun the ball. However, it was a from a game management perspective that I learnt the most. But the funny thing is it probably wasn't at the time that I appreciated what I learnt, but more a few years down the line."

In one day cricket Gareth was also part of what was, until recently, arguably the best England limited overs squad since the Graham Gooch squad of the early 90s. Michael's Vaughan's men reached the final of the 2004 Champions Trophy and Gareth was a valued member of the squad.

"We got to the final against the West Indies and had them six down for maybe 120, chasing our 200. Harmy had someone caught down the legside but it wasn't given and they ended up winning the game. We were cruising. I remember sitting up on the balcony thinking we had this in the bag but momentum shifted to them after that decision. English one day cricket was starting to evolve back then. We had Trescothick, Flintoff, Harmy and Collingwood, who was the then modern day one day cricketer. We had some good one-day talent kicking about."

Was it therefore disappointing that the one-day side couldn't push on? "If we had won, that side could have kicked on. Like anything you never really know, but it would certainly have changed the perception of English cricket for that period. Test cricket was always the most important format then, and white ball cricket always took a back seat; that only really changed last year. Winning that Champions Trophy could have changed everything."

In 2004 Gareth played his part in history as he was a member of the side that were on the end of Brian Lara's world record score of 400! "I had the tour of my life on that West Indies tour! I played a couple of warm up games and got a few wickets but we were playing good cricket as a team so I knew I wasn't really going to play so I got to see what the Caribbean had to offer - I had a great time! We were 3-0 up in the Test series and about 10 days out from that Antigua Test we heard it was going to be as flat as anything - there was no way they were going to allow a whitewash - and you could see a few boys getting a bit tetchy that it's going to be a flat one. Then Gilo did his calf and filthy off spinner Gareth gets a game! The rest is history. Lara got his 400 and there is definitely little consolation that you are part of history when you're the wrong side of it. Maybe in a few years when I retire I might feel differently. That said it was quite incredible how he went about it. He definitely isolated bowlers he knew he could take down. He smacked them and bowled beautifully well."

During that period England were beginning to peak as a side, and in 2005 reached undoubtedly its loftiest height, the famous 2005 Ashes win. I asked Gareth how good that side was. "Very good. I played against Bangladesh just before that 2005 series and was involved in the one-day stuff in 2005; you could see we were reaching our peak as an England team and Australia had probably already peaked. They were still probably man for man better than us but Vaughan's team had that hunger and desire. Yes you have the rub of the green from time to time but we'd just beaten the West indies 4-0 then gone to South Africa and won so we'd just beaten two phenomenal teams leading into that series and it's credit to Michael Vaughan how well he was able to marshal people into shape both physically and mentality; and to the players for buying into it."

With Ashley Giles the first-choice spinner in the side, how frustrating was it not to get the regular run of games as a spinner in the team. "I think at the time you don't fully realise it because you're living in the moment; if you're not picked, you're just doing whatever is needed to support the guys that are playing and that will never change. I believe that's the right way forward for any player but I do think if you're in and out of the side, because you play when someone is injured, it can be quite difficult because you're not setting your mind up for it. Graeme Hick once said that if you're always thinking 'if I don't get a hundred this game then I'm going to be left out of the next game', and it's not a great place to be. Barring that tour to Sri Lanka where I was very lucky, they stood with me - where if I'm honest they probably shouldn't have done – I never got a run of games. To get a run of games and have a crack at it is a big thing. I can't complain though, I'm not bitter it's just maybe a reason as to why I didn't play as well. The other reason, maybe, was that I just wasn't good enough which I'm also quite comfortable with."

Despite consistent seasons in county cricket, Gareth did not play Test cricket again until this Winter's tour to Bangladesh. The success of Graeme Swann was one obvious factor, but you still feel that Gareth was extremely unfortunate not to have picked up more international caps.

Back in county cricket though, Gareth made a return to the Oval in 2009. "When I left Surrey, it was never meant to be a long-term thing. I left the club on very good terms and they'd always said to go away, prove yourself and come back. When I originally left Surrey they had offered me a very good deal to stay, but it's never been about money for me, I just wanted to play. When Surrey came back in for me, I think I had reached a point where I felt it was the end of the road for me at Worcester. My wife was living in London; we were talking about starting a family and distance was becoming an issue. Tom Moody had moved on so I sat down with Vikram, who was vice captain, and I just said that for me, my sanity, to become the best I could be, I needed to move on. I will forever be grateful to Worcester for allowing me to do so. When I look back, it was 100 percent the right decision for me personally. There were probably some people at Worcester that didn't like it but it's my career and sometimes I had to decide for me. And you know what? Long term it was probably the right decision for them as it allowed Moeen to develop and play more cricket. And England are now reaping the rewards of that."

In 2011, Gareth played an important role part in bringing the CB40 trophy to south London, taking 13 wickets at 23.15. However, the next two years were two of the toughest of Gareth's life. Gareth assumed the captaincy of Surrey when Rory Hamilton Brown took time away from the role following the tragic death of promising batsman Tom Maynard. Gareth led a shell-shocked dressing room with considerable dignity and helped them avoid relegation in 2012.

"I can't really put it into words how difficult a time that was. People have said some very nice things about me, but it wasn't about me. It was about a group of people getting through an horrific time. That was how we went about it; it was about caring about one another. Cricket was very much secondary during that period. I've never seen tears in a changing room on such a consistent level and half of those tears were mine. It was horrific and it was because of what a wonderful guy Tom was and what a huge part of our group he was that we could carry on. There was certainly nothing ground breaking from me. We were just a bunch of fellas going out on to a cricket field in one way to celebrate a life but in another to get some peace for a few hours in a day. We told players that the outcome of games was totally irrelevant. We stayed up that year largely thanks to Kevin Pietersen. KP didn't take any credit for that but he was very good around a group of young players at a time when he was dealing with his own issues. I felt it was the year after that it hit us harder. But slowly but surely, we found our feet and I now feel the club is moving forward in a very good direction."

The year after Tom's death, Surrey were relegated to Division Two, but it speaks volumes for Gareth and his leadership that the team bounced back from that relegation with promotion back to Division One and back to back appearances in the final of Royal London One-Day Cup. The team is now full of promising youngsters and Gareth is excited about what the 2017 season could bring for his young troops.

"Our squad is in a wonderful place. The Curran brothers speak for themselves. Tom, the slightly older one of the two is a bit more of a battle-hardened pro like his father who gets stuck in. Sam is a bit more naturally gifted; he swings the ball and gives it a good whack. Tom hits the pitch hard and grinds out an innings so they complement each other well. They are going to be the major backbone for our team for a long time to come. Rory Burns up top has now scored 1,000 runs in each of the last four seasons and is very much the unsung hero of the group. Zaffer is developing brilliantly and Foaksey is a wonderfully gifted young keeper. It's wrong to be naming people, but I feel we have a wonderful squad: we have a few spinners, we've swing bowlers, some pace and we've got batters like Jason Roy who can smack the ball out of the ground and batters who can manipulate the field and bat for a long time."

I closed our conversation with Gareth by asking him his thoughts on how good this England side are, having spent the recent Winter months with them. "I've been watching from a far for a number of years and when the likes of Swanny and Matty P retired you feared for what could happen, but you look at how Jonny Bairstow has come in and the records he's broken; you look at how Cooky keeps going and going; Moeen is getting better by the day with both bat and ball – you can see his confidence is growing; Rash has been brilliant this Winter; Chris Woakes has had a brilliant year and then there's Joe Root and Ben Stokes, what can you say about those two. It really is a brilliant set of lads. There's no egos and as a group they are moving in a wonderful direction."

And the final question was who he named as the biggest influence on his career… "My Dad, 100 percent – in cricket and in life generally." We have a lot to thank his Dad for. Gareth may not have had the international recognition that many believe his career warranted, but so many people in English cricket are indebted to him as a player, a teammate and a captain.

28

NEIL CARTER
FORMER WARWICKSHIRE ALL-ROUNDER

Former Warwickshire all-rounder and PCA cricketer of the year in 2010, Neil Carter, was a big hitting batsman, a wicket-taking bowler and a cricketer who made his international debut after he'd announced his retirement from first-class cricket!

"It's great being the only person in the history of cricket to have retired from first class cricket and then made my international debut!" joked Neil. But jokes aside, Neil's call up for Scotland was the icing on the cake of a county career that brought championship success and a host of honours in the limited overs game. But we'll come on to all of that later.

Neil was born and grew up in South Africa (to a Scottish mother) and was a late developer in cricketing terms. "I got into cricket quite late. Allan Donald, Stephen Jeffries and Peter Kirsten were big heroes of mine. I used to get my Dad to buy me a Gunn and Moore cricket bat, because that's what Peter Kirsten batted with! The school I went to made it compulsory that you had to play lots of sports. So, as well as cricket I played tennis, squash, rugby, soccer, hockey, pretty much all sports! I never had any major representative honours in cricket growing up – I did for other sports, but not cricket!"

Yet, his love was cricket and thanks to his British passport he had a pathway to the UK. "I came over to the UK to play some club cricket in my gap year, which was great for my development, but when I returned I hurt my knee quite badly in a water skiing accident and so I was in rehab for a couple of years."

Despite this set-back when Neil started bowling again, his speed had increased and was asked to go for a net with the Boland state side and soon after that his cricket career was underway!

Neil's potential with both bat and ball was evident to all, and he soon became seen as a genuine all-rounder, so much so that it wasn't long before he was batting high up the order. "I loved giving it a bit of a whack at the top. People talk about the 'pinch hitter' today, but I was doing it for many years!"

Neil's early success for Boland whetted the appetite for a return to the UK in search of a professional county contract. "We were on 12-month contracts back in South Africa and they weren't worth very much, so people were always keen to try and get a club deal in the UK. I managed to get a 2-year deal playing club cricket and then the rules changed that if you had been born outside of the UK and had a British passport you could play county cricket as a local player. I, KP and Greg Smith were the first three who signed. KP and Greg went to Clive Rice at Nottinghamshire and I went to Warwickshire."

I asked Neil, how the Warwickshire move came about. "Former Warwickshire batsman Andy Moles was a coach of Free State, which is now known as the Knights in Bloemfontein. Andy said he had a good mate at Derbyshire, Tim Munton, who could sort me out a deal, but then a week later Warwickshire coach Bob Woolmer, who had been back home in Cape Town, phoned Andy out of the blue and mentioned they were looking at bowlers. Andy said you have one on your doorstep out here in Cape Town. Bob then phoned me as I was driving home from a club game. He mentioned he'd spoken to Andy and would like to offer me a contract and that he'd bring it to the game on Friday. It was all that quick!"

It was the start of a wonderful 12-year career at Edgbaston. Two county championships, the Clydesdale Bank 40 over league title, the Benson & Hedges Cup, and numerous other Lord's finals. What were Neil's personal highlights?

"So many! Winning the Benson & Hedges Cup in 2002 was a big highlight. I didn't play in the quarter-finals against Sussex. But, in the semi-finals, we were drawn against Lancashire at Old Trafford. They had the likes of Flintoff and Chappell in their ranks so were a strong outfit. We bowled well and then began chasing the total down. We ended up needing three runs off the last ball, when I came in at number 11 after Dougie Brown was run out by Flintoff on the boundary. Fine Leg was up on the 45, Glen Chappell bowled, and I paddle swept him over the fielder for four to win the game. That got us through to a Lord's final against Essex, which was massive for me as it was my visit to Lord's. What an amazing atmosphere!. Essex were a strong side and I remember it was start of the free hits for a no ball. Shaun Pollock bowled a no ball and Graham Napier hit him on to the roof of the grandstand with one free hit! Two young batsmen, Ian Bell and Jim Troughton, knocked off the runs to win us the game. I remember nothing about the celebrations that night though!"

That Benson & Hedges success was followed by the County Championship in 2004, a success under the captaincy of another of our interviewees, Nick Knight. "We won the championship with a week to go, which was a nice feeling not to have the pressure in the last game. Our closest opposition didn't get the number of batting points they needed. We weren't playing so I found out we won from watching Sky Sports at home!"

Warwickshire were back at Lord's a year later, in the golden Summer of 2005, but this time it wasn't to have a successful ending for the Bears. "I was pissed off after that game! When we bowled, they were allowed to change the ball; back in those days you only had the one ball. They were allowed to change it because apparently it had gone soft and brown. We then bowled with a harder ball, which was so much easier to hit. When we went out to bat, we got off to a good start. I opened the batting and hit Chris Tremlett for a massive six on to the clock tower there. Nick Knight got a hundred but towards the end he couldn't hit the ball off the square, because it got so soft. We ended up 20 runs short. If they wouldn't have been allowed to change the ball and had to bat with a soft ball, I'm convinced we'd have won that game. Afterwards, I kept our ball as I'd taken five wickets with it, and I asked if I could see the other ball as I wanted to compare it against the ball we batted with, but they wouldn't give it to me."

One amusing aspect of that final though, was Neil's dismissal. Not only was he run out; in trying to make his ground he slid in and removed all three stumps! "It wasn't an ideal way to go!"

Neil's final season at Warwickshire saw them again lift the county championship and it could so nearly have been a double. "We had another Lord's final, and we needed five runs to win from two balls. I hit a four which put the scores level, but because we'd lost more wickets, we had to win the game. So, with one run needed, I missed the ball and we lost. Gutted. There was a lot said at the time, and it would have been a great way to go out, but that's cricket."

Neil scored nearly 7,500 runs in first class, List A and T20 cricket, which combined with 648 wickets made him one of the most talented all-rounders on the county circuit.

Individual recognition came in 2010 when Neil was named as the PCA Cricketer of the Year. "That was a very proud moment as the award is voted for by your fellow players. At the time I think, across the history of the award, I was the only player to have won the award who had never played international cricket for a Test playing nation."

I asked Neil, what made that season so special? "To be honest I was just nice and fit and felt good charging in. I managed to get the ball swinging consistently and I scored a lot of runs. I think I was the second or third top run scorer that year for Warwickshire. Everything just gelled nicely. It helped I opened the batting by then in limited overs cricket as you do get noticed more, especially when you're in form. When you're on that wave you have to ride it and be confident and back your own ability."

And what made Warwickshire such a special club to play at for all those years? "Players make the environment. And we had a strong environment. There were no selfish guys and we had a good blend of experience and youth. We were very fortunate to have youngsters come through like Ian Bell, Jim Troughton and Jonathan Trott. We also had some phenomenal coaches, like Bob Woolmer. Bob was just a great man. Nothing was ever too much for him. If you had a bad day, he'd still make you feel good and perform better next up. He brought the best out of his players. The one year we got relegated, we had Mark Greatbatch as coach, but his man-management wasn't good, and the players hated it. Those same players had done well the year before, but that year everyone had a shocker. Having a strong environment is so important."

In 2008 the loyal Bear switched allegiance for two weeks when he was invited by Middlesex to play for them in the now infamous Stanford Series. The now disgraced businessman Allen

Stanford invited the domestic T20 champions from England and the West Indies to play warm up games against England and Stanford's own Xl in their own Champions Cup match. "Dirk Nannes wasn't available for the tournament and Toby Radford phoned me and asked if I would be interested in going over to play for Middlesex. I came home from South Africa and flew out with Tyrone Henderson to the Caribbean for two weeks! I wasn't going to say no. If I'm honest it was pretty much a two-week holiday! There wasn't much practice as they only had one pitch. We had a great time at Jolly Beach harbour, lots of swimming and jet skiing. It was all very much about the big game and we were just the curtain-raiser. I knew a lot of the Middlesex boys from playing against them. We played the warm up games against England and the Stanford Xl and then our match against Trinidad and Tobago. I thought we might win but we dropped a few catches. It's strange looking back at everything now. You wouldn't have suspected anything at the time. But little did we know. Stanford was quite an intimidating figure, 6ft 8 tall and came across as quite arrogant. You only had to look at the stuff with Matt Prior's wife. It was an experience that was great to be involved in, what with all of the media coverage at the time but, looking back, you feel so sorry for the people out there."

Neil retired from first class cricket in 2012, but that wasn't to be the end of his career and he nearly had the swansong of all swansongs! "It wasn't a difficult decision for me to retire from first class cricket, I was 38 and coming to the end. A few months earlier, the rules had changed regarding international qualification and it meant that if one your parents were born in a country, so for me Scotland, I could qualify with an ICC exceptional circumstances letter. And so, my international career with Scotland began. It was good fun. My first trip was to Dubai to play against Afghanistan in T20's then a trip to Edinburgh to make my ODI debut vs Pakistan. My last trip was to Dubai for the T20 World Cup qualifiers.'"

Sadly, Neil and his Scotland side didn't make it because of a net run rate mix-up.

"We played Denmark who were the lowest ranked side left in our qualifying pool in our final game. A win by a big margin would give us two bites of the cherry to then qualify. We'd play Hong Kong and even if we lost that, we'd then be able to qualify by then playing Papua New Guinea. Anyway, we got sold down the river in that Denmark game as we were given the wrong net run rate. Because Nepal who were above us had already played, we knew we had to score over 200 to win and keep them below what we assumed would be 130. We scored 203 and at the interval our manager couldn't get hold of an official to tell us what we needed to restrict them to. So, I opened the bowling not knowing. After six overs, we had them 18/1 and I came off, pretending to change my shirt as it was hot, but it was to find out if we knew the score yet that we had to restrict them to. They still didn't know. It came down to them needing 20 odd off of three overs and eventually eight or 9 off the last over. Word got around that they needed 125 so we brought players up to defend and they hit the ball over top of the field and ended up on 131. When we went off there was a voice message on our manager's phone apologising and saying that the target to restrict them to was actually 130 not 125. They ended up on 131. If we'd known it wasn't 125, we would have left the field back and would have kept them to 127 or 128. It was soul destroying knowing that one run had cost us a chance of playing at the World Cup. We ended up having to play Holland who were the second ranked team and they beat us. After that, the coach resigned. He'd always been great to me, allowed me to still live in South Africa, travel back when I needed to, miss the odd game because of work. A new coach came in and he just ignored me, I never heard from him and that was it; the end of my career. Such a shame as I really wanted a swansong at the 50 over World Cup in Australia early in 2015 in which Scotland qualified for."

I asked Neil that after this taste of international cricket, were there any regrets about not playing international cricket for South Africa or England earlier in his career. "I never really played too much cricket in South Africa, I thought I had a good chance of playing in the Hong Kong sixes. This was always a big tournament in those days. England were never going to play their current internationals, but as one of the most consistent all-rounders in county cricket in that period, I thought I might have had a look-in there"

Neil played with and against a host of talented players throughout his career, but which players were the best he came up against? "In the dressing room at Warwickshire we always talked "the Warwickshire Xl" players from other counties who all did well against us. Graeme Hick at Worcester and Mark Ramprakash at Surrey were certainly in that side. They pretty much dominated against us for many years. I remember my first five wicket haul for Warwickshire, I bounced Hick out… he was on a double hundred! We dropped a sitter off Ramprakash early on one game, and obviously he went on to make a hundred!"

And what about the best captain? "Nick Knight was good, I really enjoyed playing under Jim Troughton, who's now first team coach. He understood his players. Michael Powell was good. They were three very good captains."

Cricket has changed a lot in the last few years with a lot of emphasis on the T20 game and people questioning the longer formats. I asked Neil for his views. "Test cricket is still the pinnacle for sure in England, Australia and South Africa. It's just the world is evolving and is such a busy place. People don't have the time necessary to watch a whole day or take time off work to watch a whole day's cricket. As such, crowds are dwindling everywhere pretty much bar England, or Australia over the holiday season and in Cape Town, which tends to always get full houses days 1-4. There's just so much technology around that people don't have to get down to the ground now. Also, there is a lot more cricket played with added T20s and one-dayers. People have more options. So, it's not necessarily they don't like Test cricket, it just they can't watch everything." Some valid points.

And what about cricket in South Africa. With the recent retirements of Morkel and De Villiers, what's the state of cricket in South Africa? "It's interesting times. I suspect Amla and Du Plessis might follow after the next World Cup and there just isn't the talent coming through. Our domestic first-class competition isn't strong. The international players rarely play in it, which is probably similar in most countries, but we have issues with Kolpak players and even our domestic T20 competition only gets one or two thousand people. In two years' time there will no longer be Steyn, Philander, Amla or Du Plessis so a lot will ride on De Kock, Rabada, Aiden Markram and Ngidi. They will have a lot of responsibility on their shoulders. It will be interesting times."

It certainly will, and I think we all hope for the health of the international game, that South African cricket remains strong.

Neil's continued love of the game sees him working as the cricket professional at the Bishop's College in Cape Town. "I love it. We get a lot of touring sides come to play us and play loads of day/night games as we very fortunate to have floodlights. Because of our good indoor facilities, the Cape Cobras as well as Dale and Morne often train here. I'm also assistant coach for the Western Province U/19 team and do a little bit of work with the bowlers at the Cape Cobras, so it's great still being involved in the game."

And so, it should be. Neil brought a lot to the county game and I know for sure that current Warwickshire side would love to have him back in the ranks as they push for promotion back to the top flight.

THOSE WERE THE DAYS…

358

29

CHARLES DAGNALL
TEST MATCH SPECIAL PRESENTER

There's nothing better on a Summer's day than sitting back, beer in hand, listening to the BBC Test Match Special team talk you through a day's play. They are a British institution. From Brian Johnston, Christopher Martin-Jenkins and John Arlott to the current legends, Jonathan Agnew and Henry Blofeld. It wouldn't be a British Summer without Test Match Special. And I was fortunate to chat to one of the recent additions to the team, Charles Dagnall, or 'Daggers' as he is affectionately known.

I've loved doing all of the interviews in this book, but I must admit this was up there as one of my favourites and it's easy to see why the programme is so special, to so many people.

"Our job on the radio is to inform and entertain," said Daggers. "I like to think if we're laughing on air, then everyone else is."

Daggers joined the TMS team back in 2012, a team which now includes (in addition to Aggers and Blowers) the likes of Vic

Marks, Michael Vaughan, Phil Tufnell, Geoffrey Boycott, Alison Mitchell, Graeme Swann, Ed Smith, Ebony Rainford-Brent - to name just a few.

"You are part of a select club at TMS and that will never be lost on me. There is not a moment when I come off commentary and don't think about the legends who have been before me."

As this was me interviewing someone from the media, I thought it was only right to try and get an 'exclusive' of some sorts. I think I succeeded... The TMS team love their cakes, but is a shift happening? I asked Daggers on the kind of cake he would like us supporters to send in. His response was unexpected... "You can never fail with a lemon drizzle. But we need savoury snacks; pork pies, sausage rolls, cooked meats. Things people can pick at."

There you go, you read it here first, a world exclusive. The cake is dead. Long live the savoury snack. Of course, I'm not sure if Daggers' co-presenters would agree.

Now, before we probe Daggers about his life on TMS it would be remiss not to look back at his life as a county cricketer.

Born in Bury, Daggers was a right-arm fast-medium bowler. As a child, he played all sports but cricket was always his first love. I thought it was ironic that all three of his boyhood heroes went on to enjoy successful media careers once their playing days were over. An omen perhaps? "As a child I loved watching Michael Holding, David Gower and Ian Botham. Holding and Gower were poetic, but Botham was always the one I wanted to be like. He was sheer entertainment. I even got the Duncan Fearnley Attack with Ian Botham's name on it as one of my first bats!"

Daggers' cricketing career began in the much-respected Lancashire leagues. "I played a lot of league cricket as a junior and it was when playing in the leagues that I got selected to play for Cumberland in the Minor Counties. I loved it. It was brilliant cricket; it was always a great atmosphere and we played some really, really, good cricket. It was great to learn from some old pros like Ashley Metcalfe and Marcus Sharpe and to play against the likes of Wayne Larkins and Derek Randall."

But first-class County cricket was his dream. Having played Lancashire schoolboy representative cricket the red rose was firmly engrained in Daggers, but sadly, despite all his successes as a junior; he was never able to fulfil the Lancashire dream. "I was one of the few, if not the only one who didn't get a Lancashire contract having won the under-19 player of the year award. It was hugely disappointing as I was the red rose through and through. It was always my dream to play at Old Trafford."

Despite the Lancashire snub, Daggers was intent on not letting his goal of becoming a county cricketer die. The young seamer wrote letters to all the first-class counties asking for a trial. "I think I still hold the record for the most trials before getting a contract. I played second XI games for 13 counties!"

At the 13th attempt, he was finally snapped up, by Warwickshire. "I loved my time at Warwickshire. I played a trial game against Essex. It was always quite daunting as a trialist walking into a second team dressing room. You weren't always made to feel welcome. I got that, as a lot of the players in the second eleven are trying to save their jobs and don't want to lose their position to a trialist. But at Warwickshire it was different. Phil Neale was the head coach at the time and wanted to have a look at youth, so a lot of the regular first team players were playing in the 2's for a short period. So, I walked into the dressing room for a trial game and sat there were Gladstone Small, Tim Munton, Andy Moles, Dominic Ostler, Keith Piper and Trevor Penney; guys who had been there, seen it, done it; they didn't feel threatened by a trialist. And Moles was captain and I think he liked the fact that I was confident enough to ask for my own field placings. I remember one ball, where Moler wanted the short leg to come out; I said I think I could get this batsman out with that fielder so could we keep him in there. Moler agreed and the very next ball I had the batsman caught at short leg! I think that helped my cause!"

It certainly did, as Daggers was offered a full-time contract with the Bears. And in those early years how did he find the step up? "Bizarrely, it was and wasn't a big step up. I had been playing with and against some top league cricketers, who had recently retired from first-class cricket, so the quality in the second eleven cricket wasn't that too dissimilar. I think most of the minor counties at that time would have given second eleven teams a great game, if not beaten them. The main difference was the step up in fitness and the time spent practising."

In Daggers' league days, any kind of practice was impossible, it was just bowling - day in, day out. "I remember a seven-week stint when I played league cricket for Great Harwood in Blackburn. As a professional they pretty much expected you to bowl at one end all the way through and then bat 3. I was bowling 25 overs from one end on a Saturday and then doing similar on a Sunday. I would then play minor counties four-day cricket from Tuesday through to Friday and then at that stage of the season second eleven bowlers would get called up into the first eleven so I'd be the workhorse in the seconds and all in I'd end up bowling over 100 overs a week. The thing is I loved it and in that seven-week stint, I must have bowled 600 or 700 overs. I always felt because of that I was 'bowling' fit, but whether I was truly 'fit, fit' I don't know as Saturday nights you'd have 'some' pints and you'd rock up the next morning and get out bowling. It's very different now for the youngsters as they get taken care of. But I was 18/19 and I loved it. It's probably why I've now got a body of an 80-year-old! I never had many miles an hour to lose, but in my later years that probably cost me a few miles and the reason why I was never electric quick. I'd do it all again though!"

During his time with the Bears, Daggers opened the bowling with arguably one of the fastest bowlers of all time, the great Allan Donald. "AD was a great hero of mine. I remember watching him in a NatWest Trophy game against Somerset on BBC TV; he came on to bowl against a fellow South African, Jimmy Cook, who was opening the batting for Somerset. AD bowled a couple of deliveries and Cook didn't even get out of his stance. They hit him on the thigh pad and in the ribs. When I got to open the bowling with him it was amazing and it gave me a little insight into what Test cricket was like."

Daggers made his championship debut for Warwickshire away at the home of cricket. "I remember on my debut we had white lightening coming in from one end and let's just say persistent drizzle, me, coming in from the other! Justin Langer was opening the batting for Middlesex alongside Mike Roseberry. Although we never spoke about it, I think there was an underlying agreement between me and Roseberry, where he didn't fancy facing AD and I didn't fancy bowling to Justin Langer. I think there were an unwritten rule that Mike would only hit me for two or four, which I was quite happy with!!"

I asked Daggers of some of his most memorable games for the Bears. "Two that spring to mind would be taking my first ever five wicket haul (6 wickets in total) against Derbyshire which got us promoted to Division One and the other was playing in AD's last game for Warwickshire, in a one-day game against Derbyshire at Edgbaston; I actually took four wickets and spoilt the party somewhat, but just being near the bloke was special."

With such a high regard for Warwickshire, what prompted Daggers to make the move to nearby Leicestershire? "It was a really tough decision to leave Warwickshire. I was in the middle of a two-year contract; I'd just taken a 6-for to get us promoted and I was a mainstay of our one-day side. But Leicestershire came in and said they'd like to talk to me. I mulled it over for a quite a while, there was a small salary boost but nothing major, but I was in and out of the county championship side at Warwickshire. My games in the championship typically came at the end of the season when the first-choice bowlers had picked up injuries and I then came in. I wanted to play 16 county championship games; I wanted to know if I was good enough. It wasn't a problem if I was rubbish, but I wanted to know. I wanted to be more than a one-day cricketer. Leicestershire came in and although they couldn't guarantee me games, they said I'd have a lot more opportunities. I asked Bob Woolmer, Dennis Amiss and others for their thoughts and advice. They said they had no problems if I wanted to go. I then spoke to James Whitaker, the then Leicestershire Chief Executive and he got a contract together. Then on the day I was due to sign the contract Dennis Amiss rang me and asked if I could come into the office. Dennis said he didn't want me to go and that I had a lot to offer and there would be opportunities for me at Warwickshire, if I stayed. But I couldn't let Leicestershire down. I felt awful, but everyone at Warwickshire had said they had no problems with me going. Some people thought I got tanked by Warwickshire but that was never the case. Dennis to be fair to him admitted he did say he was happy for me to leave but he was just disappointed that I was going. I like to think I did it the right way. I just wanted to know if I was good enough."

It was a move that became blighted by injuries, leading eventually to a shin injury that was to end his career, at the age of just 28.

"Leicestershire was very different to Warwickshire. There were a lot of politics involved during my time at the club. I'm sure there were politics at Warwickshire, but they never filtered down to the players. At Warwickshire, we had much bigger backroom and office staff, whereas at Leicestershire, Chief Executives came and went, and there was just a revolving door of change at the club. I personally didn't get off to the best of starts; I got injured in my first year and had to have a hip operation. I then didn't play well at all in my second year. Philip DeFreitas, sat me down and asked me what I wanted to be, a quick bowler or a swing bowler as he (and I) just didn't know. I was playing OK but I wasn't doing anything fantastic. I was at a crossroads. Daffy grabbed me by the scruff of my neck and just said do I want to make a success of my career or not. I became twice the bowler after that conversation. In 2004 I felt good. I was charging in and I was getting more wickets caught behind; I was beating the bat at will. I felt I'd finally sussed it. We won the T20 competition which was amazing. I remember the games at Grace Road were bursting, with over 7,000 people in the ground and I found that I liked performing in front of big crowds. At 26 I felt I could be a good county cricketer."

Sadly, things went downhill in 2005, when a shin injury struck, which led to his sad retirement. "In 2005, I felt really fit. After the success of 2004, I trained my nuts off in the Winter so that I could be the best I could be in 2005. We had a new captain in H.D. Akerman. He was a brilliant captain. One day, I stupidly bowled for two hours straight in the indoor nets at Leicestershire; but I was so keen to bowl. My shins started hurting. I'd never had issues with them before. We went on a pre-season tour to India and Pakistan and I was literally screaming in pain throughout; I'd never had pain like it. I started the season, but they never got right. I tried everything from ice to rest. Nothing worked. So, for the first part of the season I was just like a vicar – coming out every Sunday to play Sunday League cricket! I would play those games, bowl well, but then wouldn't be able to walk on Monday, Tuesday and Wednesday; I would pop some pills on a Thursday; get taped up on a Friday; bowl a couple of overs on a Saturday in practice; play the game on Sunday. I did that routine for about six weeks but realised I couldn't go on like that. I had a big operation, bizarrely on my birthday in 2005, but understandably I got released by

Leicestershire; I was told I could come back if I got over the injury. Sussex were also keen to sign me if I got fit. I tried so hard to get over it, but at the turn of the year in 2006 I was still struggling massively. So, I told Leicestershire and Sussex don't go with me I'm jacking. I didn't want to take their money. I could easily have signed a contract and been injured for the entire year; that didn't fit well with me - I couldn't take people's money and not play."

And that was the end of Daggers' playing career at the age of 28.

I asked Daggers if he had regrets. "As I look back, I do wonder if I had done it too soon, but then I remember in 06 I played a little bit of league cricket and struggled so honestly, I have no regrets."

One thing that softened the blow of retirement was the opportunity to pursue a career in radio.

"I was already working in local radio in the off season so I was lucky that I had something to go straight into."

A friendship with BBC presenter (and Warwickshire supporter) Nick Owen gave Daggers his first taste of radio. "Nick used to come down and watch Warwickshire and then go into BBC Pebble Mill studios and one day he invited me along to have a look around, just for interest's sake. I wondered in and watched him do a programme for Midlands Today, but he then showed me around the radio studio and I got buzz for it. You saw all these things happening live: stories breaking, football commentary was going on – it was great. I loved things that were live."

Daggers' first break on radio came during his time at Leicestershire. "When I signed for Leicestershire, I got interviewed by the local radio station, as they did with any new player; they asked me what my other interests were outside of cricket and I said that one day I wanted to get into radio. Within a week they had me on with my own weekly cricket show."

John Shaw, a radio presenter, who delivered reports on Leicestershire's games became Daggers' mentor. "John saw something in me and my keenness for radio so I went and trained and shadowed him when he was doing sports reports at 6am in the morning. John trained me in how to read scripts, write cues, and how to use my voice etc. I remember a game we had at Southend; rain had stopped play so he printed out some sports scripts and we were sat in my Vauxhall Vectra reading through them as the lads were in the dressing rooms playing cards."

John has sadly since passed away, but to this day, not a single day passes without Daggers thinking of his mentor. "There's not once piece of radio that I do without John Shaw in my head; I always ask myself what he would have thought. He passed away way too soon. After every stint, he would always tell me what was good, what I could improve upon, what needs work etc. He was a great man."

So, was Test Match Special always his goal?

"Having always listened to TMS it was something deep down that I always wanted to do, but if I'm honest I never thought about it until I retired. At first, I just wanted to learn radio. My experience at Radio Leicester was fantastic, because as well as my cricket show I also did a lot of non-cricket stuff. I interviewed party leaders at election time and during the expenses scandal. I also reported on other sports such as rugby and football; I was presenting programmes on Leicester Tigers and Leicester City. I was out of my comfort zone but it was a great experience. Eventually I looked at TMS and they seemed to like what I was doing. I got invited to present some domestic T20 stuff, again they liked what I did there and eventually I got the nod to do a couple of one day internationals against the West

Indies in 2012."

His first international game, at the Rose Bowl, had him teamed up on the commentary roster with some of the greats of radio and cricket. "For my debut game there was me, Jonathan Agnew and Tony Cozier – I couldn't have been up with two more distinctive voices in cricket history. I thought to myself this is not good! Who are the summarisers? Phil Tufnell – that was good, I knew him; Michael Vaughan - good; Viv Richards – oh my God! It was obvious Viv did not have a clue who I was and the fact I played and stuff. He was told by the producers I'd played County cricket and I'll never forget this Viv phrase… there was a bit of rain and the players stayed on. Viv said, 'this might just grease up and give the bowlers a bit more to play with' and then turned to me and said, 'you would know, you were quick'. I just thought to myself, you never did see me play! It was a daunting first experience, but a genuine thrill."

Two years later and Daggers was commentating on his first Test match for TMS, in the 2014 home series against India, again at the Rose Bowl. "I had to catch my breath before I walked into the Rose Bowl on that first morning because the ghosts of TMS past just hit me. This was a different feeling to my previous commentating. Jonathan Agnew and Michael Vaughan helped me; Vaughany more than anyone. He really helped me feel at ease."

Another person Daggers was forever grateful to, for his words of encouragement, was the great 'Blowers'. "On the day before that first Test match, I was doing a function for Dean Headley, when I received a phone call from a number that I didn't recognise. It was Blowers. 'Daggers, my old dear. Blowers here. I understand you're making your debut tomorrow; all I want to say is good luck old thing. Be yourself and you'll be brilliant'. I thought to myself, what an utter legend. He didn't have to call me but showed just what kind of bloke he is."

And it's obvious the high regard in which Daggers holds the great man. "Whenever I hear Blowers on the radio, I know it's the Summer. His vocabulary is wonderful; he's just a broadcasting legend. You could give him a bowl of fruit to describe and he would do it in a way that nobody else could! And it's very similar with Jonathan."

I asked Daggers if he ever feels the pressure. "Commentating on Test cricket is much tougher than ODI's in that it really tests you as a commentator. When things are slow or ponderous in play, you must entertain people and keep it interesting. You'll never achieve commentary perfection, but you always continue to strive for it. There's always going to be some people who like the way that you commentate and some people who don't. You just hope that the people who have followed TMS for years and years like what you do."

And why is it people have always stayed in love with TMS, what gives it the magic? "I think it's the fact we try to entertain as well as inform and commentate on a game of cricket that's being played. If you're on air for seven hours a day for five successive days, people want more than just the cricket. They want to know about Aggers' BBQ's or what the Rio Olympics was like for him. 35 hours' straight cricket without that, would be difficult. On radio you're company for people. As John Shaw once said to me, when you're commentating on radio, you're speaking to someone who is home alone; you're their company. That's who you talk to. We'll never miss a ball in our commentary, but we will always try and entertain as well as inform."

One can only imagine the preparation that goes into a programme such as TMS, so I asked Daggers how he prepares for his commentary stints. "I always read lots of articles to get a sense of what people are thinking. It's not that I can't form my own opinion but I like to get a sense of what people are thinking about certain cricketers. I'm not a massive one for statistics. In the main I think these can be a bit boring. I don't care if someone averages 'x' in their last few Test matches, you can just speak on their recent form. I love knowing the geography of the ground, however. I do laps of the ground when I arrive to see what I can see, again because in the art of broadcasting you must be someone's eyes; if I have spotted something interesting, I might talk about it on air. I also like to talk to a few supporters to get a sense of what they are thinking. But honestly, I just like things to be organic. That way you never know where it's going to go and that's part of the fun of it. But everyone is different."

Having commentated in many countries throughout the world; it's Australia that is the country, outside of England, that Daggers has enjoyed commentating in the most. "Australia is something different. It's THE place to commentate. Each ground has its own distinct quality. I remember doing a tri-series before the last World Cup and I was the only English voice on an Australian broadcasting team – that was fun. I certainly had to fight the battles for England; what with all the grief they dish out when they are winning!"

And his favourite ground in England? "My favourite ground in the whole world is the Oval. I just adore the place. I enjoyed playing there and I love commentating there. It's more relaxed than Lord's and I just love the buzz of the place. You think of all the history that has happened at that ground – it hits you when you walk in. I will never tire of the Oval."

Since 2012, Daggers has been fortunate to commentate on many fantastic games, but which games have stood out more than most? "I recently commentated when England broke the ODI World record – that was a real thrill. The record will get beaten again sometime, but that previous record stood for a long time and to be at Trent Bridge and to get to call it, was special. Also, being at Eden Gardens for the World T20 final was fantastic. As a commentator when you get to call a player or team's milestones and must describe how it happens is truly special. I have been fortunate in 2016 to get to call a couple."

Throughout his time on TMS, Daggers has had the pleasure of interviewing some of the great names in cricket and it's an interview he did with Bumble (David Lloyd) that he cherishes more than any other. "Bumble had just brought his book out. Sky were good enough to let us interview him. It was a pre-recorded interview, but honestly, I could have spoken to him for hours. I read his book in two and a half days and just adored it. His humour and qualities as a human being are totally genuine. He does radio broadcasting on television. It was weird because, although I see him every day, I found it tough because it was like interviewing Michael Parkinson. In fact, I once did an interview with Michael Parkinson, at a Chance to Shine function and I genuinely s**t myself! There I was interviewing the King of interviews but he was a darling, just brilliant."

Other cricketers on his 'favourites' list are interviews he did with Brett Lee and Andrew Flintoff. "Both were absolute pleasures. But Bumble is the one that stood out."

Finally, I tried to get Daggers to open up on some of the biggest bloopers that have occurred in the TMS box. "There's been a couple of times where I've just lost it; someone will say something funny and you just have to laugh. Ebony and I have become like an old married couple. I adore Ebs and she's come out with some absolute pearlers. I remember setting her up and off she went! Michael and the cat are just a joy and Vic Marks has some dark humour, when his lips start to curl up you can't help but laugh. And you know what I like to think that if we're laughing, then everyone else is."

TMS really is a British institution. We are very lucky to have it.

Daggers and the team do a sterling job and there's a reason why the programme is loved by so many. It's truly magical and it will continue to be so for generations to come.

Daggers – it's been an absolute pleasure.

30

RICHARD HALSALL
BANGLADESH ASSISTANT COACH &
FORMER ENGLAND FIELDING COACH

One of the unsung heroes of England rise to number one in the 2000's was former fielding coach and now assistant coach of Bangladesh, Richard Halsall. I caught up with Richard in 2017 just days after their series with Australia, where the Tigers secured an excellent 1-1 result in the two Test match series.

"It was an excellent series for us. Our recent Test match wins over Australia and England have meant a huge amount to our playing group," remarked Richard. "The hope now is that these victories will give our Board more weight to try and develop the game in the country. Our players are crying out for opportunities to play more series. We need other countries to reciprocate offering us A team tours and academy tours."

Bangladesh are very much one of the improving sides of world cricket, especially on home soil. For many years, teams would head to Dhaka and Chittagong and series wins were a formality.

But recent Test match wins over the likes of England and Australia - and their performances in recent World Cup and Champions Trophy campaigns - have changed all of that.

"We definitely feel it's now 50:50 for us against anyone we play at home, especially against teams who have a perceived weakness against spin – we will back ourselves to win. Our challenge, however, is when we have a bad session, we have a really bad session. So, rather than lose two or three wickets, we'll lose five or 6. But we're getting more consistent. We have got three or four genuinely world class players now."

And credit to those players, because as Richard says, they've developed the hard way. "Those world-class players all came through the periods of getting heavily beaten day in, day out. But it hardened them and so our focus now is to make sure the young players coming into the side don't experience what the older lads went through and they'll step up quicker. We've got great spinners but we also have some talented quick bowlers coming through - they have just not had the cricket yet."

And the added positive for Richard, is the performance of the junior Bangladesh sides. Players are now progressing into the Test side with a winning mentality. "They have all got used to winning. When they lost in the semi-finals of the Under 19s World Cup, they were very upset because they are so used to winning. This squad beat South Africa away 5-0, they beat India 3-0 in India – the lads coming through are expecting to win. It's an exciting sign for us."

The hope now is the ICC can offer them the long-term schedules that the leading sides currently enjoy. "When I was with England, we knew who we'd be playing home and away, over a four-year schedule. As coaches we could plan. With Bangladesh, we know our next series, but right now we cannot say when we will next be playing West Indies, Sri Lanka etc and that's difficult for a coaching team and has a knock-on effect on our first-class game when we might want to offer players certain number of games for their club sides to get match ready. We don't know when we'll be playing who or when."

I asked Richard how much he's enjoying the role, especially given the reluctance of some to even travel to the country because of security concerns. "It's been fantastic. The passion for cricket in this country is truly humbling. You see people playing the game in every alley with balls made of rubber bands and bats made of any kind of wood kids can find; it's genuinely humbling."

And what attracted him to the role after leaving his post as England assistant coach, following the 2013/14 Ashes defeat down under. "I was sat in a coffee bar in St Johns Wood. I'd just been to Lord's as I was on gardening leave, they were trying to find another role for me within the set-up which was very kind of them at the time. Mushtaq Ahmed had asked me to go and work with Pakistan which was a genuinely exciting opportunity to work with him again and Waqar Younis. I've never had any kind of agent in my career; I just thought you applied for a job like everyone else normally does. But then I received a call while I was in this coffee bar from an agent who said there was a role with Bangladesh and would I be interested? I gave it a lot of thought, spoke to those close to me and did my research. Their coach, Chandika Hathurusingha was an outstanding coach, so I thought if I'm going to go on a 2- or 3-year journey into the unknown it sounded like he might be someone I could learn a lot from. I also looked at their schedule and they didn't seem to play as much cricket as Pakistan which suited me with a young family. So, for both personal and professional reasons it was the right choice."

We'll talk more about Bangladesh later but Richard has built a strong coaching reputation in the game over many years and I wanted to find out his journey that has taken him all the way to the heat of Dhaka.

"As a kid, I idolised Viv Richards and there was something about that West Indies side that I loved. I loved Viv because of his fielding and manner and to be honest just everything about how they played the game. When I was playing for Lancashire under 13s I was a ball boy at an England v West Indies ODI match at Old Trafford, when Viv Richards scored 180. After the game, the West Indies invited all of the ball boys into their dressing room, the England players didn't. They gave us souvenirs like batting gloves etc. I remember sitting next to Joel Garner, it was just incredible and those memories have stayed with me forever."

During his playing days, Richard played club cricket for Preston and played in all of the age group teams at Lancashire, but sadly wasn't deemed good enough to get a first-class contract. After playing some cricket in Melbourne and Zimbabwe, Richard moved to Brighton University to undertake a sports science degree. "When I came back to England, I played some cricket in the Sussex League and ended up captaining the second team at Sussex as an amateur – I think they just wanted an aggressive old club cricketer to come in and captain a young side! I ended up captaining them for a year. But I then went to Cambridge to do my postgraduate degree and ended up playing some first-class cricket for them before stopping playing in 2000 because of my coaching and teaching commitments."

And it was Richard's teaching and coaching at Brighton College that saw brought into the coaching set-up at Sussex under their then head coach Peter Moores. "I'd done some coaching of Sussex's under 17s and under 19s – an age group that contained the likes of Matt Prior. They were very strong sides. To be honest, my dog could have coached them, they were that strong! But the boys had gained a reputation as a tough side who fielded very well. Pete had liked the fact that the training I did was very different. He'd watched our under 19s quite a bit and he gave me the opportunity to do some sessions with the 1st XI. At Brighton College I was lucky to have two very wise, experienced teaching mentors who had seen it all but maintained a burning passion for their sport and an open mind to new methods. John Pope who was in charge of the rugby treated every person with genuine kindness and empathy whilst his gentle Welsh lilt disguised a fierce competitive edge. John Spencer who had played for Sussex loved talking about our great game and found humour and excitement in every ball. His boundless energy and enthusiasm were infectious: throw after throw after throw at anyone who wanted it accompanied by constant commentary as if it was the last ball of a tied Test match or World Cup Final. I owe them both and my then Headmaster Anthony Seldon a great deal".

There was no looking back. Richard began quickly climbing the coaching ladder. Peter Moores brought him into the 1st XI set up permanently and the team began cementing themselves as one of the strongest county sides in the country.

"We had a real mix of local players and players who hadn't done so well at other counties and who were determined to make a statement. We had the likes of Kirtley, Lewry, Martin-Jenkins, Montgomery, Chris Adams and young players such as Prior and Yardy. Sprinkled in with that was the magic of Mushtaq Ahmed. This was a group of guys who all had such a strong work ethic. That team worked so hard; they hit more balls than other county players and bowled more balls than others in training. They also knew how to enjoy themselves, which Pete encouraged."

Yet where did Richard's passion for fielding come from? "I always saw fielding as the thing you could do as eleven blokes and it's a reflection of a team's personality. Having done some analysis on fielding it became obvious to me just how important catches or dropped catches were. When I looked at batting or

377

bowling it can be quite hard to improve, but fielding was something you could improve quite easily and quickly."

Richard's success at Sussex saw him take up a role within the ECB as National Lead Fielding Coach. "Peter Moores had become head of the England academy. My role was to develop a fielding curriculum and coach coaches throughout the country. It suited me with my teaching background as I enjoyed things like building syllabuses. That wasn't daunting to me."

When Andy Flower took over as England coach, Richard was named as full-time fielding coach of the full England side and his first tour was the 2009 tour of the West Indies. "We got bowled out for 52 in that series and that was like a reset button for the national side. Everyone agreed that something had to change. Andrew Strauss was an excellent captain and he and Andy were a great pairing. What followed was a real collective 'let's roll our sleeves up' attitude and that's exactly what was needed at that time. It was actually all very simple, players knew their roles were to score runs, take wickets and in between catch balls. It was refreshing."

I asked Richard what his initial aims for the role were? "I wanted fielding to galvanise the team. That was my aspiration. When you look now at the best fielders: Smith, Kohli, Stokes, they galvanise their teams in the field. We were lucky that we had the likes of Paul Collingwood and Matt Prior who really believed in the importance of fielding. Thanks to them what I wanted to achieve became an easy sell to others. Both Strauss and Collingwood, who was one day captain, wanted their teams to be physical and field properly. Matt Prior was fantastic for me. He really drove everything on the field. He was bothered about every single throw - that was invaluable."

Richard's success in the role was down to the fact that he was given free rein to design his own fielding sessions. "I was really lucky. They must have thought I was mad at times with some of the stuff that I do – stuff like bringing the bowling machine out to give catches; they must have thought some things were lunacy, but they supported me. Andy gave coaching responsibility to me, Graham Gooch as the batting coach and David Saker and Otis Gibson as the bowling coaches. He told us that they were our jobs and thus we were responsible and accountable. We welcomed that."

One of the challenges of coaching, especially on long tours, is how to keep sessions fresh and engaging for players; how did Richard manage to achieve this? "At the end of the day it's always the same message you want to get across, watch the ball and get your head in a good position. So, no matter what the drill, the message is the same. How you catch a cricket ball will never change. However, I think my teaching background helped. Having to teach 20/30 kids for eight, nine or ten hours a day, five days a week, you learn to set up different environments to achieve the same goal. People think you're doing different things, but actually what you're doing is the same thing, it just appears different. It is a skill."

I asked Richard if he ever looks to other sports for added inspiration. "Again, going back to my teaching days, I used to study the really good swimming coaches – it was interesting to see how they would communicate to swimmers under water. I also learnt a lot from Volleyball, Basketball, Tennis, Rugby and Badminton coaches. I stole so much stuff from them. I was very lucky to be exposed to so many different coaches. Very lucky."

Back to England and for five years England had a very settled side; did that make things easier as a coach? "Absolutely. The team was set in its field placings. Strauss was at first slip, Swann at second slip, Bell at short leg and Collingwood at cover point. It's very different with Bangladesh though. With their lack of cricket, it's amazing the things they haven't yet experienced; things like fielding at slip to reverse swing bowling; where short leg should be, how deep should slip fielders be in countries like Australia. It's an element to the role I really enjoy when the captain comes and seeks my opinions on such things."

Richard enjoyed five highly successful years with England, but what were some of his favourite moments? "To be honest it was just that I genuinely couldn't believe how fortunate I was to be in the role. I was so lucky to have visited some of the ground and cities that I did. Every day was so special. But if I had to name a couple it would have been the Boxing Day Test win in Melbourne. That was just phenomenal. And during that same series, the win in Adelaide. I remember sitting at the end of the tunnel on that first morning, alongside Graham Gooch, when we took those three early wickets – Trott's run out of Katich and Swanny's slip catches. That was a proud moment for me. I was so chuffed for Trotty when he ran Katich out because I knew how hard he worked. People didn't see that he'd been out there the day before and didn't leave the session until he hit the stumps three times during the fielding drills. So, when you see people work that hard and then get the reward it makes you realise there must be a cricketing God out there somewhere. A third memory would have to be the T20 World Cup win; how we fielded in that tournament was another personal pleasure for me."

When stunning catches are taken or great run-outs occur it's a real high for coaches, but how does it feel on the flip side when catches go down, or opportunities are missed? "It's hard, of course it is. When a catch goes down it's tough as a fielder to have to stay out on the field as the batsman inevitably scores run after run. But it's been very different with England and Bangladesh. With England, the squad were very phlegmatic about dropped catches. They knew they'd done the preparation, so there was never an issue among the squad when a catch went down or there was a mis-field because they knew they'd done everything to prepare well. In Bangladesh however, it can be brutal in the media, genuinely brutal. It can become incredibly emotional, and missed chances are magnified to the extent of them becoming the focal point for winning or losing games. I remember at the last World Cup, an experienced member of the team dropped a catch at Adelaide, he honestly thought it was career ending. Thankfully we took two wickets in the next over, so all was OK, but that was how an experienced player felt after dropping a catch. I don't think an England player would be thinking that's the end of his career if he'd dropped a catch."

It's a very interesting insight into the mentality of different sides.

Richard moved on from the England role after the 2013/14 Ashes defeat – a decision which wasn't in Richard's control. "It was not my decision to move on; I got released from my contract. Peter Moores tried to find a role for me, but the side had lost 5-0 and I think they just wanted a complete clean slate. I was disappointed but I'd had five incredible years."

England's loss was most definitely Bangladesh's gain. "I really have learnt so much in the last two years. We've had some incredible moments with so many 'firsts. Our first win over England, our first win over Australia, the first time we have reached the Champions Trophy semi-finals. I have to pinch myself."

Richard has worked under a number of head coaches in his coaching career to date. I asked him how they compare. It was noticeable just how high a regard he holds all of them. "Peter Moores and Andy Flower were both very different but they both had very good work ethics; Andy's knowledge of the game was very in-depth. He was team director and didn't do too much coaching, that was down to me, Graham and David and Huw Bevan the strength and conditioning coach. He also wasn't really into the planning side or the detail but he was very much into the broad tactical stuff with Strauss and Cook. Pete meanwhile has had success everywhere. I felt he was unlucky with England in his two spells. He did the hard yards on both occasions. The first time Peter and Duncan's approach was so different. The work ethic that he'd instilled at Sussex was a genuine culture shock to some of the players who'd played under Duncan. But that's how every international team now prepares. What I find interesting though with Andy and Peter was how they were both portrayed in the media. Andy was labelled as this detailed planner but he wasn't really in to planning and the detail and Peter was labelled as this data-driven coach but that couldn't have been further from the truth for him. With Andy, it helped him being labelled that way as it was seen as a positive, but for Pete, it was sadly a negative label. I think Andy is a lot happier now in his role with the Lions where he can really coach and Pete is back being successful in County cricket. Aside from Andy and Pete there is Chandika Hathurusingha, and he is absolutely phenomenal in terms of reading games, scenarios and players."

Looking ahead to this Winter for us England supporters, Richard was part of the coaching team of England for three Ashes victories, so it'd be remiss not to ask him about our chances down under, especially having just seen the Australian side at close quarters in Bangladesh's recent series. "Smith and Warner are exceptional players. But the difference for me is that Australia will likely have four bowlers and England 5. For me, and this might sound ridiculous, but I think whoever plays the off-spinner the best will win the series. If England play Lyon well, they will win. In 2013 most of Mitchell Johnson's wickets were the tail-enders, it was Nathan Lyon who did the damage in the top order. As the Aussies will likely only have four bowlers, if England can play Lyon well, they will struggle with three seamers. On the flip side Australia will try and attack Moeen and if Moeen doesn't cope with it, some of our aging bowlers will have to bowl more overs than they should. So, I honestly think it'll come down to who plays the off-spinner best will win!"

I asked Richard, what kind of preparation will the captain and coaching team be undertaking now, in the lead up to a big Ashes series. "They will be doing all of the analysis on the opposition. They will be studying the pitches and looking at the right combinations of bowlers for the various pitches. They will be looking at how to exploit the weaknesses of the opposition and they will also be looking at how they schedule training to hit their peak at the right time. I remember in 2013 we thought we were being quite clever in bringing Tymal Mills and Harry Gurney out with us to prepare for left arm seam bowling, but that obviously didn't work out as well as we hoped! But it's a small example of how we tried to get everything in place to prepare the players. The management will also be looking at where in the tour they can offer rest and recovery and genuine time away from cricket, so the players can plan things when their families arrive etc. It's going to be a great Winter!"

It certainly is. The Ashes win of 2010/11 was arguably one of the greatest Ashes wins of all time and when people look back at that great England side the quality of the backroom staff can often go unnoticed, but it's fair to say the work of Richard (and Graham Gooch and David Saker) was so important to England's success that we should all be grateful for everything Richard did for English cricket. And to me it's no surprise that Bangladesh are now reaping the rewards of his experience. Richard – thank you.

31

CALUM MACLEOD
SCOTLAND BATSMAN

It's not often you get to speak to someone who has opened both the bowling and batting at an ICC World Cup and who in 2018 scored one of the finest ODI hundreds against England, a mightily impressive 140 not out, off of just 94 balls - Scotland's Calum MacLeod.

Calum's story is an interesting one. An out and out 'tearaway' fast bowler, who got banned at the age of 19 because of his action yet was able to completely remodel himself as a batsman to such a stunning effect.

"If I'm honest, it was the best thing that happened to me," remarked Calum. "I was a tearaway fast bowler and in my quest to bowl faster and faster I picked up some questionable habits in my action that I just never paid enough attention to. My coaches also didn't pick anything up early enough and as a result I ended having a quite a bad kink in my action which eventually got me banned."

At the time, Calum was on the books of Warwickshire, a period that coincided with Allan Donald being the first XI bowling coach and two batsmen, Ian Bell and Jonathan Trott who were entering into the peak years of their careers. "Being on the staff at Warwickshire opened up doors for me which others in my situation might not have had. There were three and a half months left of the season, so it meant I could follow the 1st XI pick the brains and chat cricket with the likes of Allan Donald and Ashley Giles and just sit and watch the way Ian Bell and Jonathan Trott went about scoring their runs, the methods they'd use, etc. It stuck with me the amount of work those two would put in. So that period, while banned, allowed me a season of 'education'. It was invaluable."

9 years later and Calum scored one of the best one-day innings as Scotland beat an England side that were ranked number one in the world. And to put that innings into context, England followed that game by whitewashing the touring Australians.

"What an absolute brilliant game of cricket. Leading into the game our captain, Kyle Coetzer, pushed us quite hard saying that someone had to beat England at some stage. Why couldn't it be us? I think that built up a bit of momentum. The way that Kyle and Matthew Cross started the game was absolutely crucial for us. Being 100 for 0 and putting them on the backfoot was one of the key things."

Scotland scored 371/5. England chased hard but their total of 365 fell just short in one of the most entertaining games of one day international cricket that has been played on these shores. "Getting the game so close meant people couldn't say England didn't turn up. They played some great cricket. I said at the time that Jonny Bairstow's innings was one you just had to walk away and learn from. He hit the ball so hard and there was so much I learnt from his levels of intent. They played well enough to beat us, but in the key moments, we managed to stay calm enough to win it."

And what was that moment like when victory was achieved? "I've never seen cricket have that much impact in Scotland. The Grange was absolutely bouncing. If you watch it back, you get goose-bumps. There was raw emotion on everyone involved in Scottish cricket. We flew to Holland a couple of days later; it's usually quite a quiet affair for us when we travel but we were having people come up to us at the airport. It was hugely exciting to be involved in and a proud moment to look back at."

Everyone now knows Calum for 'that' innings, but that innings was the icing on the cake of 9 years of re-modelling himself as a batsman. Other notable innings included a 175 off of 141 balls in a win over Canada and a 150 away in Afghanistan on a difficult spinning wicket. "If I'm honest that was probably my best innings, better than England. It was a spinning wicket, I batted to a plan and I'd put in so much work leading into that tour."

But, it hasn't all been plain sailing with the batting. "I hold the record for the most ducks for Scotland, so the game does have a funny way of bringing you back to earth!"

So how did Calum's eventful journey start?

"Growing up my heroes were all fast bowlers. I loved watching Glenn McGrath and Darren Gough. Both were quite aggressive who always gave their all. They had amazing skills and were just two players I'd always look forward to watching."

Calum's form as a bowler at Warwickshire, got him international recognition and he made his 'debut' against England. "I was in a team that played a four-day game the year before, but it got rained off.

The England game was massive. They had a lot of big characters and the first ball I faced, batting at number 11, was against Freddie Flintoff! I remember when the 9th wicket fell, I picked up my helmet, one of the old plastic ones, and it was broken! Here I was, about to go out and face Flintoff and my helmet was broken! I just stuck the broken bit back in and went out and batted. I was too nervous or shy to tell anyone else!"

Unfortunately, rain hit again, and the game was cut short.

Calum's spell at Warwickshire came to an end after five years and he left Edgbaston not long after his suspension. "By the time I left I was neither a batsman nor a bowler. I was unsure what I'd be doing, so it was the right time to leave. When I look back, I think I was very lucky with the timing."

Scotland had put their players on full time contracts and as Calum admits they were in a middle of a transitional period which gave him the time to 're-find' himself.

"Scotland had just come off of quite a successful 10-year period and a lot of players had retired at the same time. Scotland hasn't got the pool of players that England has but I was put on a part time contract for the Summer and told that there was a full-time contract here for me - show us what you have got. They showed a lot of faith in my batting which I probably didn't see myself. I thought of myself as a bowling all-rounder, but they showed a lot of faith in me. I was given the space and I probably played 15-20 games without much success, but it allowed me the time to learn my job as a batsman without the pressure of worrying about my place."

Calum rewarded the selectors for their patience. His performances went a long way to securing appearances for his country at the 2015 ICC ODI World Cup in Australia and New Zealand and the 2016 ICC World T20 in India.

"The qualification tournaments and those World Cups were the best trips I've been involved in. Kyle Coetzer's 156 against Bangladesh was a real highlight. It was probably the first time someone from an associate nation has taken a game away from a full member. It gave us all confidence."

The Scots may have not won a game in the 2015 World Cup, but they left the tournament with a number of friends, for the refreshing way they approached their games.

It is therefore extremely sad that at next year's World Cup in England and Wales, that Scotland won't be present after the ICC reduced the number of competing teams down to 10.

"The strength of cricket in the level below the top 10 has never been stronger. And when you have had the experiences like we had in World Cups it really gets to people. You go on these trips around the world, work so hard to qualify for these tournaments, it's what we play cricket for. So, for the ICC to take that away from us is so heart-breaking, not just for the players but supporters and kids in our countries. My first real memory of top-class cricket is the 1999 World Cup watching Scotland versus Australia at Worcester. Bruce Patterson clipped his first ball for four off his legs, and that memory has always stayed with me. The ICC has done so much for the associate members with the money they have put in but it's so heart-breaking that having reached the stage where countries are putting in competitive performances against the full members, that our opportunity to play on the World stage gets taken away."

It is crazy. Some of the most memorable games in recent World Cups have been giant-killings by the likes of Ireland, Afghanistan and the Netherlands. Some people may argue that some games between a full member and an associate member have been one-sided at times. "You're always going to get the odd hammering, but if you look at any team in cricket now and they suffer an absolute hammering every now and then. It's part of the game now. England and Australia have been bowled out for double figures in recent years."

It's a valid point. Cricket is a sport we all love, and that love shouldn't be confined to 10 full member countries. Our sport needs to grow and expand. Let's hope the powers that be do see sense after this next World Cup and give the associates their dream back.

Calum's form for Scotland gave him another shot at county cricket and in 2014 signed for Durham after a month-long trial. "I trialled at a couple of counties after leaving Warwickshire. I trialled at Kent for a couple of weeks but that was far too soon after I left Warwickshire and also at Northants. By the time the 2015 World Cup qualifiers came around Paul Collingwood had come on as Scotland assistant coach and that was at a time when I was playing quite nicely. He said why don't I come down to Durham and have a month-long trial to see where it leads. I had a brilliant month. I scored a lot of runs and from there I had an opportunity to go into the first team. His first XI career at Durham had its highlights. Durham won the 2014 Royal London Cup at Lord's.

"It was great to win a Lord's final. Lord's has that special feeling about it and it was an absolute showpiece. I'd played in some pretty big games for Scotland, where if we didn't win, we might not qualify for a World Cup or if lost we might lose out on funding that was critical for the game in Scotland. However, walking through that Long Room at Lord's is something else. And it got to me. I'm not afraid to say that the moment got too big for me. I ended up playing a couple of rash drives and I ended up nicking off and then walking back having got a duck."

Calum admits he found it difficult to get out of a run of low scores. "I think I'd be a lot calmer now. It amazes me to think how much batting you do in a county season. If you're in a good run of form, it's great. You cash in. But when you're in a slump of form, it's very tough. I'd never experienced a tough period in my batting career where I wasn't scoring consistent runs, so for it to happen in my second season back playing county cricket was disappointing. As sportsmen we're not the most open people. You're never going to go to the captain or coach and say I'm struggling a bit, which is of course the right thing to do and I would probably do it now and say I need a bit of help here, I need a couple of weeks out to work on some technical things. I was too nervous. I got caught up and it was purely because the games come so thick and fast. Now I'm a little bit older, I understand the game so much more.

A new county opportunity arose this year and Calum played T20 cricket for Derbyshire. "It was unexpected! We had no cricket booked in with Scotland and the opportunity came up. As a squad we were probably a little disappointed with our performances. We had the chances to make the quarter finals, but we didn't take the opportunities we had to win certain games. It was a good experience and good to be back in county cricket that bit older, where I understood my game a lot more. If an opportunity comes again next year, I'd be more than happy to do it."

As we spoke Calum had just returned from a spell in the Afghanistan T20 league. "It's a very strong league. The local talent out there is amazing and any tournament with Rashid, Gayle and McCullum is going to attract attention."

Looking ahead to next year, what does 2019 hold for him and Scotland?

"Well, welcome to the world of associate cricket, we currently have zero fixtures booked in! But, in general we've got to build on what we have done this year. It's imperative we find a way of continuing to grow the game in Scotland. We don't want 2018 to be the year that was brilliant with landmark wins and then we did nothing with it."

And what is the strength of cricket in Scotland, below the national side?

"One of the things the administrators have done is a better formalisation of a regional system. There's now a much stronger domestic game which bridges the gap between club cricket and the international team. We've also had a lot more professionalism in recent years. Players are full time and we have full time strength and conditioning coaches etc. There's a proper development programme in place. Players just below the full team now have more access to top quality coaching and we're starting to see new guys filtering through to the full squad, which is really encouraging, and more players are beginning to pick up county contracts which is great. We're in quite a strong position."

Are there ambitions to follow Ireland and Afghanistan into Test cricket?

"I'd love one day to play Test cricket for Scotland. Anybody who plays the game wants to play Test cricket. But whether that is achievable with Scotland you have to be realistic and think you might become a full member through one day cricket and T20, that's probably more realistic. But if you ask anyone whose is involved in cricket, whether it's someone who retired 30 years ago or someone picking up a bat for the first time, the majority want to play Test cricket. Ireland and Afghanistan have opened the door for associate members."

I was also keen to hear from Calum about which other associate nations are strong. "The Netherlands. The UAE as well - cricket is really growing there; there's a big passion for the game there. Nepal are on the way up. To be honest, all teams are producing good cricket. There are no easy games now in associate cricket."

It's great to see how strong the associate nations are becoming. I for one hope the ICC do see sense and give these countries the opportunities to test themselves on the World stage. They deserve it. We all want our sport to grow and now is the time to build on the strength of the associate nations. Players like Calum and his Scotland team-mates deserve it.

THOSE WERE THE DAYS…

32

DANNI WYATT
ENGLAND'S WOMEN'S BATTER

Ahead of the 2017 Women's World Cup, I spoke with a key member of England's side, talented batter, Danni Wyatt, as she and her teammates were away preparing in the warmth of Abu Dhabi. The competition was the eleventh women's World Cup tournament and it's fair to say the tournament was likely to be the best yet, given the growing popularity and strength of the women's game world-wide (and so it proved!)

"We're desperate to win the World Cup this year," remarked Danni. "But, there's some strong teams. Australia and India are always going to be strong, but the West Indies have come on leaps and bounds in recent years, South Africa are really good at the moment, New Zealand have recently gone professional and Sri Lanka and Pakistan are coming on. It's going to be a really good tournament."

The popularity of the women's game has never been so strong. As well as the World Cup this Summer we also have the

Women's T20 Super League here in England, and that's not to mention an Ashes tour this Winter and the women's Big Bash. It's an exciting time for women's cricket. But more of all that later. It's time to learn more about England's explosive batter.

Danni began playing cricket for her local side Whitmore Cricket Club in Newcastle (Stoke), a club she remains registered with, to this day. "My Dad played cricket for Whitmore Cricket Club and that's how it started for me. My brother also played but he quit after I started getting better than him! I grew up watching the Ashes on TV and my Dad and Grandad were always cricket mad, so it's always been part of the family."

I asked Danni how difficult it was starting out in the game when cricket wasn't regarded as a mainstream female sport. "When I started playing, I was the only girl at the club. In fact, I was probably the only girl in the area, but it shows how far the game has come that's there now a local girls league. I always played boys' cricket and then on to men's cricket. It was quite daunting when I first went into bat as all the fielders would come in because they didn't think I could hit the bowlers off the square, which I couldn't back then! But they accept me now - I'm now just one of the lads!"

Danni's path to international recognition was rapid. She made her debut for Staffordshire as a 14-year-old in 2005 and made her ODI and T20 debuts for England in 2010. A rapid rise. "I got spotted playing boys cricket for Whitmore, when the Staffordshire coach saw me at one of the games and he invited me for a trial and I got picked the day after when he told me that he'd like to put me in the under 13's squad. I scored three hundreds in three games and they picked me for the full Staffordshire side!"

The funny thing is despite three successive tons, Danni described herself as "more of a bowler back then"!!! "Don't laugh, it's true! I started off bowling seam but I was told I wasn't going to grow much more so I was advised to take up off spin – some back issues now mean I'm more of a batter but I still bowl a few darts now and again!"

Danni's performance with the bat (and ball!) saw her get selected for England Under 21s, at the age of just 15. "We went on a European tour to Holland and I was named player of the tournament and I then went straight into the England Academy, which is similar to England Lions, now."

At just 18 years of age Danni was making her full international debut. Her immense promise as a youngster had been recognised by the national selectors.

So how did she hear about her selection? "I was on a beach, on holiday in Sydney! Mark Lane, who was England coach at the time called and said they'd like to take me to India. I couldn't believe it! I'd never really been away before, apart from holidays with my Mum and Dad! I'd certainly never been away to anywhere like India!"

It was a memorable first tour for the talented youngster. "India really opened my eyes and it's now my favourite country to tour. Everyone is so passionate about cricket. I turned up not expecting to play and just thought I'd be carrying the drinks for a while."

But Danni got the call for the last game of the series. 3-1 down, the management decided to give her, her debut. "We'd lost the series but I was told I was going to make my debut in that last game. I was so nervous. I was picked for my bowling but I can honestly say I have never been so nervous in my whole life! I managed to get the ball down the other end so that was the main thing. I didn't really bowl that well, if I'm honest. I was 0-20 off four overs. But I remember coming into bat at number eight and just had the biggest smile on my face. I scored 28 not out and won us the game. Typical Dad though, he was on a flight over to India at the time, so he missed the whole thing! He was chuffed to bits though with how I did. I then got picked for the first T20 game a few days later and I got run out for a duck. So, I'd pretty much went from Don Bradman to Donald Duck in the space of a few days! It was a valuable lesson though that you can go from big highs to big lows, very quickly."

Despite that T20 duck the tour had shown that Danni belonged at the highest level. Her first major tournament followed in 2012 where England went all the way to the final, only to have to endure a heart-breaking defeat to arch-rivals Australia. "2012 was my real break-through year. I batted at six throughout that tournament. I'd gone to the World Cup in the West Indies in 2010, but I just carried the drinks. It was big for me to play in every game. It was fantastic that all my family came out, but I was gutted we lost the final on the final ball of the game. I cried my eyes out after that one. I remember getting home and I was properly gutted for a couple of weeks but it was a massive learning experience and to this day has given me the drive and motivation to win a World Cup. Playing in World Cups are always career highs but that particular tournament will always be a big one for me personally."

England's next global tournament was the 2013 World Cup and again England fell agonisingly short. "We didn't even make the final that year."

England lost to Australia again, this time in the semi-finals. "That was another tournament that stood out for me. I'd been in and out of the 50 over team, but in that tournament, I was given the chance to play as a pinch-hitter at the top of the order so Lottie (Charlotte Edwards) could play her natural game. Giving the ball a whack – great team player me! - has always been a part of my game so it was great to be given that responsibility. Things didn't go our way and it's always difficult to play in India and Sri Lanka with the heat, but the Aussies were on fire in that tournament."

Like the men's side the rivalry between England and Australia is fierce and while the women's team may have come up short in World Cups, when it's come to the Ashes Danni has seen victory in two Ashes series. "It's always really close between us and the Aussies. I've been fortunate to be involved in two Ashes wins which have been incredible so we know we can beat them. But I don't know what it is they just seem to beat us in World Cups. We're determined to turn that around this Summer and beat them again this Winter in the Ashes."

Australia reclaimed the Ashes in 2015, but don't bet against Danni and the team reclaiming it this Winter.

The format of the Ashes is different to the men's game. Each winner of a Test, ODI and T20 is awarded points and whichever side has the most points at the end of the series, wins the urn. "The format is brilliant. It adds something more to every game, especially with the Test match worth four points. The Test match is big one if you win that."

Test cricket is the one format Danni is looking to break into, having yet to make her international debut in the longest format of the game. "Hopefully I can this Winter as the Test is under lights, so it'll be very exciting."

And Danni is no stranger to cricket in Australia. In 2016, she made her debut in the inaugural Women's Big Bash, signing for the Melbourne Renegades. I asked Danni what the Big Bash experience was like and with her and several of her team mates building good friendships with several of the Aussies would that have any impact on the competitiveness of future England and Australia fixtures.

"The Big Bash is incredible. I love it. I love the Melbourne Summer; it's become my second home. It was a big honour and privilege to be picked for the Renegades. We finished second bottom this season so that's an improvement on the first season! It's great to play with and against the best players in the world. But for me it's made the rivalry with Australia even more intense. When you play against friends, you want to beat them even more. There's nothing better than getting your mate out!"

Last year saw the launch of our own version of the Big Bash, the Women's Kia Super League, which this year will start on the 10th August and will consist of six teams. The competition was a big success, with strong attendances throughout. Danni represented Lancashire Thunder last year, but this year will be playing for last year's champions the Southern Vipers. "I can't wait to get started with the Southern Vipers. It's a new challenge for me and it will be nice to be back playing again with Lottie. They've got a really good team so it should be a good challenge to try and win it again."

With the World Cup, the Women's Kia Super League, the Ashes and the Big Bash the women's game is on a crest of a wave. The national team is now fully professional, crowds are growing at a rapid rate and I'm not sure there is a sport that has strengthened itself so quickly. A good gauge of how fast the game has developed is the support the women's game has got from Sky Sports. Internationals are now shown live and this year's Kia Super League games will be broadcast live for the first time. "We have had a lot of coverage on TV and that's what is going to get more girls playing the sport and into the England cricket team. The more we keep winning as a national side, the more we will keep being on TV and the bigger the game will get. We also shouldn't forget the fantastic job Charlotte Edwards did as England Women's captain, a lot of the growth is down to her."

Danni is only 26 but what a journey she has had already. With many years of pinch hitting to come, I asked her what has been her most memorable performance to date? "It has to be against

Australia in a group game at the T20 World Cup. They hit 200 and we needed 10 over when I came in. I was batting with Sarah Taylor. Ellyse Perry was bowling and mid-off was up and I just thought I've got to play to my strengths so I've just gone bang and hit her for six. I don't know what happened but I just had this energy in my body and I was hitting it everywhere. After a few overs, Sarah and I walked off and we'd beaten the Aussies, despite needing 10 an over from the last 10 overs."

But, it's not about the past, it's all about the present and the future. Here is a someone who is living her dream as a professional cricketer, loves representing her country and has a real determination to help her side right the wrongs of recent World Cups. Her big hitting and sharp fielding will be invaluable this year. It's going to be exciting to watch.

As England fan's we are lucky to have her.

33

LINSEY SMITH
ENGLAND'S WOMEN'S SPINNER

In this interview I spoke to one of the rising stars of women's cricket. At just 22 years of age (at the time of the interview) left-arm spinner Linsey Smith had already appeared in two Kia Super League finals and following her selection in the England Pathway squad she was knocking on the door of the full England side. Since this interview, Linsey has made her full England debut.

"One of my aims in 2018 is to push on and give the spinners in the full England side a run for their money. You have always got to back yourself and if I can do well with the Southern Vipers again this year, the opportunity might come."

Linsey started her career by turning her arm over at her local club Aston Rowant CC and enjoyed nothing more than sending the boys back to the pavilion. "I'd grown up in a cricket family. When I was seven we moved to Oxfordshire and my Dad and brother started playing cricket at Aston Rowant, so I thought I would as well! The club had a small girls' set-up but they fast tracked me into playing for the boys, which was quite cool, albeit a bit scary. There was always good chat when you're bowling at the men, our wicket-keeper would always helpfully be telling batsmen not to get out to a girl!"

Playing boys'/men's cricket is a familiar journey taken by many in the women's game It was certainly a path trodden by our previous interviewees: Charlotte Edwards and Danni Wyatt.

Linsey's early success saw her represent Oxfordshire in age group cricket, but she realised if she wanted to continue her development she'd need to make a move to test herself at a higher level and so came about a move to Berkshire, who despite being a minor county, competed in division one of the women's county set-up (there are four divisions in total).

"I enjoyed playing for Oxfordshire, but I wanted to push myself and made the decision to play for Berkshire who at the time were in division 1. To develop I felt I needed to be playing in an environment where all of the top England and county players were playing."

Linsey's performances for Berkshire saw her called up into the Southern Vipers' squad for the inaugural season of the KIA Super League, the women's franchise T20 cricket series.

What made this rapid rise even more remarkable for Linsey was the fact that in 2015 she swapped from bowling seam to spin due to an injury.

And the move was a dream come true for Linsey. Growing up, Charlotte Edwards was a hero to Linsey, so to get the opportunity to play with one of the greats of the women's game was a dream come true. "I always looked up to Charlotte Edwards. I remember when she came into my secondary school and did a session with us; it was the moment I knew I really wanted to pursue cricket. She was a big character when I was growing up, so it was pretty amazing to get to play with this extremely experienced cricketer. In the two years I have worked with her she has shared a lot of knowledge and really helped me develop my game."

Linsey had to bide her time in that first season with the Vipers, but an injury to a team mate saw her called up for the team's second fixture against Lancashire Thunder. Having taken 1-15 from her four overs, Linsey kept her place in the side for the next game against the Yorkshire Diamonds. It was a wise decision as Linsey's 4-10 from her four overs, set them on the road to victory and for Linsey it was proof that she belonged at this level.

The Vipers went on to win that first competition, beating the Western Storm at Chelmsford. "Finals day was amazing. For a number of the team it was the first time a number of us had ever experienced anything like that and to play in front of a big crowd was great."

At the end of that 2016 season, Linsey moved from Berkshire to Sussex to further aide her development. "I wanted to join a side that were pushing for titles and I knew that Sussex would be a good environment for me to learn and develop. I probably shot myself in the foot though as both Berkshire and Sussex got relegated! But hopefully we'll fight back this Summer and be back in division one next year."

Despite the relegation at Sussex, Linsey continued to impress with the Vipers. The side went on to reach the final for the second successive year, but this year the Storm got their revenge and defeated the Vipers in the final. I asked Linsey about the impact the women's World Cup win had had on last year's competition.

"I was lucky enough to be at Lord's and to see the ground sold out for a women's game was amazing. The reaction when England won had never been seen before. It totally changed the women's game and people's perceptions of it. The first year of the Super League people didn't really know what to expect, but the crowds we got at the Ageas Bowl were amazing. In the second year however, after the World Cup, it grew and grew and to see that many people turn up for games was fantastic. I think it will grow even more this year, especially now Sky Sports will be covering more games. You also look at the women's Big Bash, the game is getting bigger and bigger around the world. It's fantastic for all the girls playing."

Linsey's performances for the Vipers has put her on the radar of the England selectors. "Last year I was lucky enough to be selected to go to Abu Dhabi with the full squad, they took five academy players over, which was really positive, and I learnt a lot from it."

Her selection for the England Pathway squad, which is the equivalent to the men's England Lions has aided her development further. "Last year the academy team joined a county boys league to get us used to playing as a team. We won that league, so we're moving up a level this coming season, which will be another test for us."

Looking ahead to this coming Summer, I asked Linsey what her goals and ambitions were. "I am hoping to keep my place in the senior academy squad and perform well for the Southern Vipers and, as I say, give the spinners in the senior England side something to think about."

The women's game is primarily built around 50 over and T20 cricket. I asked Linsey about the pressures of being spinner, particularly in the shorter format of the game, where spinners only get four overs to turn their arm over. "T20 is very pressurised, but anyone who knows me, knows that I am quite a fiery character and I never say no to a challenge! I took the new ball for the Vipers last season in the Powerplay, which was daunting, but you have to back yourself and take on the challenge. T20 is my sort of game. I love it!"

As the interview went on, I realised I had not asked Linsey about her batting. How had she got on with the bat in two seasons of T20 cricket? "Well… can you believe I've never had to get the pads on yet!" Yes, in two seasons of T20 cricket, Linsey has yet to face a ball with a bat! But she promises me she is working hard in the nets on her batting as she recognises the importance of batting and fielding and not being a one-dimensional cricketer.

We finished our conversation with Linsey naming the best player she'd bowled to. "Stafanie Taylor of the West Indies. She is pretty special. I remember bowling to her and having to look at myself and the way I was bowling. You realise you have to change things at times, or players like her will completely demolish you. She's a very impressive batter."

So, as you watch women's cricket look out for the name Linsey Smith and remember you read about her here first!

34

SCYLD BERRY
DAILY TELEGRAPH CRICKET
CORRESPONDENT

This final interview was a shift away from former players and coaches towards one of the world's most respected cricket journalists - the Daily Telegraph's cricket correspondent and former Wisden editor Scyld Berry.

Having covered more Test cricket than anyone alive (450 Test matches and counting!) one can only imagine some of the great Tests he must have covered. So, it seemed the appropriate place to start, of all those Test matches, which ones were his most memorable?

"Now that's a difficult question," remarked Scyld. "There are five that immediately spring to mind. Headingley 81, Edgbaston 81, Edgbaston 2005, the Oval 2005 and the Kingston Test of 1986 when England were bombed out by Malcolm Marshall, Patrick Patterson, Michael Holding and Joel Garner. That was the most frightening Test match I have ever seen. You genuinely thought there was a possibility of someone getting hit or killed."

It's fair to say Scyld has been extremely fortunate. Not that I'm jealous. Honestly.

We'll touch upon more of Scyld's memories and thoughts on the game today, later. But I wanted to rewind the clock. What got him into cricket and what was his journey into journalism.

"I grew up in Sheffield in the early 60s and Yorkshire were winning the championship more often than not. We had the likes of Ray Illingworth, Fred Trueman, Geoff Boycott, Brian Close, Jack Hampshire – it was a wonderful team that was good enough to beat most touring sides, including the West Indies and Australia. I always wanted to play cricket, but for one reason or another I wasn't able to until I was 17 years old and even then, I never got to bowl! I was captain and didn't dare bowl myself! So, I was 18 when I finally managed to bowl in a proper game of cricket – and I took six for 24 then immediately lost my leg break. Unfortunately, playing cricket was never going to be a career for me."

And so Scyld choose a career in journalism. If playing wasn't an option, then writing about it most definitely was. "In my last year at university I wrote to The Observer and asked if I could write some match reports for them and they said no! I asked why not, so they said come into the office and let's have a chat. A few weeks later they agreed to let me start covering some games. That was in 1976 and I've been writing ever since."

After those early years writing for The Observer, Scyld covered Test matches for the Scotsman and the Glasgow Herald. And in 1993, he joined the Daily Telegraph where he has remained to this day. For 20 years he was the Sunday cricket correspondent but for the last four years it has become seven days a week as he took on the daily as well as the Sunday reporting duties.

"It's all year round now. 41 years of Summer and Winter – or more often perpetual Summer!"

So, what's a typical lead up to a series for a journalist and what does a day at the Test involve? Personally, I always feel for a journalist who must be all prepared to write a piece, then a flurry of wickets fall in the last over or two but the deadline for filing the piece hasn't shifted!

"Before any series I like to write a lengthy preview for the Sunday Telegraph five days before the Test begins. I then go to the ground the day before the game to see both sides practise and attend the press conference by both sides. I like to get a feel for which side will be stronger and more likely to win. I then write up the piece in the afternoon. If the Test is in England, I hope to have covered one of the warm-up games before the first Test to do some research on the opposition. On the day of the Test itself, the thing about being a cricket correspondent is not that the days are very arduous, but they are very long - 10/12-hour days is the norm. I get to the ground at 10am for an 11am start. I'm someone who watches a day's play as closely as possible. I like to think I miss less than an over a day, maybe two or three balls. Then come the close of play I'll start writing which takes me an hour or two. I normally have to file the piece to the Telegraph by 8pm. About half an hour after sending it I like to re-read it one more time on my iPhone to check there are no silly mistakes. Then it's back to the hotel, something to eat and time to switch off for the evening. I basically repeat that every day for a Test match. On tour, weeks can go by without having days off, but that's the nature of the job."

And what if those late wickets fall, which can ruin your planned piece? "To be honest the real challenge is not so much the Test match as I don't start writing until just before close, but the one-day games that take place on a Saturday as the Sunday papers have an earlier deadline. You have to pretty much file as soon as the game finishes so that can involve some skill to know an hour before the game finishes which side will win and to write accordingly. There's nothing worse than having to tear up and start again. It takes me about an hour to write 900 words so those Saturday one-day games are probably the biggest challenge of the job."

In Scyld's time as a journalist technology has evolved and social media has been introduced; I was keen to know how life has changed for Scyld as a journalist?

"The means of transmission. We used to have to type out our report for someone to phone it through to copytakers or take it to a telex office abroad! Now it's all about the laptop, and in the last few years the internet and connectivity have been good in all countries that we tour. But I remember even five years ago getting a signal in a hotel on some tours could be challenging. Social media has also been a useful tool to keep an eye on everything going on. For example, being told by someone when a record is about to be broken because the Test Match Special guys have sent a tweet with an interesting statistic can be useful. And of course, just the amount of information that is now in the public domain because of social media is a plus."

We spoke earlier about the memorable games Scyld has covered, but what about the most difficult story? "For me it was Kerry Packer and the World Series. It was completely unprecedented. No one knew where the game was going to go. Would there be anything left after Packer had creamed off the best players? No one knew where it would end. Would there be any more international cricket against the likes of Australia and the West Indies?"

In 2008, Scyld was appointed editor of the Wisden Cricketers' Almanack, one of the biggest honours for any cricket writer. It was a role he was in for four years. "It was heaven and hell! It was heaven in that in the Summer there was very little do to apart from commission the odd piece, but it was hell in January and February when most correspondents had left it until the last moment to file their piece and having to chase them up, edit and proof read. There were definitely two extremes to the role. It was intense, but I was very glad to have done it for four years."

One of the things I wanted to get from this interview with Scyld was to pick his brains on the state of cricket today, starting with where he sees the future of Test cricket?

"If I'm honest I do think it's a bit alarming. I think the popularity of Test cricket has passed its peak. I'm sorry I've come to that conclusion but the Ashes illustrated that to me. The ICC has had a role to play in this. The World Test Championship should have been implemented in 2013 and 2017. The ICC said it would do this, but then they cancelled them. I think history will look back and see that as a pivotal moment when T20 cricket overtook Test cricket in its popularity. Test cricket needs context."

And with Alex Hales and Adil Rashid being two recent players who have turned their backs on red ball cricket, is this a trend that Scyld thinks will grow?

"Yes, I'm afraid the dam has broken. Unless the ICC and ECB greatly increase the payments for Test matches many more will do the same. I think every young player still wants to play Test cricket, but once they have failed to crack it, they'll give up red ball cricket and specialise in T20. It's where the money is."

Is there something that the ICC can still do? "They could make sure minimum payments for every Test match are subsidised to a satisfactory level, but the Test Championship planned for 2021 of just one Test match in England between the first- and second-best countries is pitiful and too late. It should have been the top four teams playing against each other. That would have a been a lovely grand finale to a four-year cycle. A one-off Test which can be decided by the toss of a coin and virtually over in an hour won't revive the game."

After a Winter where the England Test side has struggled, and the one-day side has revelled, how does Scyld see the state of the current England sides? "The 50 over side is the most advanced of the England sides across the three formats. They have real depth with 14 or 15 players now competing for those 11 places whereas the Test side has only nine or so confirmed players. They haven't got that squad of 15 that the one-day side has. In T20 our team seems to be lagging a bit behind the 50 over team."

Does this bode well for the 50 over World Cup next Summer in England? "I think the trajectory towards the 2019 World Cup is encouraging but we never seem to win the crunch knockout games. The Champions Trophy semi-final was the biggest set-back in that regard. England would have been full of much more self-belief if they had won that 2017 Champions Trophy."

And what about the Test team this Summer? "Pakistan in May should be an England win, but we did think that last time and Pakistan managed to draw the series 2-2. As for India, the fascination is can Virat Kohli cope with the ball swinging and seaming around? If he can't you'd expect England to win; if he can, such is his appetite for run scoring then India will probably be favourites. Especially now they have a very good pace attack as well as their spinners."

I always love to listen to Scyld and picking his brains on the state of play of the game. You always receive insightful views. But like with all of my interviews I had to ask him about the best players he has witnessed live.

Let's start with the bowlers. "Malcolm Marshall has to be up there. He swung the ball both ways, cut the ball both ways and bowled so fast. In terms of a spinner you can look no further than Shane Warne. What I look for in a cricketer is someone who is never defeated. I never saw Warne defeated. He reached a stalemate with Collingwood and Pietersen in the Adelaide Test of 2006 but he was never beaten from what I saw and nor was Marshall."

And the batsmen? "Viv. For the simple fact that no one ever got on top of him. A good rule of thumb: does a cricketer leave a team stronger than he joined it? Viv did that with every team he joined. The Leewards, West Indies, Somerset and Glamorgan. The energising and transforming of a team into winners is the best rule of thumb and he was better than anyone else that I know."

One thing people may not be aware of is that away from writing Scyld is heavily involved in promoting cricket to people who don't have easy access to proper cricket grounds. "I launched the Wisden City Cup, which is now the ECB City Cup, as a competition for youngsters in inner cities who want to play cricket but don't have access to a ground. Because I wasn't able to play the game when young, I don't want others to suffer the same frustration."

Journalists can come and go, but there's a reason Scyld has covered more Test matches than anyone else: people love reading his articles. It was a pleasure to interview Scyld, but I suspect my interviewing skills come a distant second to his! Scyld - thank you!

THOSE WERE THE DAYS…

CLOSE OF PLAY

And that brings a close to all of the interviews. I hope you found them to be an enjoyable read. I certainly enjoyed each and every one of the conversations.

For more interviews please visit our website www.addisarmycricket.co.uk and subscribe to our mailing list. I aim to continue interviewing more figures from in and around the game and who knows in a couple of years there could be a sequel!

Finally, thank you once again for buying the book. All profits are being donated to the Ruth Strauss Foundation. A charity that has touched so many people.

Sir Andrew Strauss' wife, Ruth, had been diagnosed with an inoperable form of lung cancer that attacks non-smokers. The foundation has been launched to provide emotional, psychological and wellbeing support to patients and their families going through a similar experience and to fund research into rare lung cancers.

To find out more information, or if you would like to donate further money, please visit: www.ruthstraussfoundation.com

Michael Gegg

THOSE WERE THE DAYS...

Printed in Poland
by Amazon Fulfillment
Poland Sp. z o.o., Wrocław

51727789R00247